Fifty Years Below Zero

P9-BIH-122

Courtesy New Bedford Whaling Museum

LEFT TO RIGHT: TOM GORDON, FRED HOPSON, AND CHARLIE BROWER
AT POINT BARROW IN SEPTEMBER 1898

Fifty Years Below Zero

A Lifetime of Adventure in the Far North

CHARLES D. BROWER

IN COLLABORATION WITH
PHILIP J. FARRELLY
AND
LYMAN ANSON

WITH PREFACE BY
TERRENCE COLE

UNIVERSITY OF ALASKA PRESS

Library of Congress Cataloging-in-Publication-Data

Brower, Charles D., 1863-
    Fifty years below zero : a lifetime of adventure in the Far North
/ Charles D. Brower, in collaboration with Philip J. Farrelly and
Lyman Anson ; with preface by Terrence Cole.
       p. cm. -- (University of Alaska Press' Classic reprint series
; v. 3)
    Includes index.
    ISBN 0-912006-68-4 (acid-free paper)
    1. Alaska--Description and travel. 2. Barrow, Point, Region
(Alaska)--Description and travel. 3. Frontier and pioneer life-
-Alaska. 4. Eskimos--Alaska. 5. Brower, Charles D., 1863- .
6. Adventure and adventurers--Alaska--Biography. I. Farrelly,
Philip J. II. Anson, Lyman. III. Title. IV. Title: 50 years below
zero. V. Series: Classic reprint series (Fairbanks, Alaska) ; v. 3.
F909.B8 1994
979.8'03--dc20   94-9812
                                                                CIP

Originally published and copyrighted in 1942 by Dodd, Mead and Company, Inc.
Reprinted 1994 by the University of Alaska Press
Preface and Index ©1994 University of Alaska Press

International Standard Book Number: 0-912006-68-4
Library of Congress Catalogue Number: 94-9812

This publication was printed on acid-free paper which meets the minimum
    requirements for American National Standard for Information Sciences—
    Permanence of Paper for Printed Library Materials, ANSI Z39.48-1984.

Cover design by Dixon Jones, IMPACT Graphics, University of Alaska Fairbanks.
Front cover photograph: the cutter *Northland.* Back cover photograph: Charles D.
    Brower, photograph by Alfred M. Bailey, BA21-799, All Rights Reserved, Photo .
    Archives, Denver Museum of Natural History.
Map of Alaska, facing page 12, by Jan Neimeyer. Map of the Arctic Coast of Alaska,
    facing page 13, by Dixon Jones, IMPACT Graphics, University of Alaska
    Fairbanks.
Production and publication coordination by Debbie Van Stone.

Fifty Years Below Zero is the third volume in the University of Alaska Press'
    Classic Reprint Series. This series—edited by Terrence Cole, associate professor
    and chair of the History Department, University of Alaska Fairbanks—brings
    back into print highly regarded, classic works of enduring excellence. Other titles
    in the series include:

        Arctic Village. A 1930s Portrait of Wiseman, Alaska, by Robert Marshall
        Exploration of Alaska 1865-1900, by Morgan Sherwood

These volumes are reproduced from original editions with material added.

Several people helped with the preparation of this volume. We thank Grace Berg
    Schaible and Michael T. Cook for their assistance in obtaining copyright and
    historic information. Eva R. Trautmann compiled the index. We extend our
    thanks and appreciation to Grant and Dorcas Thompson and the rest of the
    Brower family for their encouragement and support.

To My Devoted Wife,

My Fine Sons and Wonderful Daughters,

this book is affectionately dedicated.

CONTENTS

LIST OF ILLUSTRATIONS

PREFACE TO THE 1994 EDITION

THEY called him the "King of the Arctic." For more than half a century Charles D. Brower lived on top of the world near Point Barrow, Alaska, the northernmost point of the northernmost possession of the United States. Among explorers he was a legendary figure. The shrewd trader was the first non-Native—and for years the only one—to live year-round with the Inupiaq on the Arctic coast of Alaska. He learned the Native language, traditions and customs as well as any outsider ever could. "You wouldn't think, when you had your back turned and listened to him talk," his daughter once said, "that he was a white man."[1]

Fifty Years Below Zero, first published in 1942, is Brower's recollection of his life in the Arctic. One of the most widely read memoirs ever written about Alaska, his book was reprinted at least nineteen times over a period of forty years by its original New York publisher. Brower was renowned as a good story teller; he once held his own swapping hunting yarns with Teddy Roosevelt in the White House. His book is a classic adventure story describing the daily struggle for survival in the Arctic, the continual battle between life and death in the most unforgiving climate on earth.

His account of the wreck of the *Navarch* in August 1897 is a harrowing chapter in Arctic literature. After abandoning the ship in the ice pack about thirty miles off shore, Brower led thirty-one men across the ice for twelve days without any food or extra clothing. He could not save everyone. Of the thirty-two men on the death march from the *Navarch*, only sixteen survived, half of whom were barely conscious when rescued, and three of whom lost one or more legs from frostbite and gangrene. The dead disappeared below the ice or were left behind when they could walk no further.

"For years afterward I didn't want to talk about this experience," Brower once said. "The recollections of hearing the voices of the men we had to leave behind. There was nothing we could do to relieve them and we couldn't take them along. To have a man begging you and to hear his voice dying away in the distance asking you please not to leave him, was awful. It was utterly impossible for us to do anything for them. It was as much as we could do to take ourselves along."[2]

Charles DeWitt Brower lived to tell the tale, having learned at an early age what it took to survive.[3] He was born in Manhattan on March 6, 1863, while his father was away on a Civil War campaign. Brower loved to read and excelled at school in history, Latin and physiology. At age eleven he bought a Civil War muzzle loader with which he loved to roam the wooded hills around his childhood home in New Jersey outside of New York City. "As a boy I always liked to be by myself," he said, "and what spare time I had was away hunting or fishing."[4]

With his father's grudging approval Brower left school at fourteen to sign up as a cabin boy on a sailing ship bound for South America. He earned eight dollars a month. On the return voyage to New York he nearly drowned when his ship collided with another vessel and sank off the Atlantic coast. Back home in New Jersey, he enthralled his old school friends with tales of his trip. Brower would never again feel content with the routine of settled life in civilization, a trait he claimed he inherited from his footloose father. "I think in all probability that I took after him," Brower once wrote, "as he was always a wanderer even in his old age, when he had the price...."[5] For seven years Brower sailed around the world, growing up in Calcutta and Liverpool, Melbourne and Montevideo, and earning a lifelong supply of sea stories.

A favorite yarn from Brower's seafaring days concerned the last fateful trip of the *C.C. Chapman* from Antwerp around the Horn to San Francisco in 1883. When the vessel was some distance off the coast of Chile, a fire broke out in the hold; a load of blacksmith coal had ignited. Efforts to douse the fire only fanned the flames. "I stayed with the fire as long as I thought it was any use," Brower recalled, "but we could all see we were making no headway...so finally I had to call the men out of the hold, and put all the hatches on to try and smother it."[6]

The captain refused to put ashore in Valparaiso, since the authorities there would have probably condemned the vessel, which would have meant loss of the entire cargo. So the ship sailed on. Twelve days later, by which time the fire appeared to have gone out, the hatches of the ship suddenly blew off their hinges and the flames roared higher than before.

The ship had become a steaming volcano. "During the next month the hatches were blown off every few days," Brower said, "and every time the fire took a new lease, and spread further aft." Ultimately the *C.C. Chapman* was afire for fifty-two days and 6,000 miles at sea. Miraculously, the ship made it safely through the Golden Gate, only to blow up and sink in the mud of Mission Bay as they were preparing to land in San Francisco.

The voyage of the *Chapman* convinced twenty-year-old Charlie Brower to find a safer line of work. "I was glad to think that I was through with the sea and ships," Brower wrote, "as I thought forever...." But try as he might, "It seemed as if I did not fit these shore jobs. If I got one in a store I wanted to be outside, and if I was outside there was something else that was not right."[7]

Brower went back to sea in 1884–1885 on a voyage to the north coast of Alaska for the Pacific Steam Whaling Company, a trip that changed both his life and the course of Arctic history. Like the giant oil companies that drilled Prudhoe Bay a century later, commercial whalers in the late 19th century struck it rich on the north coast of Alaska, but instead of crude oil they were after whale oil and particularly baleen, the flexible substance found in great abundance in the jaws of the bowhead whale. Used primarily to manufacture items such as corsets, hats, umbrellas, fishing rods, and buggy whips, baleen was the closest thing in the 19th century to plastic. Each whale was a floating treasure chest; the baleen from a single bowhead could sell for the price of a mansion in San Francisco, and whalers butchered nearly 19,000 whales in the Arctic by the time the industry ceased in 1914.[8]

Pacific Steam Whaling Company, the innovative San Francisco firm that hired Brower in 1884, revolutionized the Arctic whaling industry in the 1880s; besides building more efficient steam whalers, the company opened the first baleen and whale oil refinery on the west coast, and in 1884 established the first shore-based whaling station in the Alaskan Arctic near Point Barrow.[9] A shore-based operation could hunt with small boats in offshore leads in the early spring or late fall as the Natives had done for generations, while ships would have to wait months for open water before they could follow migrating whales into the Arctic Ocean during the brief northern summer. Brower's first task for Pacific

Steam Whaling in 1884–1885 was to investigate the Corwin Coal Mine, the exposed coal seam east of Cape Lisburne where the U.S. Revenue Cutter *Corwin* and other vessels blasted fuel out of the hillside. During his first winter in the Arctic, Brower traveled extensively along the Arctic coast and even accompanied a Native whale hunting crew on the ice at Point Hope. Afterward, he returned to San Francisco in the fall of 1885 intending to head to a warmer climate. "I had made up my mind," he said, "to go to Africa."[10] Before he could leave for the jungle, however, Pacific Steam Whaling convinced Brower and his friend, George Leavitt, to return to Alaska in 1886 to operate their Point Barrow whaling station, housed in the former U.S. Signal Corps observatory near the village of Utqiagvik, the largest Inupiaq settlement on the Arctic coast.

Located on a promontory twenty-five to thirty feet high—which explorers had named Cape Smythe—above the flat Arctic coastal plain, the ancient whaling village of Utqiagvik would prove to be a natural site for a commercial whaling station. Offshore lay a stretch of deep water in which sea mammals congregated, while the higher elevation of the village protected it somewhat from being crushed by the wind-blown Arctic ice pack. Situated only about ten miles southwest of Point Barrow, the narrow sandy spit that juts into the Chukchi Sea at the top of the continent, Utqiagvik, or Cape Symthe, was subsequently renamed Barrow when a post office opened because it was easier to pronounce (causing endless geographical confusion over the years between Point Barrow—the sandspit—and Barrow—the community ten miles away).[11]

When he arrived in Utqiagvik (Barrow) in August 1886 at the age of twenty-three, Brower expected to remain for only a winter or two at the most until he had pocketed enough baleen money to move on. In fact, Barrow turned out to be Charlie Brower's last port. His two-year stay lasted a lifetime. For nearly sixty years, long after the demise of the whaling industry which had lured him north, Brower made his home on the Arctic coast of Alaska.

He stayed in part because where others saw only a desolate frozen wasteland, he envisioned unparalleled opportunity on the Arctic shore. At the time he landed in Barrow in 1886, not a single white man resided permanently among the Alaskan Inuit, and Brower quickly foresaw the profits that an ambitious entrepreneur, willing to adapt to life in the Arctic, could reap in the whaling and fur trading business. Furthermore life with the Eskimos on the edge of the Arctic Ocean offered personal freedom and satisfaction he could not find anywhere else. "This was the country, and these were the people for me," Brower said.

"They seemed to be happier than any folks I'd ever seen. They hadn't forgotten how to play. They faced life with optimism, laughing and joking and always more content with their lot than the crowds down south."[12]

Married twice during his life in Alaska, Brower fathered fourteen half-Inupiaq children. His first wife, Toctoo, a Point Hope woman he met in 1884, perished in the measles epidemic of 1902. Afterwards he married Asianggataq, his remarkable partner for forty years and mother of ten of his children, most of whom grew up to be influential leaders in the Native community. Tom Brower, his oldest son by his second wife, calculated in 1977 that Charlie's descendants totaled by that time "over 100 grandchildren and over 150 great-grandchildren, living mostly in Alaska."[13]

Brower's firm, the Cape Smythe Whaling and Trading Co.—still owned today by the Brower family—eventually controlled a string of trading posts across the Alaskan Arctic. When changing fashions doomed the commercial whaling industry, Brower turned to fur trading and other enterprises, including reindeer herding. Browerville, the site of Brower's main store on the outskirts of the village of Barrow, was the shopping center for northern Alaska, where Inupiaq exchanged furs and whalebone for all the fruits of the industrialized world, from canned food and coffee to oysters, figs, pineapples, candy, or anything else in a well-stocked grocery store.[14]

Perhaps the ultimate secret of Brower's success was his lively curiosity about the world, and a willingness to adapt to the environment. Despite dropping out of school at fourteen, he never quit learning, and insisted all of his children get some education. Reading history, natural history, literature and anthropology were lifelong pursuits. His home-made education came from the a three-foot shelf of world history—the Grolier Society's "Book of History" series—and a complete set of the Harvard Classics, which he claimed to have read from cover to cover. "You can get a book," he once said, "to teach you almost anything."[15]

He developed a taste for classical music, opera and fine singing. On cold winter nights visitors might hear the scratchy sounds of Enrico Caruso or John McCormack on Brower's old wind-up phonograph. He taught himself the basic principles of business, law and medicine. When necessary he pulled teeth, set broken arms and legs, and even performed operations; equipped with only an old razor and a pair of forceps, he once carved a .44 caliber bullet out of a man's thigh. He was the official census taker for northern Alaska in 1900, and as postmaster and U.S. Commissioner, for many years Charlie Brower was the law north of the Brooks Range.

Above all else, however, Brower learned from the Inupiaq people. Many traders lived with the Natives for decades without learning to speak the local dialect. With the help of his first and second wives—whom he called his "sleeping dictionaries"—Brower mastered Inupiaq and spoke with no trace of an accent. In fact he conversed with other whites so rarely, he said he learned to speak Eskimo better than English.[16] He studied the Native way of whaling and may have been the only white man ever to accompany an Inupiaq whaling expedition equipped exclusively with aboriginal hunting gear. An accomplished ivory carver, he helped create a new Eskimo art form when he introduced the Natives at Barrow to weaving baleen baskets, modeled after the style of Athabaskan willow baskets.[17]

Some modern accounts tend to stereotype traders like Brower as ruthless exploiters of the Native people. Even one of Charlie Brower's grandsons, Billy Neakok, a militant proponent of Native rights, has called his grandfather "the first crook who was up here."[18] Like any successful trader, Brower saw no shame in giving little to get much. That was the nature of the business. With the only store in town he could drive a hard bargain, and stare down anyone who came through the door.

Certainly by today's standards not everything Brower did would still be considered ethical. For instance, in 1912 Brower and explorer-anthropologist Vilhjalmur Stefansson wanted Barrow Natives to assist with the excavation of archaeological remains from nearby village sites. They found a novel method of payment—chewing gum. Stefansson explained that at the time Barrow was suffering through "a chewing gum famine, and men, women, and children were willing to do anything to get a little gum. When therefore Mr. Brower put at my disposal the unlimited credit of his firm and the resources of his storehouse, and when I announced that I was willing to pay in chewing gum for the excavation of the native village sites of the neighborhood, every one from the children to the most decrepit turned out to help me in the work." In exchange for the chewing gum, Stefansson's workers dug out 20,000 artifacts which the explorer boxed and shipped to the American Museum of Natural History in New York.[19]

To condemn Brower out of hand simply because he does not always meet modern expectations grossly distorts the historical record. When he smashed stills in the village to stop the manufacture of bootleg whiskey, and threatened to cut off the supply of flour to the entire village if any of his employees used their ration to make hooch, he may have been acting in a high-handed, paternalistic fashion by today's standards. But he saw direct action as the only way to save the Inupiaq from self-extinction.[20] To no avail he warned the Inupiaq not to abandon their warm—but to foreign senses dirty—sod igloos in favor of drafty frame houses, as the missionaries were urging them to do. "I tried to get them not to buy lumber," Brower wrote. "I knew they would not be as comfortable in a small frame house as they were in their own style igloos, [which] it has taken them centuries to develop."[21] When large numbers of Natives crowded into these ill-heated wooden shacks, many caught pneumonia and died.

Likewise Brower opposed the missionary-inspired destruction of the Native dance houses, which were torn down and used for fuel. He thought it criminal to teach the Natives not to hunt whales on Sunday, as it "may be the only day during the season they have a chance to get their meat and blubber to last them for a year." In a similar vein the missionaries wanted to keep the Natives off the trapline, so that villagers could more readily attend church services at least three times a week. "I thought that they could be religious out in the country as well as here and still make a living," Brower said, admitting that he "had to almost force" Native trappers out of town during the trapping season.[22]

Archdeacon Hudson Stuck, the enlightened, circuit-riding Episcopal priest on the Yukon who once claimed that the worst thing in Alaska were the "low-down white men," stayed with Brower for several weeks in the course of a 1917–1918 dog sled trip across the Arctic. Stuck found

Brower to be a realist, who cherished "no delusions about the Eskimos, [but] his attitude towards them was entirely kindly and sympathetic." According to Stuck, Brower's long and intimate association with the Eskimo people "had given his observant mind a penetrating insight into their character, and into their manners and customs, past and present" superior to almost anyone he had ever met.

Visiting scientists would echo Stuck's pleasure at finding Brower to be a virtual one-man arctic research institute. The archdeacon called Brower "the best informed man on all Arctic matters that I found on this coast.... He had met every man of note, explorer, traveller, scientist, who had visited these parts for more than a quarter of a century.... I found him a mine of information, a mine that I dug in a good deal during those two weeks and I sit here today wishing I had dug in more."[23]

Naturalist Alfred M. "Bill" Bailey of the Denver Museum of Natural History became acquainted with Brower on an arctic collecting expedition in 1921, and launched Brower on a notable career as an amateur ornithologist and biologist. Bailey taught Brower and his sons how to preserve specimens of birds and small mammals for shipment to museums across the United States. Over the next quarter-century the Brower family added sixty-three new species or subspecies to the list of known birds in arctic Alaska, contributing more "to the knowledge of Arctic birds than...all other collectors who have visited the north."[24] In 1929 the University of California Museum of Vertebrate Zoology published a pamphlet entitled "Mammals Collected by Charles D. Brower at Point Barrow, Alaska," detailing the ninty-seven shrews, weasels, foxes, marmots, squirrels, lemmings and voles, which Brower sent them to "add to the meager information available about the fauna of northern Alaska." Yet another tribute came from the Chicago Academy of Sciences. In 1933 Brower was second author on a paper with Alfred Bailey, entitled "Birds of the Region of Point Barrow, Alaska." The prestigious academy cited Brower's "notable contributions" in building its fine collection of arctic birds.[25]

Brower's keen interest in archaeology, history and ethnology, and his expertise in the Inupiaq language, made him a natural colleague of anthropologist and explorer Vilhjalmur Stefansson. From their first meeting in 1908, the two men remained friends until Brower's death thirty-seven years later. Though vastly different in age and educational backgrounds, the Harvard-trained anthropologist and the self-taught trader shared a strong work ethic and a love of learning. Brower interpreted for Stefansson when the explorer first came to Alaska, and instructed him in Arctic lore and history. When Brower came south for the winter every seven or eight years, he and Stefansson would renew their old friendship, sometimes at the Explorer's Club in New York, where Brower became a member under Stefansson's auspices.[26]

In the 1920s Stefansson, a prolific author with about two dozen books and hundreds of articles to his credit, convinced Brower to write a memoir of his life in the Arctic. Once the trader started typing his whaling stories, he did not stop until he reached nearly nine hundred pages. Though rich in historical and ethnological detail about whaling and trading in the Arctic, the huge manuscript he mailed to Stefansson in 1928—later entitled "The Northernmost American"—was plainly not publishable in its original form. Only the strongest readers could have possibly endured even half of its nine hundred pages, and Brower readily admitted the weaknesses of his writing style. "I realize that it is bum," he said, "the spelling bad, and the punctuation worse, and that to be of any value it will have to be rewritten by someone that knows how...."[27]

The first publisher whom Stefansson consulted about the manuscript identified the most obvious defect; though Brower could spin yarns all day about Native life, and remembered every fight he ever had and every animal he ever killed, he obviously had not felt comfortable writing or reflecting about himself. Despite the enormous bulk of the manuscript, he revealed precious little about his personal life or his family, never mentioning his second wife Asianggataq, to whom he had been married at that time for nearly twenty-five years, and ignoring most of his fourteen children. Stefansson told Brower that publisher William Morrow read the manuscript and "thinks you are a little bit self-conscious when you are talking about yourself and hopes you will get over it, reminding yourself of the manner in which you wrote the Eskimo yarns and trying to do the rest of your writing as much as possible in that spirit."[28]

A naturally private man, Brower seldom spoke of his personal life to anyone, especially to strangers. "I had seen a reporter try to get information from Brower," teacher Leon Vincent once wrote. "Seated on the edge

of a counter, notebook in hand, he had fired questions at the old king for
half an hour. Each thrust was parried with masterful evasiveness. His
queries met a stone wall of polite nothingness."[29]

Brower's bird-watching friend, "Bill" Bailey at the Denver Museum
of Natural History, edited and serialized some portions of the memoir
in 1932–1934 for *Blue Book*, a men's adventure magazine. But the style
and size of the manuscript continued to scare away book publishers, all
of whom wanted a ghostwriter to re-work it as a romance or a novel. As
the years passed Brower grew more disillusioned. "My book has been to
allmost (sic) all the big publishers in New York," Brower wrote Stefansson
in February 1941, "so have just about given up hopes that it will ever be
published."[30]

Just a few months later, in June 1941, Dodd, Mead and Co. in New
York finally agreed to publish Brower's autobiography. Released in
1942, fourteen years after Brower had completed the bulk of the
original manuscript, *Fifty Years Below Zero* had been substantially
shortened and polished by two collaborators whose names shared the
title page: Philip J. Farrelly, an old friend of Brower's from San
Francisco, and Charles Lyman Anson, a professional rewrite man.
Farrelly and Anson deleted hundreds of pages from the original
manuscript, including Brower's sea stories of his life before Alaska,
intending to put those out in a separate book for boys—which was
never released. At Brower's request Farrelly used as an introduction
the remarks Stefansson had previously written for the *Blue Book*
serialization of Brower's life. Stefansson had never seen the final,
much-shortened version of the book, but nevertheless he predicted that
if Charlie "writes with a third of his conversational zest and charm, it
will be literature."[31]

Only after the book appeared did Anson and Brower actually meet for
the first and only time, when Brower came south to Chicago in 1942 to
help promote the book. According to Anson, Brower claimed that when
he had received his initial copy, he stayed up all night reading his own
autobiography to "see how it 'came out.'" Though clearly pleased with
the book and delighted to see it finally in print, Brower commented to his
long-distance collaborator, "Somehow I don't seem to remember a lot of
that conversation you put in."[32]

The book was well received. A reviewer for the *New York Times* in 1942 called it a "markedly straightforward and modest" account by a unique individual. "Being alone in the snow brought forth no philosophy, and trekking in bitter weather brought forth no lyrical prose about snow and ice, but he got where he was going."[33]

Three years later, in February 1945, Charlie Brower died of a heart attack in Barrow. He was eighty-two. At the time of Brower's death Stefansson was planning a trip to Barrow with a group of military historians so they could meet the "King of the Arctic" first hand to hear his "fascinating narratives and philosophizing." When he heard of Brower's death, Stefansson called off the trip. Without Charlie Brower to greet him at the store, Barrow would never be the same.[34] Nevertheless, thanks to Stefansson's prodding in the 1920s, which had forced Brower to sit down at a typewriter, the generations who never had the opportunity to hear him yarn away about old times in the whaling trade can still catch a glimmer in *Fifty Years Below Zero* of the way it used to be.

—*Terrence Cole*

Notes

1. Margaret B. Blackman, *Sadie Brower Neakok: An Inupiaq Woman* (Seattle: University of Washington Press, 1989), 45.

2. "Memorandum as to the Wreck of the *Navarch*," Box 3, Folder 7, Brower Papers, Stefansson Collection, Dartmouth College Library.

3. The major source on Brower's life is his original 895 page unpublished memoir, "The Northernmost American," from which *Fifty Years Below Zero* was drawn. The published book was heavily edited and rewrittten in parts by Philip Farrelly and Charles Lyman Anson, and constitutes just a small portion of the original work. Both the Stefansson Collection at the Dartmouth College Library and the Rasmuson Library at the University of Alaska Fairbanks, have copies of the complete typescript. The Charles D. Brower Papers in the Stefansson Collection and the Alfred M. Bailey Papers in the archives of the Denver Museum of Natural History both contain valuable Brower correspondence.

The title page of "The Northernmost American" stated—apparently erroneously—that Brower's middle name was David. Both his application for membership in the Explorer's Club and his obituary in the

New York Times (13 February 1945, 23) record it as DeWitt. See also Charles Lyman Anson, "Arctic Man," *The Alaska Sportsman*, December 1949, 20.

4. Brower, "The Northernmost American," 4-8.

5. Ibid., 1.

6. Ibid., 103.

7. Ibid., 108, 110.

8. The best overview of the whaling industry in the Alaskan Arctic is John R. Bockstoce, *Whales, Ice & Men: The History of Whaling in the Western Arctic* (Seattle: University of Washington Press, 1986). See also John R. Bockstoce, *Steam Whaling in the Western Arctic* (New Bedford: Old Dartmouth Historical Society, 1977).

9. Bockstoce, *Whales, Ice & Men*, 27-29.

10. Brower, "The Northernmost American," 202.

11. For the impact of shore-based commercial whaling on Barrow see: Joseph Sonnenfeld, "Changes in Subsistence Among Barrow Eskimo," Arctic Institute of North America, 1956. For the ethnology of the Barrow area see: John Murdoch, *Ethnological Results of the Point Barrow Expedition* (Washington: Smithsonian Institution Press, 1988).

12. Leon Vincent, "King of the Arctic," Part 3, *The Alaska Sportsman*, November 1959, 20.

13. Quoted in Alfred M. Bailey's preface to "The Charles Brower Journal," Bailey Papers, Denver Museum of Natural History. The Brower family's life is most fully treated in Margaret B. Blackman's excellent oral history of Charles Brower's daughter Sadie, entitled *Sadie Brower Neakok: An Inupiaq Woman*.

14. Blackman, *Sadie Brower Neakok*, 48.

15. Leon Vincent, "King of the Arctic," Part 2, *The Alaska Sportsman*, October 1959, 41.

16. Leon Vincent, "King of the Arctic," Part 4, *The Alaska Sportsman*, December 1959, 37; Blackman, *Sadie Brower Neakok*, 257.

17. Blackman, *Sadie Brower Neakok*, 15; Molly Lee, "Baleen Basketry of the North Alaska Eskimo," (M.A. Thesis, University of California Santa Barbara, 1982), 16.

18. Quoted in: David Boeri, *People of the Ice Whale: Eskimos, White Men and the Whale* (New York: E.P. Dutton, 1983), 256.

19. Vilhjalmur Stefansson, *My Life With the Eskimo* (New York: Macmillan Co., 1924), 387-388.

20. Brower, "The Northernmost American," 494.

21. Ibid., 573.

22. Ibid., 694.

23. Hudson Stuck, *A Winter Circuit of Our Arctic Coast* (New York: Charles Scribner's Sons, 1920), 213, 214.

24. Alfred M. Bailey, *Birds of Arctic Alaska* (Denver: Colorado Museum of Natural History, 1948), 40; see also Alfred M. Bailey, *Field Work of a Museum Naturalist* (Denver: Denver Museum of Natural History, 1971), and the Brower-Bailey correspondence in the archives of the Denver Museum of Natural History; Alfred M. Bailey, Charles D. Brower, and Louis B. Bishop, "Birds of the Region of Point Barrow, Alaska," *Program of Activities of the Chicago Academy of Sciences*, Vol. 4, No. 2, April 1933.

25. E. Raymond Hall, *Mammals Collected by Charles D. Brower at Point Barrow, Alaska* (Berkeley: University of California Press, 1929).

26. For information about the relationship between Brower and Stefansson, see the collection of Brower-Stefansson correspondence in the Brower Papers in the Stefansson Collection, Dartmouth College Library.

27. Brower to Stefansson, 25 February 1928.

28. Stefansson to Brower, 20 April 1928; Blackman, *Sadie Brower Neakok*, 37-38.

29. Leon Vincent, "King of the Arctic," Part 3, *The Alaska Sportsman*, November 1959, 18-19.

30. Quoted in Blackman, *Sadie Brower Neakok*, 37

31 Philip Farrelly to Stefansson, 10 June 1941, 21 June 1941, 14 July 1941; Stefansson to Farrelly, 13 June 1941; Stefansson Collection, Dartmouth College Library.

32. Charles Lyman Anson, "Arctic Man," 22.

33. *New York Times*, 13 February 1945, 23; "Uncle Sam's Most Northerly Citizen," *The New York Times Book Review*, 4 October 1942, 30.

34. Vilhjalmur Stefansson, *Discovery: The Autobiography of Vilhjalmur Stefansson* (New York: McGraw Hill, 1964), 353.

Courtesy Dartmouth College Library

CHARLES BROWER (STANDING) AND VILHJALMUR STEFANSSON (SEATED)

INTRODUCTION

ON AND off for the last half century Charlie Brower has been Uncle Sam's most northerly citizen. The honor was taken for a spell by his partner an old friend Tom Gordon, who had a house three miles farther north; at another time Charlie Klengenberg camped six miles beyond, towards the Pole. But Klengenberg moved to Coronation Gulf and Gordon to Demarcation Point— both places farther east but also farther south. That left Brower what he had been earlier—America's most northerly pioneer.

Brower is what a loyal American likes to think of as a typical American. He is what you might expect of Manhattan Island born somewhere around Twenty-third Street when that street was far uptown: he is the logical development of a boy who was admitted to Annapolis but who left that road of gold-braided promotion for the paths of high and free adventure on unknown seas and shores. Meet him at the City Club in New York, and you think him what in a sense he was born to be, a typical successful and genial New Yorker; meet him at the Explorers Club of New York, to which he also belongs, and you will have difficulty in localizing him among that far-traveled company. For he talks Africa, and Australia of the Ballarat days, till you think him a Tropic rather than a Polar-man.

I write this to introduce a book which I have read in its original and rough draft, but I shall read it again with eagerness when it comes from the press in its finished and, I understand, more compact version. For if Charlie finally imparts a third of what he knows about whaling, pioneering, and about the Arctic, it will be a source-book on frontiering and high adventure; if he writes with a third of his conversational zest and charm, it will be literature.

But in any case the tale will be to me the life-story of one of my oldest and dearest friends—and in subscribing myself a friend I speak for most of the explorers, whalers, traders and missionaries who have reached or passed the north tip of Alaska since 1884. I speak, too, I am sure, for many captains and officers of the U.S. Coast Guard, for reconnaissance workers of the U.S. Geological Survey, for teachers whom the U.S. Bureau of Education has been pushing up toward Barrow of comparatively recent years, and for nearly everyone else who for any reason has come within reach of Charlie Brower's help and his cheer at any time during his fifty-eight years of keeping open house to all comers about three hundred and thirty miles north of the Arctic Circle.

Vilhjalmur Stefansson.

PROLOG

"So Charlie Brower is going to retire!"

This rumor, perennially floated by well-meaning friends in the States, is groundless.

True, I am nearing eighty and for the past fifty-seven years have lived north of the Arctic Circle—mostly right here at Point Barrow, eleven hundred miles from the Pole. Also, the long winter nights seem better suited than formerly to such mild pastimes as writing, preparing museum specimens or carving a bit of ivory. Finally, I'll have to admit that I don't bounce the way I used to after taking a tumble.

But retire? Why?

If there *were* any basis for the rumor, my friends might point, perhaps, to the haze of distance—it must be that—which is beginning to turn my few pre-Arctic years at sea into a thing apart, the misty prolog to a clear-cut play.

I have no recollection at all of a first brief period in New York City. But there, according to family reports, I was born in 1863 while my father was serving a second enlistment during the Civil War. It seems that we moved to—for some reason or other—Prairie Du Sac, Wisconsin. Here a baby brother first saw light, my older sister having been born in New York after Father, a natural wanderer, had come home from Japan at the outbreak of the war. How he managed next to lose all he had in a fling at Pennsylvania oil is still a blank.

But sometimes, working over a piece of ivory at night, my mind dreams back to flashes of the trip we made by lake and canal to rejoin Father in the east. Clearer yet is our settling at Bloomfield, New Jersey, followed by school—playing—swimming—fighting with other boys—learning a dollar's worth via the well-known newspaper route. All so many years ago . . .

1

I go at the ivory carving again, but only to picture myself at thirteen dragging my scanty "ship's boy" dunnage aboard the brigantine "Carrie Winslow," bound for Montevideo.

Then in no time, it seems, we are sailing back into New York harbor under a starry sky, my head crammed with six months of unbelievable yarns to spin the home folks. Suddenly there are shouts—looming lights too big for stars—the crashing and ripping of timbers as the "Carrie Winslow" is cut squarely in two by the "British America." Somehow I find myself floundering around in very wet water, grabbing desperately at a piece of wreckage . . .

Dim recollections follow of a rescue, months of recuperation at home; finally the start of another voyage, this time on a full-rigged, two-thousand-ton ship.

I can still feel that breath-taking thrill at my first sight of the "C. C. Chapman." Nor have I forgotten my reason for selecting her to sign on as ordinary seaman for a trip to Australia. It was the naive reason of a boy of fifteen—simply that she was the biggest boat I could find along the New York waterfront at the moment.

A beautiful ship, the "C. C. Chapman," despite the mixture of bitter and sweet she dealt me. Certainly much too fine a vessel for the end she was to meet.

My memories of her form the highlights of five years spent almost continuously at sea. Melbourne and Callao parade colorfully before my eyes. And there is a Peruvian hell-hole called Huanillos that stands out as the place where I go swimming off the ship and beat a shark back to the gangway by inches.

Rounding Cape Horn for Liverpool and Calcutta under fair winds makes me lose respect for the "hardships" of the Horn. I regain my respect with interest, though, on a subsequent voyage from Dublin to San Francisco. We are carrying railroad iron and iron car-trucks, and this time the Horn is ready for us.

We never do get around. After bucking a five-weeks' gale, suddenly those iron car-trucks break loose and start battering the daylights out of our wallowing craft. Then comes a nightmare period below decks, dodging wheels and axles as they roll drunkenly around in the shadowy light of swaying lanterns. But we discover a trick to this. After skipping aside or jumping over them when they lunge towards us, we learn to stand still on the equal chance that they'll not come all the way. It seems to work just as well, and after two days and nights we manage to secure them, one by one.

Meanwhile, the "Chapman," listing badly, comes about, turns tail on the Horn and scuds *eastward* for a run that takes us practically around the globe. And so, with a crew weak from scurvy and a captain gone stark mad, we make port, after all. Two hundred ten days, Dublin to San Francisco! A record of some sort, no doubt, even for those times. . . .

I pick up my ivory carving again for another try. The little piece is nearly finished. So also, in retrospect, are my sailoring years. For it is the "C. C. Chapman's" last cruise, and now at nineteen I am third mate of her when we leave Antwerp and stand out to sea, bound once more for San Francisco.

No iron car-trucks in our hold this time to break loose at a critical moment; nothing but good safe scrap-iron, blacksmith's coal, furniture, sulphur, plate glass, gin—things that stay put. It looks like an easy trip ahead.

It is—at first. The only shifting of cargo occurs when some of the gin shifts from the hold into our new first mate. But in spite of a drunken mate things go fine until we run into a sudden blow well down the coast of Patagonia. The gale itself is nothing. But just as we are letting go the main, a coil of rope, running free, catches the captain's leg and throws him to the deck, breaking his hip.

We patch him up as best we can. Finally the "Chapman" rounds the Horn in good shape. We head north with fair winds. A time even comes when the Old Man is able to hobble about on deck. Luck, it seems, is with us still.

Then one day, far off Valparaiso, somebody notices a smell of gas coming up the fore hatch. Presently smoke issues from a ventilator in the fo'castle. We find the captain.

"Get the main hatches off and locate the fire!"

Easier said than done. Only one hatch gives access to the bottom of the hold past that plate glass, and we know by the smell that the fire isn't there. Unfortunately, it's in the blacksmith's coal where nobody can get to it.

The captain, hobbling about, barks out orders, one of which is to keep pouring water down, just the same—tons of it. Too slow in passing empty buckets up, the men begin tossing them. Then someone misses, an empty hits the captain, knocks him down and breaks his hip again in the same place. We carry him below in agony. And the best we've done to the fire is fan it into a fresh start by opening those hatches.

Hurriedly they are slammed on tight again. For the next few days all hands are busy stuffing putty and oakum into every crack that smells of smoke. Although this seems to hold the fire under control, San Francisco is still six thousand miles away. Shall we head for some South American port while there's time? It's up to the Old Man to decide. With all his money invested in the ship, he takes a gambler's chance. The word comes up from below:

"Keep on to 'Frisco!"

We hold our course. When nothing happens, day after day, the men breathe easier. Twelve days now since discovering the fire. Maybe we've got it licked, after all.

Early next morning the main hatches blow off with a bang and some of us are overcome by the rush of gas. Others heave the hatches back into place and batten them down. Too far off South America to turn back now, there's nothing to do but set every foot of canvas that she'll carry and drive on.

We cross the line. A few days later the deck grows too hot to walk on barefoot. Pitch melts in the seams and oozes out. Our shoes track it over the ship as we work. Next, the main fresh-water tank heats up until the water boils. Every day or so the hatches blow off without warning. We expect the whole ship to go sky-high any minute.

There come times when it seems we can't stand the strain another hour. All the boats long since have been made ready, but somehow nobody mentions launching them. To abandon ship would mean almost certain death for the Old Man in his condition. So we sail the ship, sit tight and hope the fair wind holds.

It does better, finally whipping up to a gale that tears our light sails to shreds. The end, we feel, is near. It isn't a matter of days now, but of hours—of minutes. Yet seamen scramble recklessly aloft to bend on spare canvas. For the next three days and nights the old "Chapman" travels as she hasn't traveled in years.

As we near the California coast at last, still outwardly intact except when a hatch blows off, the wind lets down some. We sight the Farallones one afternoon, pass them a little after five. We cross the bar. We sail up the bay into San Francisco, rounding to smartly, as though nothing were wrong. At ten that night we anchor off Long Wharf, our destination.

It seems like a miracle. The men, too exhausted to dwell on miracles or anything else, stagger below. What do they care? Fifty-two days and nights they've been sitting on a volcano. Now, come what may, they'll risk a few hours' sleep.

Luckily, we rout them out at four next morning. About five the fore and main hatches blow off again, and for the first time flames roar up through the main, with more fire licking through our port side just abaft the fore rigging.

Two fireboats lying at Vallejo Wharf spot that flare and hurriedly steam alongside. Still playing their streams on the doomed old "Chapman," they tow us down the bay behind Mission Rock and there pump water into us until we settle ignominiously into the mud, our deck barely awash. So the voyage ends. . . .

So, too, the curtain drops on this brief but necessary prolog. What follows is the main Arctic performance that has been unfolding ever since. It will keep right on, I feel, for some time yet.

That is, if I don't retire.

CHAPTER I

To A boy not yet twenty-one but already fed up with the solitude of seven years at sea, the bustling San Francisco of 1883 looked like the Promised Land.

"No more lonesome places for *me!*"

That was my one thought while elbowing through the crowds in search of a job. I turned down the first one offered because it came, ironically enough, from the City Fire Department and I'd had enough fire for a lifetime.

It was some months later while working for a newspaper that the old lure of wide horizons and far places began to stir. Africa, for example. I'd always wanted to see what Africa was like inside.

Gradually the conviction took hold that somehow Fate would set me in Africa yet—little dreaming that ladies' corsets even then were shaping my course in exactly the opposite direction.

Ladies' corsets! For without them there would have been no demand for whalebone, hence no great whaling fleets of sturdy wooden vessels, sail and steam, manned by men the like of whom the world had never known.

The importance of whaling in those days can be understood when you remember that whalebone was worth around five dollars a pound and that a self-respecting whale was likely to be carrying anywhere from five to ten thousand dollars' worth of corset stays "in the rough." Result: A far-flung Arctic industry with hardship, disaster and violent death on one side of the ledger, balanced by fabulous profits on the other.

Profits were never so large, however, that an alert outfit like the Pacific Steam Whaling Company didn't try to cut operating costs in every way. And since one aggravating source of expense was the high cost of shipping coal to the far north for use of its

6

fleet, reports of certain coal veins near Cape Lisburne, Alaska, on the Arctic Ocean, called for immediate investigation.

Which was Fate's way of turning me into what some of my more romantic friends call "the most northernly citizen of the Western Hemisphere."

Quite unexpectedly, the Pacific Steam Whaling Company had offered me a chance to accompany a small party to Arctic Alaska on this coal mining proposition. They were also to trade with the Eskimos for furs, whalebone and ivory. I was mulling it over, my thoughts still leaning towards Africa, when my old shipmate, George Leavitt, hove into view. I blurted everything out.

"Going to take it, Charlie?" he asked.

"Would you?" I countered.

Somewhat to my amazement, George not only would but *did*. And so did I.

In the Company's office shortly afterwards we were introduced to a Captain Ned Herendeen who was getting ready to leave for Point Barrow to start a new whaling station for the same outfit. It seemed he had just spent two years up there with Lieutenant Ray of the United States Army Survey, and had convinced the Company that Point Barrow would be a fine place to whale when the ice broke up in spring.

Our little coal prospecting party consisted of four in all. J. J. Haverside was in charge. The others were George Leavitt, a man named Henry Woolfe and myself. Knowing nothing of the Arctic, George and I were busy boys those last days before sailing, trying to round up what we considered essential to such a venture. We made plenty of silly mistakes. But among my few sound hunches was a trip to San Leandro for an Eskimo dog that somebody wanted to give away. Mark proved a fine, big fellow and I kept him in the north as long as he lived.

We put out of San Francisco early in June on a little schooner, the "Beda," under command of Captain Gage who had never sailed the Arctic before; our main cargo, coal and other supplies for the fleet.

Heading across the North Pacific, we made Atka, one of the

Aleutian Islands, two weeks later. Then, after landing four copper prospectors on Solonois Island, a pin-point of land so tiny
that I've never found it on any map, the "Beda" turned northward up Bering Sea for the Pribilof Islands. This was the run
that gave me my first taste of Arctic fog and storm.

In those days mail went to Alaska by any craft headed in that
general direction, and since we had a load of it for precipitous,
wind-swept St. Paul, one of the Pribilofs, we tried hard to land
it somewhere near the settlement. With the wind wrong, there
wasn't a chance. The lee of the island was bad enough because of
high surf.

I was used to surf landing, however, and promptly volunteered
to try it with the small boat and one other man.

As we neared the beach, we regretted our rashness. Only the
eager looks of the waiting populace kept us on until it was too
late to quit, anyhow. There was nothing to do but wait for an
enormous roller, then start in, rowing desperately.

As soon as we hurtled, ker-blam, on to the beach, men rushed
shoulder-high into the water, grabbed the boat on both sides and
landed us in the midst of as extraordinary a setting as I ever saw
before or since.

It wasn't the Aleuts themselves that astonished me, deliriously
happy though they were to get long-delayed mail from "outside."
What made my eyes pop was the sight of seals—seals—seals.
Millions of them, it seemed, in every direction!

We had been too busy trying to keep right-side-up to realize
that we were heading straight into the center of where these
numberless females had their pups, one to a mother. Only here
and there was an old bull who had hauled out early in the season,
gradually gathering his harem around him as they arrived later.

No matter where we went, there was nothing either way but
these breeding rookeries. I never could have imagined such a sight.

It was curious to see how the young males kept together in a
section they had set apart for themselves. I noticed, too, that a

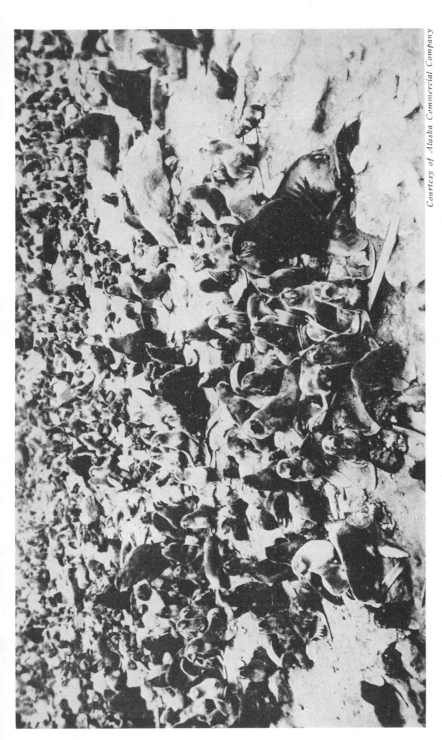

Courtesy of *Alaska Commercial Company*

ST. PAUL, ONE OF THE SEAL ISLANDS, HALFWAY BETWEEN THE ALEUTIAN ISLANDS AND BEHRING STRAITS. THE SEALS ARE MOSTLY FEMALES WITH THEIR PUPS, BUT HERE AND THERE IS AN OLD BULL

Courtesy Arnold Liebes

ESKIMO KAYAK

good many of the pups seemed alone, and asked if they were orphans.

The man laughed. "Their mothers are off fishing, that's all. Sometimes leaves 'em alone for two days at a time. But you take the old bulls, now, they're different. No, sir, you don't catch an old bull quitting the island till the breeding season is over."

Pondering over the private life of the seal, we finally remembered the "Beda" lying offshore and came to with guilty consciences. Friendly hands helped launch the little boat through the breakers and presently we climbed aboard our schooner thoroughly soaked, to be welcomed by Captain Gage with choice remarks about "three hours to put a mail sack ashore." But it was worth it.

After breaking anchor, we headed north again, our destination distant Point Hope where we were to meet the whaling fleet and give them their coal.

Raising St. Lawrence Island days later, we finally entered shallow Bering Strait and, leaving the Diomede Islands to port, skirted Cape Prince of Wales where Cape Mountain marks the westernmost tip of the continent. At this point the Strait is only fifty-six miles wide, and it gave me a strange, exhilarated feeling to see North America on one side of me and the dim outlines of Siberian hills on the other.

Creeping northward into the Arctic Ocean, we encountered our first scattered ice, a new and disconcerting discovery for good Captain Gage. So disconcerting that, instead of heading direct for Point Hope, he went over to the east along the edge of the ice. The result of his unnecessary caution was that on July 1, 1884 we anchored under the lee, not of Point Hope but of Cape Krusenstern, miles south. It took another two days to work our way north to the fifteen-mile finger of sand which forms Point Hope.

There was plenty of ice offshore the whole distance, but long before reaching our rendezvous the sight of some seventy whaling ships of all kinds encouraged Captain Gage to hold his course.

Presently, two of our Company's vessels steamed up and piloted us through small strips of ice until we anchored on the south side of Point Hope in a good lee.

The direct water route from San Francisco was about thirty-five hundred miles. The actual distance we had sailed was anybody's guess. I only know that Captain Gage wasn't the only one to heave a sigh of relief as we set about distributing mail to all the ships' boats which promptly surrounded us.

As fast as they got it, away they went, leaving the captains of our own ships aboard to settle in what order they would get their coal. Captain Everett Smith of the steam whaler "Bowhead" drew first chance, so that same night—it was light all the time now—we warped the "Beda" alongside the "Bowhead" and gave him his fuel.

Captain Smith was a fine man and an old-timer at the whaling game, and it happened that he and his crew were feeling extra good over getting eight large whales. Just the same, I thought it a rare kindness for him to insist on steaming all the way back to Port Clarence for an Eskimo and his wife who were to cook for our coal prospecting party.

Third in line for her fuel was the "Orca," under command of Captain Colson. It had been arranged that the "Orca" was to take us the rest of the way to those coal veins north of Cape Lisburne, and we lost no time transferring all our supplies and equipment to Captain Colson's vessel. Considering the complete "knocked-down" house we had brought along from San Francisco, this proved quite a job. But we heaved and tugged and got the last piece stowed just in time, so we thought,—only to find ourselves camped there for three more long days and nights while the deck swarmed with Eskimos trading whalebone. The guttural hubbub never stopped.

What impressed me was the air of prosperous independence of these natives. But whalebone was selling at the time for more than four and a half dollars a pound. So why shouldn't they feel cocky —at least compared to a handful of white adventurers in search of some half-mythical coal supply?

The crew, meantime, were entertaining us with tales intended to be helpful to greenhorns. For years, it seemed, whenever a ship was wrecked in the Arctic the Eskimos had always been allowed to do with it as they pleased, even to ordering the crew off. Hence, their present reputation for being a bad lot. What they might do to a small party of white men wintering among them was a question. Some advised us to give up the idea entirely.

"At any rate," they warned, "if you ever see a bunch of 'em heading your way without their women and children, *lock yourselves in and be damned sure your guns are loaded*."

We promised.

In spite of their ominous predictions, we were glad to be on our way at last, and relieved when the "Orca" managed to steam up the coast as far as Cape Lisburne without meeting serious ice. When I mentioned our luck to Captain Colson, his square, grizzled face cracked into a grin and he pointed ahead.

Just around the Cape, we now made out what looked like a compact mass of ice.

George and I had been at sea together for several years but ice navigation was new to both of us. We watched the "Orca" tackle the job with something more than casual interest.

A deep bight made in north of Cape Lisburne, it was twenty-four miles to where we were to erect our house, and the first twenty-two were packed by broken ice through which we twisted and turned to every point of the compass.

It was early evening when we entered the bight. By midnight all headway stopped. The captain now climbed into the crow's nest for a personal survey. His report: A strip of solid ice two miles wide separated us from clear water.

"That ends it for tonight," I said to George, secretly relieved. "I'm going below for a little rest."

Hardly had I pulled off my clothes when the engine-room bell rang for "astern." Then came "full speed ahead." Too tired to pay attention, I was about to crawl peacefully into my bunk when suddenly the "Orca" hit the Rock of Gibraltar and I landed in a heap against the forward partition.

Clawing on my clothes again, I rushed on deck, prepared for a scene of utter confusion. But nobody seemed disturbed or even excited as the "Orca" backed off preparatory to ramming the ice again.

This battering-ram procedure went on methodically the rest of the night. Sometimes the ship would slide up ten or fifteen feet on the ice and lie there, rolling a little from side to side as though catching her breath before plopping back into deep water. Occasionally her sheer weight would break the ice. More often it required repeated ramming. But always we made some progress, anyhow, and several hours later we crashed through the last of the floe. Then, nothing lay ahead but clear water to our destination.

Long before reaching it, however, I had acquired great and sudden respect for whaling captains. You couldn't help it after watching that night's work.

Captain Colson was no exception to dozens of others with whom I became intimately acquainted later. They hailed mostly from eastern states but all the old whaling centers were represented. Whatever else anyone may say about those two-fisted whaling captains of the Arctic, believe me they were *men*.

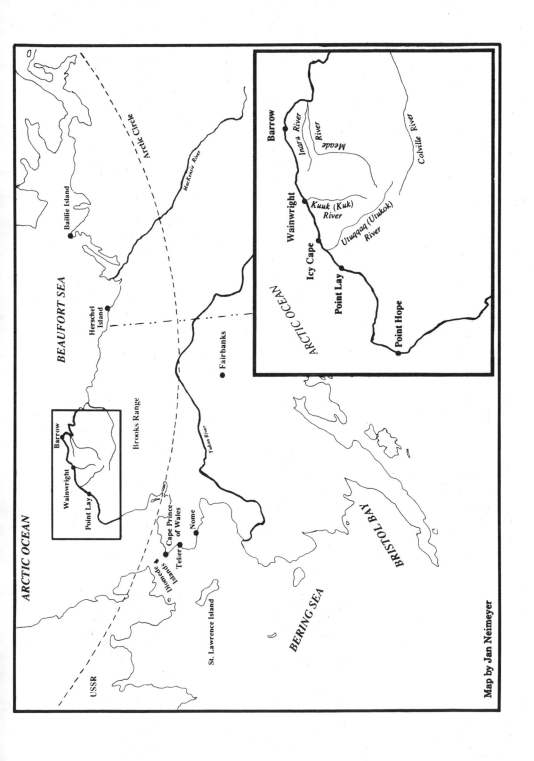

Map by Jan Neimeyer

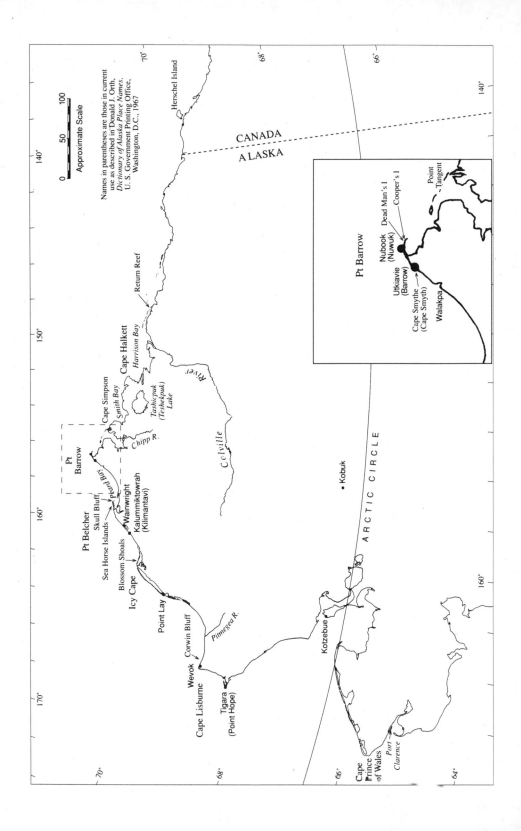

Approximate Scale

0 50 100

Names in parentheses are those in current use as described in Donald J. Orth, *Dictionary of Alaska Place Names*, U.S. Government Printing Office, Washington, D.C., 1967

70°

68°

66°

140°

CANADA
ALASKA

Herschel Island

Return Reef

Cape Halkett

Harrison Bay

Cape Simpson

Smith Bay

Tashicpuk
(Teshekpuk)
Lake

Chipp R.

Colville River

150°

Pt
Barrow

Skull Bluff

Peard Bay

Pt Belcher

Sea Horse Islands

Wainwright

Kalummiktowrah
(Kilimantavi)

Blossom Shoals

Icy Cape

Point Lay

Corwin Bluff

Pitmegea R.

Wevok

Cape Lisburne

Tigara
(Point Hope)

160°

170°

ARCTIC CIRCLE

Kobuk

Kotzebue

Cape
Prince
of Wales

Port
Clarence

70°

68°

66°

64°

160°

Pt Barrow

Nubook
(Nuwuk)

Dead Man's I

Cooper's I

Point
Tangent

Utkiavie
(Barrow)

Cape Smythe
(Cape Smyth)

Walakpa

CHAPTER II

CAPTAIN COLSON said that the place we were to land was called Corwin Bluff. We took his word for it.

It was a bluff, all right; too much of one to look very inviting. But half a mile south of the bluff proper we could see a gully with a small stream emptying on the beach. We pointed this out and the captain nodded.

"There's your spot."

The "Orca" had seven small boats. Two of them lashed together formed a sizeable raft for carrying lumber, and on top of the lumber could be piled all sorts of other supplies, including the house itself in knocked-down form.

Even before our crew landed the last load, Haverside and I hurried off for a first glimpse of the precious coal we had come so far to inspect.

There it lay, the larger veins cropping out on the beach itself. Each vein dipped two ways, one about forty-five degrees on the face of the cliff, the other pitching downward from the cliff. Eagerly we measured the biggest vein. Fourteen feet wide! Several others ran from six to nine feet. The rest were much smaller.

When two more Company vessels came in and all three crews set about erecting our house, we went at the coal again for a coldly calculating examination. Haverside finally shook his head:

"Never be able to mine that stuff to advantage. Get some out, maybe, working from the face of the cliffs. Want to try it?"

We did—and the earth came down in an avalanche.

Thinking us greenhorns, some of the crews from other ships tried getting an extra supply of coal, and nearly lost two of their men in the landslide that followed.

That settled it. Haverside decided to return to San Francisco at the first opportunity and report that coal mining at Corwin Bluff

13

was a lovely dream. George, Woolfe and I would hold the station in case the Company still wished to proceed. Nothing suited me better than the prospect of a long, care-free winter in that remote Arctic wilderness—unless, perhaps, it were Africa.

A day or two after the whalers had pulled out, leaving our house up but far from finished, the "Bowhead" put in from the south bringing Joe, our new cook, and his wife. Captain Smith also had aboard Captain Herendeen and all his equipment for the new whaling station at Point Barrow.

Joe proved to be a Port Clarence Eskimo married to a half-breed Russian woman. Joe's long suit was cooking, not cleanliness. Marenka made up for this, though, and kept the house neat enough, once we had it completed.

But putting on the final touches resulted in one of the most painful experiences I ever had. Working with a chisel, I was fool enough to use my hand as a mallet and soon raised a blister in the palm that turned into a felon. I wanted Woolfe to lance the thing, but he lost his nerve and wouldn't.

For three days and nights I walked the country for miles in every direction trying to lessen the pain. One morning, as the others were about to eat breakfast, a steamer hove in sight from the north. This turned out to be the "Baleana," another of our vessels, under command of Captain Bouldry.

When he came ashore I thought the pain in my hand must have driven me crazy because there beside him stood Captain Everett Smith. Hadn't I seen Captain Smith go north in the "Bowhead" just a few days before?

What brought him back was an incident all too common in those early whaling days; an incident of which I was to see many a more terrible example in the years to come.

After leaving us, the "Bowhead" had joined the other ships waiting at Icy Cape for the ice on Blossom Shoals to move. Captain Smith should have waited, too. He knew that now. For when he tried to get around the Shoals ahead of the others the ice suddenly came together, crushing in the "Bowhead's" starboard side and flooding her engine room.

"It held us up for three hours, anyhow," he explained, philosophically, "then, sudden-like—"

His downward gesture was eloquent.

"But, Captain," I asked, "what happened to your crew?"

Most of them, it seemed, had found their way to the other whalers still at Icy Cape. Herendeen with them, no doubt. Too bad about losing all his supplies for the new whaling station.

"What I want to do," he went on, "is leave the rest of my crew here with you. Most of 'em are on the 'Baleana.' "

"Here—with us?"

"Well, it won't be long. The 'Corwin' is due most any time now and—what in hell you been doing to your hand?"

He insisted on lancing the felon at once and I was more than willing. That over, the relief was so overwhelming that I went to sleep just sitting there on a box.

When I finally woke up the "Baleana" had sailed, leaving Captain Smith, his mate and several members of the ill-fated "Bowhead's" crew on our hands.

I shall never forget our first sight of strange Eskimos heading our way. "Lock yourselves in and be damned sure your guns are loaded." That was the warning which flashed to mind, only to be discarded sheepishly when the newcomers calmly set up camp near by.

There were two families. One from Wevok, a native settlement at Cape Lisburne, consisted of a huge, friendly fellow whom we nicknamed Baby, and who was accompanied by his sister, a smart looking girl of about twelve, named Toctoo. The other family comprised Unocoluto, his wife and their two small children, both adopted.

No invasion could have been more peaceful, no friendships more sincere. Physically the strongest man I ever knew, Baby was never to leave me for any length of time as long as he lived, while his little sister—but more of Toctoo later.

Corwin Bluff was a secluded spot even in that region of vast loneliness. Most of the whaling fleet—including sailing vessels called "crowbills" because only their "wings" carried them along—went by far offshore.

During this summer period, Captain Smith and his old Sharpe rifle introduced me to a basic Eskimo superstition that I later ran into in many forms. Schools of beluga, or whitefish—really a specie of small whale sometimes fifteen feet long—would often swim along the beach. These made fine pot-shots for Captain Smith who always managed to kill two or three out of a school. Although they sank at once, their white color was so easy to see in three fathoms that our Eskimo neighbors would spear the bodies from an oomiak and tow them ashore.

I happened to be there when they landed the second one killed. I wanted to cut it up at once but they wouldn't let me. It seemed a small request and their sudden firmness was surprising. As I stood watching silently, the women brought fresh water in a bucket and carefully poured some on the spouthole of the dead whitefish. The rest they sloshed over its head. Replying to my questioning look, they explained that the whitefish lived in salt water and therefore must have a drink of *fresh* water before being cut up.

Why?

Because otherwise its spirit would tell the rest of the whitefish and no more would ever be killed. The same great truth, it seemed, applied to any animal taken from salt water.

The "Corwin" arrived from the north in August and scooped up all our guests except a former shipmate of mine named Ed Black who had been on the lost "Bowhead." Black was anxious to stay with us and we were mighty glad to have another white man in the party. So, when Haverside returned briefly on the "Baleana" he engaged Black under the same arrangement that George and I had.

The "Corwin" gone, we dug out enough coal for our needs and settled down for the winter with little to do but explore our surroundings.

At first I was content to collect a lot of fossils from the adjacent cliffs. I took several boat-loads back to the house and the following summer sent them "outside" by Captain Mike Healy on the "Bear." Thus began my lifelong hobby of shipping Arctic specimens of flora and fauna back to the museums of civilization.

Getting more ambitious, I began to wander farther and farther on hunting trips. Then, late in August, with scattered ice still floating around outside, the male eider ducks began coming from the north. We built blinds on the ice and got a lot of these for winter use, preserving them in snow banks at the foot of the cliffs above our house.

After one long trek with Baby, I even shot my first bear—a Barren Ground grizzly. This success, coupled with a two-day hunting trip with Unocoluto and his family, gave me the idea that I could easily become a wonderful hunter all by myself.

To prove it, I started off alone one day, taking only a small lunch as I intended to be back by evening. All went well until I passed the first chain of hills four miles inland. Then suddenly fog closed in thick. However, I kept on, expecting it to lift any minute. When it didn't, I headed for the house, taking what I imagined was a short cut.

The Lord only knows where I wandered that day until stopped by darkness. Next morning I started for home again, pretty hungry by now. Although the fog was thick as ever, making the tundra appear like a featureless plain, I was sure I knew just where the house was now.

Several times that day I suddenly dropped ten feet or more over a bank, and once walked straight into a bluff covered with snow. It was a most curious sensation, not knowing where the next step would land me. But I kept on, moving cautiously, playing a game of blind man's buff in which I seemed destined to be "it" forever.

Darkness caught me stumbling along the bed of a small stream. There I kicked a hole in a snowbank, snuggled in and tried sleeping with the rifle underneath to keep it dry. But lying, hungry, on an old .44 brought little sleep, and morning was welcome even though the fog seemed thicker than ever.

So I groped along through the third day. Only now I had a stream-bed to follow which, I reasoned, would have to hit the ocean some time, some place.

It did—just as pitch darkness reenforced the fog. At least I'd reached a beach strewn with driftwood. I'd saved a few matches, too. Whittling some shavings, I soon had a fire blazing, its flames lighting up a hole in the all-pervading fog.

Awakening was like the sudden rise of a curtain on some brilliant stage setting. The day dawned cold and clear, with seagulls flying up and down the coast. I followed them with my eye and got quite a jolt on making out Cape Lisburne far to the south. Just why I should expect to find it *north* of me is something I never could explain.

Those gulls made my mouth water. Had any flown close I should have tried a shot. The hundreds of tom-cods washed up on the beach at my feet—that was another matter. All were frozen hard. If Eskimos ate them this way—crunching them down like potato chips—why couldn't I? At last I picked one up and shut my eyes tight. . . . It tasted good.

When I opened them again I distinctly saw a girl standing a little distance up the stream-bed. I blinked hard. She was still there. Suddenly, I recognized Toctoo, the sister of Baby, coming towards me.

It took a vast amount of chatter and pantomime for her to give me even a rough idea of what had happened.

When I didn't come home that first night, everyone grew anxious, and next morning all the Eskimos began looking for me. Toctoo had finally picked up my trail and followed it alone for two days and nights until—well, here she was.

Here, too, was hardtack and a can of meat she brought from the house. I don't believe she'd eaten a mouthful of anything the whole time.

Now, however, she proceeded to fill up on frozen tom-cods, after which we started home together along the beach.

Toctoo was only a little girl, but she knew how to take care of herself. Had I wandered through that fog in another direction, I have a feeling that she'd have found me, just the same.

It was an experience I'll never forget as long as I live.

CHAPTER III

SNOW covered the ground by the middle of September and my first attempts to navigate on snowshoes left the Eskimos weak with laughter.

Another source of constant amusement to them was our Siberian-made skin parkas which the "Corwin" had brought us. They were much longer than any made on the American side. The figure we cut in these cumbersome garments wrung the last drop of hilarity from the natives.

The tables were turned, however, when it came to dog-sleds. We had brought two hickory sled-frames with us fitted with steel shoeing, and I put them together at the first good snowfall. Crude as they were, they drew such admiration from all the Eskimos, who probably had never even seen a hardwood sled before, that soon we were basking in the reflected glory of white man's handicraft.

Returning home one night, we found another Eskimo family at our place. They had come ninety miles down the coast from Point Lay, and their reports of caribou only one short day north of us had all the Eskimos stirred up and eager to start immediately.

I had discarded the notion of ever becoming a great white hunter among the natives—getting lost in the fog had completed the deflating process—but if these caribou were half so plentiful as rumored, here, perhaps, was a chance to redeem myself.

I talked it over with George. Neither of us had ever taken a crack at a deer. And, after all, there wasn't much to do around the house.

"Why, sure," he said, carelessly, "I wouldn't mind bagging a few just for the fun of it."

So we went along with the natives, Baby insisting on acting as our body-guard and general factotum.

Whatever else that caribou hunt accomplished, it taught me

20

how to build a temporary snow shelter. These were quite distinct from the sod-covered igloos framed of driftwood or whales' ribs, that the natives of those regions used for permanent homes.

The shelter our Eskimos threw up for the duration of the hunt was rectangular, the longer dimension providing comfortable living space for a party the size of ours. The door was in the middle, with sleeping quarters at either end separated by a small open space where the stone oil lamp was kept. It didn't take long to build.

After choosing a snowdrift deep enough to dig out for the body of the house, they cut big blocks of snow and ranged them around the hole, placing one row above another so as gradually to slant towards the center of the house. When the walls were pretty well up, they cut top blocks so as to meet, forming a sort of gable roof.

Then they shoveled snow over everything. For the time being, not an opening was left. Next they dug away from one side down to the level of the bottom, and here cut their door through from the outside. We carried in our possessions and stowed them at either end. All that remained was the door itself.

This was a job for the last Eskimo who entered. He simply cut a final block of snow, attached a dog harness to it, crawled inside and hauled the door into place behind him. Now, everything was ready for the night.

Though lacking frills, our house was comfortable enough for the two weeks that George and I spent with the Eskimos hunting caribou.

I use "hunting" advisedly. We hunted. The natives killed. Our lack of success wasn't due to any scarcity of game. The place teemed with caribou. But where the Eskimos got over forty, George and I seemed unable to connect at all.

Finally, George quit in disgust. Perhaps I didn't possess George's independent spirit, but I did stick it out a while longer and managed to shoot three caribou. That helped.

Finally I grew tired of hunting, too, and on the fifteenth of November, according to my diary kept all these years, Baby and I returned to the station with our meat.

Up to this time I had been content to explore the vicinity of the station while awaiting the Company's decision on the coal. Now something I learned from a chance Eskimo visitor changed all this. He told of native villages far north, along the coast between us and Point Barrow. The fact that apparently no white man had ever traveled that bleak coast in winter lent added glamor to an idea slowly crystallizing in my head.

Why not visit those distant settlements, find out first-hand what the natives were like—perhaps, if all went well, even push on to Point Barrow, the extreme tip of the continent?

Both George and Woolfe were dead against any such scheme. Five or six hundred miles in the dead of winter without charts was crazy enough. But who knew what treatment a white man would receive from those distant tribes? Even if I got through to the top of the world, what, they pointed out, would I live on coming back?

"You forget," I argued, "that Captain Herendeen is probably at Point Barrow by now setting up the whaling station."

"What you forget, Charlie," they said, "is that his whole outfit went to Davy Jones' locker along with the 'Bowhead,' and God knows where Herendeen is himself."

"I'll bet on Herendeen getting through somehow. And if he's there, he'll give me plenty of grub to get back on."

"Suppose he isn't?"

"Well, if the natives can live along that coast, so can I."

When they found my mind made up, George and Woolfe reluctantly agreed that I might as well go—"and get it out of your system."

CHAPTER IV

It was decided that I should take two sleds and three Eskimos, including Baby if he cared to go. He did—emphatically. For the remaining two he recommended Kyooctoo, a good hunter living at Wevok on Cape Lisburne; also an Eskimo named Chipic who, he said, had once traveled along that north coast in winter and could find his way in any weather, like a fox.

Difficulty arose as soon as I broached the matter to Kyooctoo. Unlike Chipic, who looked forward to trading a wolverine skin at Utkiavie which he hadn't visited in several years, Kyooctoo was just plain scared. He told us over and over that the Innuit at Utkiavie were very bad people and would kill him.

But after much soothing and coaxing we finally got his half-hearted promise to go along.

The women seemed most concerned over my long Siberian parka. Figuring, perhaps, that I'd disgrace them among strangers, they suddenly got busy remodeling my outfit into something more in line with what the well-dressed Arctic traveler should wear. A pair of new sealskin pants was the finishing touch.

Meanwhile, sleds had been overhauled, dog harnesses and sled covers made and provisions gathered for the trip. By November twenty-fifth I couldn't think of another thing to do but start. So we might have set out lacking one great essential if, at the last minute, Baby hadn't tactfully mentioned food for the dogs.

We got off the next day, anyhow.

Camping that night at our recent hunting grounds where some of the Eskimos were still shooting caribou, we headed north along the coast at daybreak and made good time.

At dusk the natives threw up a hasty shelter of snow, using our sled covers for a top, then built a five-foot ledge of snow blocks on which to prop up the sleds overnight. Had the dogs ever reached them, there would have been nothing left of their hide lashings by morning.

My main job throughout the trip was to make a fire outside and do the cooking. Later, whenever a gale blew I always had to build a windbreak first. Trouble followed even then until I learned to use pieces of birch bark which had drifted in during the summer. These would light with a match, and once lit would never blow out.

Tonight was calm, so that a fire gave no difficulty. My trouble lay elsewhere. We were to have bean soup and hardtack, I remember, with tea a side dish. Everything got pretty well smoked up, but since no one kicked I considered my cooking satisfactory until I tasted the stuff myself. After which I followed the Eskimos' example and finished up on some raw frozen deer meat we had along.

Kyooctoo had been trying all day to tell me something that sounded like "Ah-kun nel-la-rog-a-mute took-a-roo." Finally I appealed to Baby. It was hard even for him to make me understand, although he went through all sorts of pantomime. First he would show me a piece of meat, then talk a streak and end by lying down with his eyes shut, at the same time repeating *"took-a-roo!—took-a-roo!"*

At last I caught on. What Kyooctoo had been endeavoring to drum into me all day was that *a white man would die in the cold weather.* That meant me. But why?

Again Baby fell back on alternate talking and gesturing, and after about an hour of this I was able to piece together the incident which had prompted Kyooctoo's warning.

It seemed that two summers before, three white men had deserted a whaler somewhere along that coast and managed to exist until winter when two of them died from exposure. The third, rescued by Eskimos and carried to their village near Cape Lisburne, developed pneumonia.

The natives of that region, according to Baby, never let a person die in one of their houses if they could possibly help it, since that meant abandoning the house forever. To avoid this, it was their custom to put the sick one out in a tent in summer, or a snow shelter in winter, there to die alone or recover, as the case might be.

But this dying white man presented a new problem. What to do with him they didn't know. As a last resort, the village devil-doctor beat his drum and went into a trance to find out. The result was that four of their women put the dying man on a sled—he was too weak to walk—slid him over to the Cape as gently as possible, then mashed his head in with rocks.

I resolved not to get sick.

Ever since leaving our caribou camp behind we had noticed the hills receding more and more. By the third day, I couldn't tell whether we were on land or ice. Whichever it was, the going proved good and we fairly ran to a village called Kukpowruk on a river of the same name. Nobody was home. We spent the night in one of their empty houses, anyhow, and next day found the populace camped in eight igloos at a bend near the river's mouth.

Their amazement was almost laughable as they never had seen a white man on that coast in winter. Everything they had to eat was trotted out for us and that evening all the men crowded into the igloo where I was staying to learn if I cared to trade for fox-skins.

Since good ones were then worth only two dollars each and it didn't take much merchandise to get one, I spent most of the night buying their entire supply. These I stuffed into a sack to leave there until I could pick them up on the way back. I had learned by now that in a deal of this sort Eskimos were absolutely honest.

Chipic urged that we stay here several days. He said the natives wanted us to and would be only too glad to feed our dogs. But I had no idea of the distance between villages and decided we'd better push ahead. As soon as it grew light, I called to Baby to get the others, then went outside to lend a hand loading the sleds.

One look at our dogs nearly gave me a fit. They resembled a bunch of Fourth of July balloons. Since I had refused to visit as long as they wished, the women had simply fed our dogs so much the poor animals could hardly waddle, let alone draw a sled.

I lost my temper and stamped around in the snow angrily telling the grinning natives what I thought of such a trick. They only grinned all the more. Finally, I joined in the general laugh.

But next morning before daybreak we got away in a northeast gale, the dogs traveling well from having eaten nothing since their recent gorge.

As daylight filtered through, the gale increased, whipping snow into our faces like blasting sand and making it impossible to see any distance ahead. Chipic, taking the lead as usual, led on unerringly until long after dark, when we reached another village on the inside bank of a long lagoon. Chipic seemed to know all these places. But how he ever found this one in weather which obliterated landmarks completely was a mystery.

Here again the people were away hunting, so that we had our choice of empty houses to make ourselves comfortable in until the gale should blow itself out.

It was going hard as ever next day. Along in the afternoon, however, a man and his wife struggled through from the hunting camp somewhere inland. They had run out of seal oil and had faced the storm to return for more. Their advent helped me out of a great inconvenience.

Since we were traveling on salt ice with no easy way to get a drink, I had been bothered continually by thirst, and Baby took it on himself to tell the woman about this. As a result, when we set out the second morning she presented me with an Eskimo "water bottle."

It was nothing but a seal's hind flipper. The meat and bone had been taken out and the skin dried. When starting on a long journey it was filled with fresh water. Then, whenever anyone took a drink, the skin was stuffed full of snow and carried under the attiga, or parka, next the body where the snow soon turned to water.

My flipper-canteen was a mighty handy item all the way up the coast. Ordinarily, the water tasted terrible, but if you were thirsty enough it was grand.

We found only one family home in the next settlement somewhere back of Icy Cape. They made up for it by feasting us and our dogs. This time, though, I saw to it that they didn't put the dogs out of commission entirely.

The sun had been below the horizon for some time now and the shortening days cut down the distance we could travel at a stretch. But driftwood fuel strewed the coast, often piling up several feet high, so we didn't mind camping wherever night caught us.

One afternoon, just before dark, we stumbled on quite a settlement, Kalummiktowrah, and for once the natives were all home. They poured out of every igloo, urging us to stay with them a long while. What white man's town, I wondered, would act the same to wandering strangers?

But when they let fall that there was an even larger village a few miles north I made up my mind to push on next morning. Still they persisted. As a last inducement, they politely offered me my choice of any of their young girls, and when I refused seemed to think me a very curious white man, indeed.

A rather startled one, I'll admit. It was the first time I'd run into this hospitable custom which later I found common enough all along the coast. The girls themselves didn't seem to object. It was a gesture of courtesy, little more.

The village they spoke of farther north proved interesting for several reasons. One was the flattering way its young men and girls pounced on us and dragged us, sleds and all, into their headman's igloo where meat and fish awaited us—along with the rest of the population.

Another worthwhile reason was the proposal made by Arngning, the headman. If we'd stop a while, he promised to go with us as far as Utkiavie, the biggest Eskimo settlement in Alaska and only eleven miles this side of Point Barrow itself.

I agreed to stay two days, but largely to placate Kyooctoo who had been getting more and more scared and was always urging delay. When our host, by way of small talk, described how badly the people of Utkiavie were treating Eskimos from the south, poor Kyooctoo nearly died. A couple of days' rest, I thought, might brace him up.

In general, Arngning's village resembled the others we had visited on the coast. But a few miles back beyond some hills I witnessed a really remarkable sight. Here were many veins of coal, some on the surface. I remember measuring one of them eight feet thick. Not only was all this coal on fire, but they said it had been burning for years, having started one summer long ago from the campfire of a careless hunting party. For all I know, the stuff is burning yet.

"But why don't you use it for fuel?" I asked, innocently.

That was considered a joke of the first water. What could they burn coal in but stoves? And who wanted *them?*

We lingered in that village an extra day, after all. I had forgotten for the moment the quaint Eskimo amenity of over-feeding visitors' dogs. But the next morning, having refused the customary offer of my choice of girls, I was relieved to start north again with Arngning and his dog-sled now added to our party.

Long before reaching Point Belcher and Sedaroo, its ghost-village of mostly-abandoned igloos, we began to notice empty casks along the beach—hundreds of them. Also, we passed the remains of several wrecked vessels, their battered hulks shoved high on the shore by ice.

The mystery was cleared up that night in Sedaroo. Keawak, the fine old headman of this once-populous settlement, told me the tale—a strange one of unavoidable shipwreck but needless human destruction.

It happened a number of years before when numerous vessels were wrecked in a great storm. According to custom, the Eskimos were soon ransacking their cargoes. Since white man's food meant nothing to them, they dumped flour all over the ice, using the flour sacks for sails and snow-shirts.

Ignorant as they were of white man's food, the natives knew all about white man's alcohol. They even believed that anything coming in a bottle was whiskey. When they broke into the ships' medicine chests, they promptly gulped down whatever the bottles contained.

Many died in their houses. And because none of the surviving Eskimos would ever go in to take them away, the bodies were still there even while Keawak was describing the catastrophe.

Much later, while visiting Sedaroo one summer, I found the houses falling apart—but those bodies still there.

It was anything but summer-like the morning we pulled out, joined now by Keawak who had suddenly decided to go a distance with us towards Utkiavie and Point Barrow. The weather was bitterly cold, brilliantly clear, with a full moon that threw everything into sharp relief over a two-mile radius.

All that day the crowd of us made excellent time along a huge lagoon back of Peard Bay. Finally, Keawak emitted a grunt of farewell and left us abruptly, heading inland. Our pace then slackened due to the nervousness of Baby now, as well as Kyooctoo. Neither knew just what the people of Utkiavie would do to strangers from the south.

We took three sleeps to cover that final stretch to Utkiavie. The last day our travel was very slow, indeed. We were always stopping to let Chipic and Arngning tutor the other pair on what they should do in the approaching crisis. One man was to follow each of them as they neared the settlement. Finally, they must make a run for it. If they could get into some house before any of the villagers knew they had come—especially if they could manage to *eat* something there—it would entitle them to be treated like guests for the time being, and at least stave off the inevitable rough stuff.

Utkiavie was situated on a bluff fifty feet above the ocean. A way this side we left the sea-ice and clambered up narrow paths to the top. From there, a trail led straight to the big cluster of houses five hundred yards ahead.

I stood there catching my breath from the steep climb when suddenly all four Eskimos started for the distant igloos as fast as badly-scared Eskimos could run, leaving me alone with the three sleds. Next instant our dogs spotted the village, too, and leaped forward excitedly, but couldn't keep up with the Eskimos.

Meantime, I had got out my old Colt revolver and strapped it under my parka—just in case. There was nothing to do then but hop on one of the sleds and let 'er go.

Whisked in among the igloos, I found myself promptly surrounded by what seemed hundreds of surprised natives, all talking and laughing at once. Some of the older ones shook hands with me as I sat there on the sled looking around. Then one of them, called Ooshalloo, invited me into his house where he insisted on my peeling off my parka. He was equally insistent that I get up on a shelf in the back of the room.

I hesitated a little, but did so. It wouldn't pay to let the old boy see that I was in any way alarmed. But, looking down at the crowd of natives who had wormed in after us, I had the distinct impression of being on exhibition for no good purpose.

Next, one of Ooshalloo's two wives took my shirt and cleaned it of snow, after which she silently handed me some black whaleskin, or muctuc, to eat—a sinister action like offering the last meal before an execution. I had finished one of the tough, rubbery slabs and was starting to gnaw the other, when all at once a powerful hand reached out from the crowd, grabbed me by the collar and yanked me clear to the middle of the floor.

I let go the muctuc and was fumbling desperately for my gun when a voice boomed out in perfect English,

"Drop that damned blackskin and come over to the house!"

No sight will ever be more welcome than the grinning, bewhiskered face of Captain Herendeen.

CHAPTER V

"COME on," he urged, enjoying my expression, "unless you prefer blubber to decent food."

I scrambled to my feet, pushed through the good-natured crowd and followed him until we came to quite a civilized wooden house half a mile from the village.

"You seem pretty much at home with that crowd," I said, as he ushered me in with a proprietory sweep.

"Why not? I lived here two years with Lieutenant Ray. He built this house for a magnetic observatory, you know."

Then I remembered how Herendeen had been with the International Magnetic Expedition as hunter in 1881 and 1882 before convincing the Pacific Steam Whaling Company that this was just the place to start a farthest-north whaling station. So here he was back, despite shipwreck and loss of supplies.

When the "Bowhead" went down off treacherous Blossom Shoals, he had taken to the ice with officers and crew and managed to reach another vessel of the fleet which had finally landed him exactly at his goal. Then, canvassing other whalers in the vicinity, he had succeeded in accumulating another outfit.

He said that as soon as Ooshalloo took me into his igloo, the young men had brought my sleds directly to him and told him that another white man had just come up the coast. So he had hurried over—and I knew the rest.

One thing I didn't know, and it worried me. Chipic and Arngning would probably be safe enough among these Utkiavie natives because they seemed to understand them. What would happen to the terrified Kyooctoo—and especially to Baby whom I thought the world of—was another matter. My last glimpse of them racing for cover was not encouraging.

"They're holed up in some igloo safe for a while," Herendeen guessed. "I doubt if you'll set eyes on them for a couple of days."

I didn't.

But there were plenty of other things to see. The period of dark days had brought all the Eskimos flocking into the village, which meant native dancing every night. All three dance houses were kept packed except for a cleared space in the center just large enough for two, or maybe four, to perform at a time.

I never saw more enthusiastic dancing. The men sat at the back of the house singing and beating tomtoms on their kelouns, or native drums. Presently, everyone in the place would be singing. Then, suddenly, a man would leap up and start dancing, going through all sorts of antics with his arms, yet always keeping perfect time. Next, a woman would join him, weaving her body sidewise from the hips up while her shuffling feet never missed a beat. Rhythm personified!

Twice I went to Nubook, a small nearby village out on the tip of Point Barrow, to see the dances there. At my second visit they put on quite a show.

It revolved around a ravenskin and a white foxskin fastened to a board in such a way that they could be worked by somebody in the background pulling strings. In trying to escape the fox, the raven hopped all over the board in realistic fashion. The story represented something out of their folklore, doubtless centuries old. I couldn't catch the fine points of the plot, but the way they did it was really clever.

One day a lone Eskimo came up the coast from Icy Cape. A poverty-stricken specimen he seemed, his sole wealth consisting of one turquoise bead and a couple of dogs hitched to a broken-down sled. He said he was on his way to Nubook to trade. I turned to Captain Herendeen:

"What can he get for one bead?"

"We'll see when he comes back."

Although many of the dancers sported beads, sometimes three or four heavy strings of them across their chests, I had noticed that they were of just two kinds—one a turquoise, the other made of blue glass with a white heart. Handed down through countless generations, their origin a mystery, they stood for wealth and affluence.

But that lone Eskimo's reappearance in Utkiavie, after concluding his trade with the headman at Nubook, showed the part these beads played in the economic life of the natives all along the coast. In exchange for his one turquoise bead, the fellow showed up with a new sled, five dogs, ten large slabs of whalebone, five cross foxes and one silver foxskin, *the value of which was well over a thousand dollars.*

On the afternoon of the thirteenth poor Kyooctoo came to me looking as if he'd been through a thrashing machine. Half the village was with him, everyone chattering excitedly. Learning that we'd be leaving for home shortly, the natives had assembled in two parallel lines and made Kyooctoo run the gantlet. Baby they had let off, since he belonged to a tribe south of Point Hope where this sort of thing was not customary.

In such a "game," the men's job, it seemed, was merely to keep the victim in line and prevent his breaking away and gaining the sanctuary of another igloo before finishing his run. They depended on their women to get in the real licks.

That the ladies had come fully up to expectations this time was evidenced by Kyooctoo's gory appearance. Scratched and gouged from head to foot, his clothing in shreds, he was a mess. I wondered what implements were responsible until I saw the women proudly displaying their fingernails, notched and sharpened especially for the event.

Reflecting on the probable outcome had these women been in anything but a playful mood, I got Kyooctoo patched up and mended and soothed, both physically and mentally. Three days later, on the sixteenth, we left Utkiavie with expressions of great good will from the natives, and—more to the point—an ample food supply from Captain Herendeen.

CHAPTER VI

REACHING the station some two weeks later, after a trip marked chiefly by Kyooctoo's relief at putting Utkiavie behind, I tried to settle down for the rest of the winter.

No use. Successful completion of that cold walk up the coast to Point Barrow and back brought on a restlessness which grew worse as I saw winter slipping away. What did the coast look like *south* of us?

When I broached the matter to Baby, he explained eagerly that if we went where he was brought up, two sleeps south of Tigara, we'd have fine hunting in the hills. Also his relatives, who were "good Eskimos," would undoubtedly sell me all the furs I wanted.

That last really settled it so far as I was concerned.

No sooner did Woolfe find out that Tigara on the tip of Point Hope was then considered the largest native village in Alaska, next to Utkiavie, than he wanted to go along that far himself to trade with the headman of so important a place.

That was all right with me. To insure added help in emergencies, I decided to take along a strapping young Eskimo named Awaclak, besides, of course, Baby. Then, on second thought, Woolfe persuaded Unocoluto to join the party in order to bring him back from Tigara with all his fancied booty.

Getting away at last, the five of us made Wevok that first night. Then, rounding Cape Lisburne in crisp, clear weather, we hurried south for two days and drew close to Tigara just before dark.

Unocoluto now revealed a great secret. Tigara, he announced, was his home village and we must stay at his house while there.

We might have done so except for being met at the outskirts by one of the strangest, most paradoxical specimens of the human race I ever encountered before or since. He was the headman, Attungowrah by name.

When this surly, thick-set brute with cunning eyes and Neanderthal jaw indicated that we would lodge with him, there was nothing more to be said. It was funny, though, to see the expression on Woolfe's face as he sized up the man he'd hoped to do some really profitable trading with.

We soon discovered that the whole village was scared to death of Attungowrah. Not only did the natives believe him the strongest man in the world, they were firmly convinced that he had the power to kill anyone he didn't like by *devil-driving*. To them, he was the greatest devil-doctor of all time. And, naturally, Attungowrah didn't go out of his way to argue otherwise.

After we had made ourselves at home, the Attungowrah household proved somewhat crowded because he kept four secondary wives there too. His head wife dwelt in a house by herself from which, however, she ruled the rest with a firm hand.

One day, for reasons I didn't understand at the moment, Attungowrah asked me to walk with him to the graveyard, which extended for miles and looked like a vast forest of small trees with their tops cut off. But instead of wood, the uprights were jawbones of whales to which were lashed the lower jaws of walrus. These last supported wood platforms and on them rested most of the bodies.

A few, though, still lay on the ground where they had been dragged on old sleds belonging to the deceased. All were wrapped in sleeping skins, and around each grave I saw articles that the person had used in daily life. For example, in the case of a woman there would be her sewing gear, her colura, or woman's knife, her cooking pots; perhaps even her personal ornaments.

A man's body was indicated by hunting implements, a pipe, now and then the keloun on which he had pounded out many a tomtom for dancers now long dead. If a child were buried, his toys littered the place. Whatever was left at a grave had been thoroughly smashed so as to be of no use to anyone alive.

With many of the bodies decayed and fallen down, the place took on a gruesomeness exceeded only by Attungowrah's purpose in taking me there. After showing where the members of his family were laid up to dry, he led the way to a private rack and pointed to the four bodies it held—all men, he explained, significantly, whom he had murdered.

The fact that one of them was a fresh arrival added to the effect he wished to convey. Namely, that he, the great Attungowrah, was a very tough guy, indeed, and what was I going to do about it?

Much to Woolfe's disappointment, the old boy refused even to look at his trade goods, although we were at Tigara several days. Finally, Woolfe came to me in disgust and said it wasn't any use, that he and Unocoluto were going back.

"With all those goods?" I asked.

"Listen, Charlie, I'll leave the stuff here for him to look over by himself. Why don't you leave yours, too, and we'll go back together?"

When he saw that I was determined to continue on south and take my goods with me, he and Unocoluto pulled out for home.

Their going brought a change in Attungowrah. I have always thought it was because I refused to give up my outfit. At any rate, next morning he suddenly told me to get out of the village, that he didn't want me there any longer.

We were in his house at the time, and coming out of a clear sky it gave me a jolt. All I could do for a minute was stand there and look at him.

Now, seven years at sea had taught me the earmarks of a bully and what surprising things can happen when somebody calls his bluff. Whether or not this scowling giant fell under that category, a sweep of anger made it easy to take the chance.

"I'll quit your house," I said, "but I won't leave your village 'til I get damned good and ready."

Without a word he left the igloo. I lost no time getting my belongings together and pitching them out after him. But before following, I strapped my Colt revolver under my attiga.

He was waiting close beside the entrance when I emerged. I brushed past without taking the slightest notice, dumped my stuff in front of the next house and sat down at its entrance to see what would happen next.

Thinking, perhaps, that only a misunderstanding could possibly account for such foolhardiness, Attungowrah then came over and told me again that I'd have to clear out, adding, pointedly, that he'd kill me if I didn't.

Remembrance of that newest body in his private graveyard convinced me that he really intended adding me to his grizzly collection. It seemed time to act. I reached for the Colt, and, pointing it at his stomach, made him understand that if he went into his house for a rifle I'd plug him the second he came out.

At this, the amazement that came over his face would have been laughable in a lighter situation. It was a new experience for the great Attungowrah. He just didn't know what to do. But neither, for that matter, did I.

Finally, he turned and walked off slowly to the other end of the settlement, leaving me sitting there, revolver in hand, for a good half-hour. He must have talked things over with some of the others because when he returned it was to assure me that I was a good man, after all, and could live in his house again as long as I liked. I repeated that I intended to stay in the village a while but would have nothing more to do with him or his igloo.

This seemed to hurt his feelings a lot.

After a discreet period Baby and Awaclak put in an appearance, both greatly worried. Perhaps we'd better leave, they said, *before the season got too late.*

Long after we had shaken the snow of Attungowrah's bailiwick off our feet and were well along towards Cape Thompson, two days away, Awaclak and Baby were still making face-saving remarks about wanting to get south before spring thaws set in.

A third day's travel down the coast brought us to a ruined village where Baby used to live before he and his sister moved north to Wevok. Showing no surprise at finding the place deserted, he told of wide-spread death by starvation and sickness—flu, from his description—some years before which had scattered the population. We'd be sure to find a lot of his relatives "up the river."

So up the river we headed next day, and entered country thick with willows, some much higher than our heads. When about thirty miles from the coast we suddenly threw a native camp into an uproar. None of them, it seemed, had ever seen a white man in this region before.

Baby had been perfectly safe in guaranteeing us a welcome from these relatives of his. There was nothing in the line of food they didn't offer from their abundance of fish, ptarmigan, rabbits and deer meat. Most of all I enjoyed a piece of mountain sheep which tasted like mutton.

What gave the camp an odd look was that the houses, instead of being built partly underground, were framed of willow poles stuck up and tied together at the top to form an arch. On this framework they placed a six-inch layer of smaller willows which, in turn, was covered by dried grass. Finally, they shoveled snow over the whole thing.

I had always considered the igloos on the coast plenty warm with their oil lamps going. These willow houses were *hot*. And all they burned was a single seal-oil lamp for light.

It was a well-ordered community. The men hunted all day, their women keeping busy patching clothing or snaring rabbits and ptarmigan. They used two methods for getting these grouse. One was to set snares of braided deer-sinew among the willows where the birds had favorite runways. The other used long nets laid on top of the snow, often stretching several hundred feet. Women and children got behind and drove the birds slowly ahead. If the driving wasn't too fast, sometimes a whole flock got tangled in the meshes. They fished with weighted deer-sinew nets set under the ice.

The longer we stayed among these friends and relatives of Baby's the less cocky I felt at being a white man. Did the complexities of civilization, so-called, yield more downright satisfaction than learning to make the most out of one's environment, however crude?

But when we broke away and traveled on to Cape Krusenstern

ESKIMO WOMEN CARRYING THEIR CHILDREN "PIGGY-BACK"

FULL-BLOODED ESKIMO WOMAN (AT RIGHT), MARRIED TO A WHITE MAN AND HER FAMILY OF HALF-BREED CHILDREN

and found there two half-starved, utterly forlorn families, my picture of life in the raw turned less rosy. With the ice closed in solid, they were now reduced to the scanty remnants of last summer's seal-meat so horribly rotten than only an Eskimo could keep it down.

It was a relief to hear of better prospects in a river settlement farther south. Here, they said, we'd find at least plenty of fish for men and dogs. Why they didn't go there themselves was beyond me.

Their reports of fish had been so eloquent that we cached most of our own grub along the way—a bad mistake.

Several miles south of Cape Krusenstern we wheeled inland and hours later plunged into the first real timber I had seen in Alaska. Here the going got tough on account of the soft, flour-like snow, but turned better after reaching the river.

Something black was moving on the ice from one bank to the other. Awaclak grabbed his rifle and shot the first land otter I had seen. It was about four feet long. Pausing only to throw it on a sled, we were following the river when suddenly ahead of us loomed a number of houses built of good-sized logs. One even had a log porch.

It was owned by another relative of Baby's—a big, friendly native named Tutisic who welcomed us all like long lost brothers. By now I was so hungry for palatable food, after caching our own supply far back, that I could hardly wait for the family to prepare supper.

Here was fish aplenty! My mouth fairly watered at the sight. But all of it was so rotten that I couldn't touch a mouthful.

Our land otter, skinned and cooked on the spot, was a Godsend.

Tutisic's house, like all the other log cabins there, reminded me strongly of some peculiar Russian ones I had seen much farther south. This was interesting. Hadn't they copied them from the Russians? I inquired, eagerly.

Nobody knew. All they were sure of was that when people lived in the timber they always built houses like this.

There followed another day's journey, another village, another welcome—another offering of rotten fish.

I turned in hungry that night and arose, hungrier still, for a thirty-mile trek that landed us at an isolated house thoroughly occupied by an ancient Eskimo, his three sons and their wives.

But it wasn't the furs I bought here that caused the place to linger pleasantly in memory. It was because their fish, while tainted, could nevertheless be gulped down by a famished white man.

Both Baby and Awaclak advised heading home now because April was on us and soon the overflowing streams would make crossings difficult. But when our ancient host described a famous native meeting place on a peninsula only two or three sleeps away, I thought we could risk that much additional time.

Had I known that much of the distance lay through timber with soft snow deep enough to bury the dogs, I never should have attempted it. All the way to the Koobuk River the three of us had to break a trail by the intermittent process of wading ahead single file, then trampling down a return path to the dogs. That was the only way they could wallow through with their load.

Those three days it took to reach the river were the hardest three days' travel I had ever experienced. It was the only time I really wished myself back in civilization.

Once on the river ice, though, two easy days brought us to a big settlement on the end of the peninsula where the town of Kotzebue now stands.

Here the natives were accustomed to gather from points as far north as Tigara, and south to the mouth of the Yukon. Which accounted, no doubt, for the unusual wealth of the headman with whom we stayed. His racks were loaded down with bundles of Siberian deerskins, bales of Russian tobacco and furs of all kinds —a veritable gold mine for trading purposes, and well worth the whole trip.

What made our three-day visit particularly pleasing was the innate courtesy of the old chief himself. He was a natural host, thinking up all sorts of little things to have the women do for us

—mending and such—and finally insisting that his boys give our sleds a thorough overhauling. To have offered pay would have been an insult.

Sorry as he seemed to have us leave, he, too, pointed out that melting snows would soon make travel impossible—a warning which threw my two Eskimos into a fever to get away.

This time we avoided that inland timber country like the plague and made fine time northward along the coast, finally picking up our cached grub near Cape Krusenstern.

That was one night when I gorged on white man's food until I couldn't look another slapjack in the eye.

Stopping only to trade powder and lead for foxskins brought in from the hills by several parties of Eskimos, we went on rapidly for three more days. The fourth morning started out fine and we hoped to round Cape Thompson by dark. But the nearer we got, the worse the weather became. By late afternoon we could hardly face the wind which threatened to roll our dogs over any minute.

It seemed a great find, then, to run across a small igloo where a Point Hope family had already taken shelter. We crowded in thankfully, but had hardly made ourselves snuggly comfortable when two more sled-loads from Point Hope arrived on the scene.

The igloo was only ten feet square. After the last Point Hoper had squirmed in among us, there wasn't room to lie down. All we could do was sit there in a huddle. The fact that human bodies occupied even the fireplace was of no concern, however, since nobody had any food.

Very early next morning I crawled outside for a breath of air and Baby followed. What we found was a gale that put travel out of the question. Since neither of us had eaten the night before, we got out some beans from the sled and chopped off frozen portions to thaw in our mouths before swallowing.

That night, on visiting our bean sack again, it was empty. Seemingly, everyone who ventured outside had stopped and helped himself.

While willing enough to recognize their native custom of sharing one's last food, I made up my mind next day that there would be no more camping with anybody until we made Tigara.

For that reason it was around midnight when we neared the place, and so inky dark we couldn't see where we were going. Our only luck, it appeared, was that darkness would at least enable us to avoid Attungowrah.

We had scarcely stumbled in among the first igloos when somebody grabbed the leader in my team and took us right up to his house before I knew where I was going.

CHAPTER VII

AT the same instant the old boy came out and invited me inside.

It was the last thing in the world I had wished. But I was about done up by the long day, so finally crawled in after him with all my things.

Attungowrah seemed genuinely pleased to have me in his house again. He routed out all five wives to prepare my favorite slapjacks. Then he had them spread out my sleeping skins. Nothing was too much trouble this time. The perfect host!

Just the same, I slept fitfully the rest of the night and it wasn't until next day that my misgivings began to wear off.

I had arrived at a moment of great excitement. One or two whales had been reported far out, the first that year, and the whole village, including Attungowrah, was too excited over thoughts of spring whaling to feel badly disposed towards anyone.

What really convinced me that the old boy had nothing up his sleeve was his unexpected invitation not only to whale with them, but to become a member of his own boat crew.

There were two reasons why I wanted to accept. First, whaling was something I knew nothing about. Second, these people were still using methods handed down by their forefathers and I doubted any white man had ever had a chance to "go native" to quite this extent. So I snapped up his offer, at the same time making him understand how great an honor it would be to join his personal crew.

From that time on, Attungowrah and I got along fine.

"But first," I said, "let me go up seventy-five miles to our station beyond Cape Lisburne for more food and ammunition. When do you leave?"

He said in six sleeps sure. Maybe I could make it in time if I hurried—*maybe*.

I hurried, all right, bringing back Unocoluto, several Eskimos

43

from Wevok and two heavy sled-loads which contained, besides my shotgun with plenty of ammunition, a coal-oil stove and a case of oil. We got in in plenty of time to have enjoyed the last of those six sleeps. But there was no sleep for me that final night—nor for anybody else in Attungowrah's house.

In a way, it was my own fault. When Attungowrah explained why I'd have to sleep out in the entrance hall, the thought probably never crossed his mind of a white man wanting to witness the native rites which always preceded each whaling season. But I argued that, since they were taking me whaling with them anyhow, I might as well be in on the devil-driving, too.

He refused. The other two devil-doctors would object, he said.

"Who are they?"

When he admitted that Unocoluto was one, I hunted up my old neighbor and got him to say that it would be all right so far as he was concerned. After a while it was all right with the others, too. They cautioned me, though, not to talk or make any sound because the devil, or Toondrah, wouldn't like it.

When I entered Attungowrah's igloo at the appointed time I found all openings closed, the gut window covered with deerskin and every lamp extinguished but one. Its flickering flame revealed the three devil-drivers sitting on the floor, stripped to the waist. Each held his native drum. The heat was unbearable. Luckily, I had left my boots, squirrel-skin shirt and sealskin pants out in the hallway and wore nothing but the lightest clothing.

As I stood there, blinking uncertainly, Attungowrah motioned me up on the platform at one side and told me to watch closely. If I saw the devil I wasn't to be afraid because they were all very powerful medicine men, and would protect me from harm.

Things started with the singing of some of their medicine songs, slowly at first, then faster and faster until at last they were shouting and making all kinds of outlandish noises. It was a good show, all right.

But gradually their earnestness, the gleam of their glistening bodies, the din, the hot, heavy air of the place—these things began to envelop me in an eerie spell. By the time they had worked themselves into a sort of trance, rolling around on the floor, yet never letting go those drums on which they kept up a monotonous tattoo, I was certain the whole lot had gone crazy—and not so sure about myself.

Anyhow, I was so downright scared that it took their next act to remind me what it was all about. Having fanned their emotions into a proper clairvoyant state, they suddenly dropped their drums and lay about on the floor as if dead. Now came the prophecies.

First one would predict something, then another would take his turn until all three had had several tries at telling what was going to happen. Unocoluto, I recall, declared that the omalik, or headman, would get three whales this spring. Another said the devil had told him that the coming whaling season would be a good one and everybody have plenty to eat next winter.

When it came Attungowrah's turn, the personal nature of his remarks must have made me start because I was quickly aware of the old boy eyeing me shrewdly from his prone position on the floor.

Mostly, his predictions concerned my clothing. The devil, he reported, told him that all of it was to be taken from me and that I must have a new lot. He said it had been revealed that a squirrel-skin shirt like mine would never be allowed on the ice during whaling because no whales would come near if they discovered such shirts being used. My sealskin pants, the pride of Corwin Bluff, were pronounced taboo as well. They must all be replaced by new.

As I waited to see what magic would bring this about, all at once the seance ended. Presently, the women returned to perform their usual job of filling, trimming and lighting the stone lamps. That done, Attungowrah and the other devil-drivers sat around the rest of the night, eating and enumerating the endless things I mustn't do while whaling.

For example, no white man's food could be taken on to the ice. Nor would I be permitted my sleeping gear; nor any extra clothing, even a change of socks. And my only shelter would be a snow wall to act as a wind-break. Above all, I must keep very quiet day and night. The slightest sound of hammering or pounding would be fatal to success.

Silly as all this seemed, now that the spell of the seance was wearing off, I considered their warnings as a sort of "trial by fire," and, more eager than ever to take part in the whaling, accepted these various taboos as solemnly as they were offered.

It gave me a queer feeling, though, to return to the entrance hall and find that all my skin clothing had vanished into air.

Although I never set eyes on any of it again, Attungowrah's head wife gave me a complete new outfit of deerskin which caused me to look and *feel* more like an Eskimo than I had thought possible. Even the natives jokingly made out that I was no longer a Cabluna, or white man, but an Innuit like themselves.

But never did an Innuit have more to learn about the primitive art of whaling from the ice—or, for that matter, about the ice itself. Let me first explain the ice situation along that coast.

Permanently attached to the mainland during the whaling season, "shore ice" may extend out several miles, depending on the depth of the water. Then comes a stretch of "flaw ice" formed when portions of the great floating pack become temporarily frozen on to the shore ice. The outer edge of this flaw ice is known as the "flaw," with a lead of open water beyond.

It was along the flaw itself that the various Eskimo crews camped during the season. Here they sat day and night watching for whales passing north through the open lead, at the same time keeping an eye shoreward for dangerous breaks that might set their flaw-ice "camp" adrift any moment.

All this I was to learn from experience. At the start, even the sled used by each crew for carrying their oomiak to the flaw had features new to me.

Its runners, eight inches high, were held eighteen or nineteen inches apart by lashed cross-pieces which projected on either side and made a broad support for the boat. Each runner was shod with ivory cut from walrus tusk. Ivory, they said, made the best shoeing for salt-water ice because it slipped more easily.

All such details were justified by the importance of the sled in hunting whales. The ice was almost always rough, and when the pack came in with a bang many a fine skin boat would have to be abandoned except for a good sled on which to haul it to safety. Sleds were the one thing the Eskimos never forgot.

During my quick trip to the station for supplies, Attungowrah's boat had been re-covered with sealskin and other essential preparations made so that we could start at a moment's notice. It meant merely lifting the oomiak from its winter rack and lashing it on to the sled.

Most of our crew of eight, including myself, then lined up on either side with harnesses over shoulders and commenced the four-mile haul over the ice to the flaw.

So great a man as Attungowrah did no work himself, of course, but stalked majestically behind, both arms inside his attiga. With one of his wives bringing up the rear carrying a bucket of fresh water, we made quite a procession. I dropped back after a while to ask for a drink and thought it odd when she snatched the bucket out of reach. Presently, I forgot the incident in examining the gear carried in the oomiak at my side.

At the bow was a small ivory crotch to rest the seven-foot harpoon shaft in. All our whaling gear was probably prehistoric. The ivory harpoon had a cutting edge of slate about ten inches long fitted in the end of the shaft. A thong of walrus hide fifteen fathoms long formed our whale line. One end was fastened to the harpoon head and the line then led back down the shaft, at the middle of which a small sinew lashing held it tight until a strain came on the line. Then it automatically pulled loose.

When a whale was struck, only the head of the harpoon stayed in the animal. The shaft, floating free, could easily be picked up for future use. At the other end of the line they fastened a number of floats, each made from the entire skin of a seal. Blown up with air, these floats offered a serious drag on any whale trying to get away.

The other weapon commonly used for the kill was a twelve-foot lance. The flint heads of these murderous things were beautifully made. Often as large as a man's hand, they had edges so sharp that a casual cut from a lance head was one of the most painful wounds I ever got. Lances were never thrown because, when used, the boat was always so close to the whale that a man simply jabbed in where he thought it would do the most damage.

Among the Eskimos' whaling *tools,* as distinct from weapons, were knives with handles from eight to ten feet long well adapted to the tough job of cutting up dead whales. The cutters of these knives consisted of pieces of flint, very sharp and set into a bone at the end of the handle. They formed regular saw teeth. It was marvelous how quickly a whale's carcass could be sliced up with such knives. Then, for hauling chunks of meat out of the water they had developed a sort of boat hook, or nixie, made from a piece of ivory lashed to a pole. About the only other gear stowed in the oomiak were paddles, unless one included the charms always carried along to bring success.

Four miles of the hardest kind of sledding brought us to the flaw at last. Here we lifted the boat off and set it gently on the edge of the ice, convenient for launching. Somebody laid the harpoon in its ivory crotch, another saw that the line was in place, the rest set about blowing up their sealskin floats. When all was ready, Attungowrah's wife performed the final rite by pouring her bucket of fresh water over the bow—the one reason she had been lugging it all that distance.

Their explanation was that everything killed in salt water needed a drink of fresh water after death. Otherwise they would report the oversight to others of their kind and no more would ever be taken.

It took me a minute to see where this applied to a *boat,* however "dead" it might be. Then suddenly I remembered that our oomiak was covered with *sealskin.*

Ready now to cruise along the open lead in search of a likely place to camp for whales, we launched the boat and held it steady while our harpooner took his place in the bow, the rest seating themselves two on a thwart.

Attungowrah, afraid the devil might see that I was a novice and send us bad luck, assigned me a place way aft where I'd do the least harm.

A couple of miles south he spotted a small bight where a long, level stretch of flaw ice extended well inland. I never should have chosen it for a camp-site, but the place suited him fine. Here, he explained, whales coming along the flaw would be apt to run under this ice and rise to spout in the bight where we could strike them easily. All my visions of whaling crews wildly pursuing their prey over the ocean fell flat. They waited quietly, it seemed, until the whales obligingly came to *them*.

Later, I discovered that both methods were practiced; that, while "good ice" often brought whales close in, "bad ice" made it necessary to go out after them.

Since ice conditions were pronounced good today, we hauled the oomiak out of the water with its bow overhanging about three feet for a quick getaway, then made the simplest camp imaginable. After cleaning the ice off boat and paddles and blocking up the stern with a small chunk to prevent the craft freezing tight, all hands threw up a four-foot snow wall around the stern. True, we had the sled to sit on behind this wind-break, and the sea to gaze at for amusement. But no fire or other creature comforts were permitted during the two cold days and nights we waited there before anything came our way.

How I longed for my coal-oil stove and some good, hot tea!

CHAPTER VIII

THE only food we had brought on the ice was a slab of muctuc and a little frozen deer meat, and I began to think that starving must be another essential of their whale-hunting technique. I didn't know that each day some woman would come out from the village packing cooked meat on her back.

One of us stayed on watch continually. Meanwhile, the others slept or talked, or just squatted there on the sled staring out to sea. Not even the occasional sight of a distant whale caused much stir.

But towards the end of the second day one emerged nearby from under the ice and spouted a couple of times. Next instant we were lined up along the oomiak, waiting for the whale to come close enough for our harpooner to strike. However, the animal went down and we resumed our dull watch.

Hardly an hour passed before another whale came from under the ice in exactly the same place. This time Capokti, our harpooner, clambered over into the bow and, grabbing his harpoon with both hands, braced himself for a mighty shock.

Along came the whale swimming quietly, leisurely, spouting every little way and raising its head two feet out of water. I'd never seen one so close before and it looked like a mountain.

Finally, it reached a point directly in line with our oomiak.

At a word from Attungowrah, the Eskimos now picked up the boat and practically *threw* it at the whale—harpooner and all.

Capokti made no attempt to hurl his weapon. He didn't have to. The weight of the boat behind him drove the old stone-and-ivory harpoon head over a foot into that black body.

Although not more than the forward half of the oomiak had touched water, before we could haul it back the whale gave a tremendous kick and went down in a smother of foam, carrying our line and floats with it. Into the boat we scrambled, pell-mell, to give chase. But before shoving off from the ice, the sound of Attungowrah's guttural sing-song caused every Eskimo to stop dead and sit there as if hypnotized.

Nothing could show more clearly what importance they attached to magic. For consider: Their first whale of the season making rapidly out to sea—and here they sat like wooden men, listening to their headman chant a whale song handed down through the years as a powerful charm that never failed.

Only after he had finished was it permitted to pick up the floating harpoon shaft, grab paddles and start offshore with a belated burst of speed.

Several other boats, hearing the song across the ice, were on the alert now, too. For some reason—Attungowrah's charm, no doubt —the whale only traveled a mile or so, then came up to spout. The sealskin floats seemed to be bothering it some as we drew near because it swam around in circles. "Gallied," as the whalemen said.

By this time the bewildered monster was surrounded by a number of boats, and although all took turns jabbing in harpoons, nothing seriously affected its speed for an hour. Then suddenly the whale turned and swam under the flaw ice, taking all those drags down with it as if they didn't exist.

So long a time passed that it seemed we'd lost out. The Eskimos knew better. When the animal reappeared, more tired than before, our harpoon struck home again. Incidentally, we attached the twenty-first float to its body. I counted them.

Wishing only to be left alone now, it went under the ice again and repeated this until it just lay on the surface, completely exhausted. This was the moment long awaited by our crew. With Attungowrah steering, our best lance expert ready in the bow and the rest of us paddling hard, we moved in close enough for the bow man to use his lance near the animal's flukes in an effort to hamstring it. He was only partly successful, yet managed to do enough damage to prevent the whale from going down.

Backing off a way to get a good start, our next maneuver was full speed ahead and this time we never stopped until our bow had climbed right up on the whale's back. Then the lance expert cut loose with all his skill. A stroke here, another there. Lightning speed! Deadly precision!

Still the whale wouldn't die.

The Eskimos had one last trick. Shoving the oomiak along until part of it lay fairly across the whale's back put our expert in position to lance a large artery similar to the jugular vein in a man. Poised for a mighty effort, he jabbed deeply at this vital spot and a great fountain of blood spurted high and crimsoned the water all about. We backed away in a hurry.

A dangerous moment! For in dying, the animal went into his death flurry with such a thrashing of fins and flukes that any boat would have been stove in and its crew injured or drowned.

Yet, with the breath of life gone at last, nothing looked more utterly helpless than that floating carcass towards which the other boats came racing.

Lashing the fins across its belly for easier towing, the Eskimos made fast a line to the head, and, all crews paddling, slowly towed their prize the quarter-mile which separated us from the edge of the ice.

It was during this towing that I witnessed another example of native reliance on charms. The harpooner went aft while Attung-owrah sat down amidships where he suddenly produced from some hidden source the dried skin of a raven. This he solemnly hung down over his back. And there it stayed, I noticed, until after the last of the whale had been cut up and divided hours afterwards. Just what this charm was supposed to accomplish I never found out.

Once alongside the flaw, the first thing was to haul all the boats up on the ice; the second, to send a messenger to the village with a piece of the whale's skin tied to a paddle. Thus the women would be informed, and one of Attungowrah's wives bring out some fresh water to give the whale the customary drink.

By the time we had finished chipping a long ramp in the edge of the ice to facilitate hauling the carcass partially out, women began arriving with sleds, dogs and children. Then for a while it was bedlam. Sleds everywhere under foot—women yelling—children shrieking—dogs fighting! Stern measures finally restored order and work began. But not until the women had poured their fresh water on the whale's spouthole.

After thus preventing word reaching other whales of what had happened to this one, some men fastened walrus lines around the small of the carcass and, men and women pulling together, the flukes were hauled up the ramp as far as possible. In this position they could be cut off and dragged back, giving everyone a chance to saw away at the body proper.

First they cut off pieces of blackskin with the blubber attached, being careful not to disturb the under side which would serve as a sled for sliding the carcass farther up. All this was only following a trial-and-error technique developed through untold generations of whale hunting. Getting the whalebone out alone must have taken a few hundred years of experiment.

It was a long, hard job at best because the head, heavy with all its tough skin and blubber, sank deeply into the water. How they could ever raise it high enough to get at the bone was difficult to see.

Once the lips were off, they slit the skin in two places on the back of the head, then cut toggles in the ice about ten feet from the edge. Next, two four-foot slabs of ice were set up. After a walrus line had been rove several times through the head slits, over the four-foot slabs and back through the toggles in the ice, their rig resembled a number of huge violin strings stretched over the bridge-piece. The only thing needed to operate this powerful "Spanish windlass" was a piece of driftwood rammed between the lines and twisted around and around until the whale's head rose clear of the water and offered easy access to the whalebone on one side.

The "Spanish windlass" had been worked with the whale float-ing alongside the ice. Now it was rolled over in the water and the other side of the whalebone reached in the same way, after which they severed the head itself.

Working from boats, they removed everything else they could get at above or below water. When the whale was once more hauled up the ramp it was much lighter, yet too heavy to haul all the way out without some new kind of purchase.

So to the backbone they fastened a strap to which was attached a short piece of round wood crosswise of the whale. Then from "eyes" cut in the ice, a line was passed around the wood and back again ready to be hauled taut at a given signal. The line was wet and, slipping nicely over the round wood, turned it into a sort of pulley.

This, then, was the primitive "block and tackle" with which they moved what was left of the carcass well up on the ice where the ribs were disarticulated and shoulder blades and jawbones saved for sled-runners. All remaining now was the backbone and it didn't take the old women long to disjoint this with their coluras, or women's knives.

Nothing was lost. The women of all ages saw to this, cutting away every scrap of meat from the bones and going at it so recklessly that it seemed they must surely hack each other to pieces.

Cutting and disjointing finished and everything sorted out, the meat and blubber were divided equally among the boats' crews— with one exception. We got the flukes and the small as extras. After which each boat divided its share among the crew so that everybody who had worked on the whale got something.

When it came to dividing the valuable whalebone our boat was allowed a full quarter of that, besides all the short bone from the nib end of the whale. The other crews took the balance, share and share alike.

That the hardest physical labor was yet to come didn't concern the men. It was the women's job to sled all the meat and blubber home and even stow it in the great holes fifteen feet deep that served as family "ice boxes." Those women with only a dog or two were the worst off. They had to harness themselves alongside in

Courtesy Arnold Liebes

WHALING SCENE. THE DARK MASS EXTENDING OUT FROM THE BOAT IN THE FOREGROUND IS A WHALE ALREADY KILLED

Courtesy Arnold Liebes

A WHALING CAMP LOCATED OUT ON THE ICE

Courtesy Arnold Liebes

WALRUS HUNTING ON THE FLOATING ICE

order to get their loads home.

While this back-breaking work went on, we, too, had a few items to take care of before going home for a much-needed night's rest.

Oomiak and paddles must be cleaned of ice—paddles placed in straight line across stern—eagle-skin charm stuck up on stick in boat—small slab of whalebone from each side of head placed in bow under lashings, to be left there as long as the whaling lasted.

Why all these silly chores? Because no more whales would come near our boat if one detail were omitted.

Our final and most important duty, though, was to assemble the whale's end pieces on the ice. This called for high art.

Corners of the flukes, properly spaced, outlined the tail. A piece of blackskin with blubber attached represented the animal's body, rendered more realistic by arranging pieces of the fins alongside. We laid the actual spouthole just where it would have come in real life and, for a final touch, placed bits of the animal's nib end in front of everything.

Viewed through half-closed eyes, the outline bore striking resemblance to a full-size whale lying there on the ice. I had no doubt the natives actually believed that it would fool the devil, too.

Of Attungowrah's credulity I wasn't quite so sure. An incident had occurred earlier which showed the headman in a new light. It was while all hands were busy dividing the meat that he took me aside and made a practical suggestion. This:

Since he was a very powerful devil-driver and we had already killed one of the three whales promised him by the devil this year, he saw no great harm in sending one of his wives four miles to the village for my coal-oil stove and a little tea. He thought if we lighted the stove *well back from the edge of the ice* the whales would never know anything about it.

That was all right with me and our tea tasted fine—Attungowrah's and mine. For no one else got a taste. The old fraud brazenly explained that he alone stood in with the devil enough to do some things forbidden ordinary Eskimos.

CHAPTER IX

A FEW days later, Attungowrah became very angry at life, and at the devil, and particularly at several other crews hunting far north of us.

The long wait for our second whale was getting on the old boy's nerves. When news reached us that these other boats had killed *three* he fell into a rage. Apparently, the thing that hurt most was having to hear about it first from one of his own wives when she brought us cooked meat.

He glared back at the poor woman through smoldering, half-closed eyes, then, with a burst of gutturals, bundled all hands into the boat and started us paddling madly up the flaw in search of a luckier place to haul out and wait.

So far as I know, I escaped the full blast of his wrath. His only direct reference to me was something about the devil punishing him for having let me make that tea on the ice.

It took another day before the devil was appeased, and then he wasn't—quite. For next morning, although we spotted a tantalizing run of whales, they were all too far out. Frightened now that the devil might not give him two more, as promised, Attungowrah decided to take matters into his own hands and go after them the hard way.

So we launched the oomiak and chased whales all day long without a letup. And just when I thought my arms would drop off we drew close enough to one big fellow for our harpooner to get ready in the bow. After a final burst of speed which shot the boat right up on the whale's back, I watched the stone harpoon sink into its body out of sight.

Then things happened fast. As we slid off the animal, one kick filled the boat with water and nearly swamped us. But this seemed only to weld the Eskimos into a single machine that responded

56

perfectly to Attungowrah's orders from the stern. No sound or
ripple marked their powerful paddle-strokes, no fear showed on
any face. Wonderful whalers, those old-time Eskimos!

I did my best to follow their example, and when the whale submerged I, too, waited motionless for him to reappear and spout.
Silence was important, they had explained, because a whale can
hear better under water than on the surface.

When this one came up half an hour later, he was close to several
other crews who managed to get in some fancy lance-work before
we arrived for the kill.

It was a much larger whale than our first and the cutting up job
left everybody ready for a rest ashore.

That first night something happened that I shall never forget. A
woman had just died, and before we arrived in the village they had
put the body on a sled and hauled it two miles up the sandpit. What
made it more tragic was the fact that she had been pregnant.

Nevertheless, it seemed unlike Attungowrah to carry on quite
so violently over the death of a woman who was no relative of his.
Did his mixture of bluff and ferocity really conceal a soft heart,
after all? I began to think so until he dolefully confided that nothing worse could possibly happen *during whaling*. It might even
mean depriving him of his third whale for the season—which
would be going just a little too far on the devil's part.

After a half-hour's sullen reflection, however, he decided that
something might still be done about capturing that third whale if
he consulted the devil and followed directions to the letter. There
was no time to lose, though.

Without waiting for dim lights or any such frills, he proceeded
to work himself into a trance on the spot. As I stood by watching
his dark, contorted features while he writhed on the floor, it wasn't
hard to believe that the instructions issuing forth came straight
from the devil in person.

They were gruesome enough. The woman's body must be opened
and the child taken from it, wrapped in sealskin and buried sepa-
rately. Otherwise, warned the devil, speaking through Attungow-

rah, *no more whales would be taken that year.*

Snapping out of his trance remarkably soon, the old boy delegated four women, including two of his wives, to do this carving. They demurred. It was the first time I'd seen any of them stand up to him for even a moment. But he brushed their terrified protests aside and insisted that everything must be done exactly as ordered.

I hardly know why I asked permission to watch the proceedings except that strange customs always fascinated me, and certainly here was something I'd never witnessed before.

Although surprised, Attungowrah said I might look on if I were particularly careful to make no noise. So I tagged along after the reluctant women, all four walking single file.

Two carried razor-edged flint knives set in handles a foot long; the others had fashioned themselves nixie hooks out of forked pieces of willow. When we came to the body on the sled, they unwrapped it and removed the attiga. Then, hesitating a long moment, one took her knife and made a long, deep cut up and down the abdomen.

Another hooked the body of the child with her willow nixie and, by pulling hard, succeeded in bringing it out through the incision. Just at the last she had to cut away something that held it back. This was too much for one of Attungowrah's wives, named Kinmurunna, who promptly fainted. Stopping only to drag her out the way, the others went ahead with the operation.

When all was over, the infant's body was gently wrapped in sealskins as the devil had ordered, the attiga replaced on the dead woman, her body again wrapped in skins. Next, they arranged her sewing gear and a few beads alongside. Their last act consisted in breaking the sled beyond repair.

"Let's get out of here," I said, helping Kinmurunna up despite her weak protests, and she and I walked slowly back to the village. What the others did with the child's body I never found out.

But I hoped fervently that the devil was satisfied.

Attungowrah seemed so certain of it that he took life easy a couple more days before going on the ice for the last time.

It was the twentieth of May, and the camping spot chosen was a wet one due to melting snow leaving pools of water all over the ice. But here he waited confidently through four days and nights for his good friend, the devil, to send along that third whale.

Seated in the boat to keep our feet dry, most of us were dozing in the sun when the lookout sounded an alarm. There was no novelty for me now in helping heave an oomiak at a passing whale, seeing the harpoon sink in, then paddling after the struck animal for the usual kill. But this whale, a small one, kept us from closing in by a most unusual performance.

Striking well aft, our harpoon had cut some tendon that prevented the whale from sounding. At each attempt to dive only the head went down, leaving its flukes thrashing in air as the animal stood on its head.

The first time this happened we were so close that the wind from the flukes almost knocked me overboard. Had it kicked sidewise instead of up and down, we should all have found ourselves in the water. Other boats had come up, but they kept discreetly away from that acrobatic whale until it tired itself out. Then we severed the jugular vein, let the animal bleed to death and towed it in.

As we stood about, tired and blood-covered after the laborious cutting up, I asked Attungowrah anxiously if this were the last. He nodded. Yes, now that the devil had fulfilled his promise we'd go ashore and this time take the boat with us.

It was good news. I'd had enough whaling for a while and felt like letting out a whoop. But unnecessary noises were taboo until the season ended for all

So we silently put the oomiak on a sled and dragged it back to the village, there to be propped up on two sleds turned on edge to put it beyond reach of the dogs. Just before leaving, Attungowrah remembered to put an eagle skin in the stern and to make sure that the two small pieces of whalebone were placed under the lashings of the bow.

My immediate wants centered around white man's food, prohibited on the ice. Another thing was a white man's bath.

Since the whole village had moved for the summer into tents scattered over the sandspit, I picked out an empty igloo, heated some water and, to Attungowrah's amusement, took my first real scrub-down in many weeks.

After that, I roamed around the deserted village for a couple of days, then went out to see what the graveyard looked like now.

It was even more harrowing than in winter. Absence of snow revealed skulls and bones all over the ground, together with numerous bodies never, for some reason, put up on racks. Squirrels furnished the one cheery note. They were scampering everywhere and watching me from every dry knoll.

I shot a few and carried them back to the tents. But all the women looked askance. They wouldn't think of cooking anything that grew fat feeding on dead bodies.

It was just about then that I lost my taste for squirrel meat, so it didn't matter.

At last the fast-softening ice brought the remaining crews ashore and whaling from the ice ended. All oomiaks were hauled on the beach and propped up the way we had left ours. An eagle or raven skin stuck in the stern indicated which boats had been successful. While twelve whales had been taken in all, ours was the only crew to kill more than one.

This caused Attungowrah to load his chest with beads, tuck his arms inside his attiga and strut around among the tents with all the patronizing smugness of the devil himself.

CHAPTER X

SINCE the devil had been kind this spring, laughter and good nature prevailed everywhere at Tigara. Even Attungowrah could afford to unbend now and again, secure in the knowledge that no one would outshine him at the feast and whale-dance for which preparations were already under way.

Having picked a big, smooth place on the beach, they dug up from somewhere the split skin of a walrus and threaded a line of walrus hide around the edge so that it could be grasped anywhere through the lacing. Two long diagonal lines, crossed beneath the skin and lashed to each corner, led out seventy-five feet to anchors formed by logs buried deep in sand.

Hauling the lines taut over driftwood crotches set up about twenty-five feet from each corner raised this skin "stage" five feet off the ground, at the same time stretching it tight enough to bounce a person like a fire net when jerked by willing hands. "Nelakatuk," as they called it then—and do yet—is a cross between a sport, game and dance.

Three oomiaks turned on edge to act as windbreaks and a few old boat covers spread over the sand for the orchestra to sit on completed the preparations.

As each boat-header who had caught a whale gave his dance, the small and flukes of his particular whale were brought out for all to feast on.

His family fared excellently, gorging on whale meat plain, whale meat fermented, whale entrails, and finally the whale's heart. That these items were considered great delicacies was proved by the enthusiastic belching which ensued.

For all that, the big dance itself was what the younger folks were waiting for.

The morning it started every man, woman and child was on

hand for the fun; and as I sat down with the rest, the orchestra, composed of very old men, took its place on the boat coverings prepared to sing slow songs and beat drums all through the dance.

Suddenly, a crowd of excited men and women of all ages rushed to the nelakatuk skin, each grabbing hold of the laceline with at least one hand. When a song started, some grinning youngster would dart out of the crowd and climb into the skin. Then everyone would jerk together and he would be tossed up and down until unable to keep his footing. Once they had him sprawling helplessly, the crowd went wild. This happened more often with men and boys than with girls. I saw girls repeatedly tossed twenty feet into the air and still retain their balance.

Eventually, the giver of the dance allowed himself to be tossed like the others, but not so high. While performing on the skin, he must also hand out a gift. Usually the recipient was some old man or woman. But sometimes all the dancer had time to do was toss his present into the air and let the crowd scramble.

Attungowrah, whose turn came the second day, had to give three dances—one for each whale killed by our crew. True to his dramatic flair, he had let it leak out beforehand that he would give away a fine wolverine skin. Consequently, his appearance on the "stage" brought a rush of women, each fighting for a vantage point close up.

Any thought I may have had of seeing the old rascal lose his dignity for once quickly vanished. Although pretending to give him "the works," it was clear that they were handling him very gently, indeed, as became so exalted a leader. A few conservative leaps, and with a flourish he yanked the wolverine skin from under his attiga and sent it flying into the crowd. That skin never touched the sand. Snatching it from hand to hand like animals, the women cut it to pieces in no time with their sharp knives.

Towards evening of the third day they laid the nelakatuk skin flat on the sand in front of the orchestra. Younger men now took over the kelouns. Women banked themselves behind to join in the singing. The dancers themselves made a far more colorful spec-

tacle than before. I noticed several wearing the heads and bills of
loons, others with headbands of beads, spiral shells and beaver
teeth. Both sexes displayed all their fanciest skin clothing, complete with gloves or mittens brilliantly trimmed.

In the dancing, two or more men would start together, then be
joined by some of the women, all dancing twice before quitting. I
had never seen such gyrations as the men went through. Hands
wriggling, arms waving, heads jerking to the rhythm of song and
drum, they hopped about, stiff-legged, until it must have jarred
their teeth loose.

All this in marked contrast to the grace of the women. Except
for a curious twisting motion of the hips, their dancing was con-
fined to bending knees, moving feet sideways and rising rhyth-
mically on tip-toe.

And throughout I never saw one of them raise her eyes from the
ground.

This sort of thing kept up until along towards morning, when
all at once the faster beat of the drums 'roused me out of my semi-
dormant state. Women were falling out now, leaving the men to
keep pace with the rapidly quickening rhythm.

Most of them succeeded—especially devil-drivers like Unocoluto
who had reputations to sustain. These men never stopped until
they had danced themselves into a frenzy and dropped, their places
taken instantly by others.

To add to the weird effect, later in the morning a fog closed in
which distorted everything. People nearby looked small, those farther off loomed like mountains. As the drumbeats rose to final
madness it seemed as if the dancers were fastened to strings ma-
nipulated by the devil and that the rest, sprawled grotesquely on
the ground, were denizens of hell.

The last dancer to collapse was hardly less done up than I, a
spectator, walking back to Attungowrah's empty igloo for some
sleep.

One of the few outsiders to whale at Tigara that spring was
Kyooctoo, who earlier had gone with me to Point Barrow. Know-

ing him for a fine hunter, I made him a proposition shortly after the whale-dance.

"Kyooctoo, how about trying for a bearded seal? Or is it too early?"

His face brightened. No, it was June now and he was sure we could shoot one asleep on the ice.

Borrowing white attigas, nearly the color of sea ice in spring, we headed south next morning, accompanied by another Eskimo who also owned a gun. His, however, was an old-fashioned, smooth-bore, muzzle-loading double-barreled affair. I didn't know until later that only one barrel carried a bullet, the other being loaded with shot for a possible duck.

We had covered perhaps six miles along the coast when Kyooctoo and I stopped at a water hole well out from land. The other man left us in order to search farther inshore. As we rested, I felt a sharp nudge from Kyooctoo. Then I saw what he saw.

Three polar bears were coming leisurely towards us from the direction of Cape Thompson, two of them a mile out on the ice, the third about in line with where our friend had paused to examine another water hole.

Rough ice enabled us to hide easily, and the northeast wind prevented the animals from getting our scent. But we hardly expected the fine target they presented, coming up to within fifty feet of where we lay huddled on the ice with rifles aimed.

Our first volley was enough. My prize proved to be a year-old cub. Kyooctoo had killed its mother.

Whether the third bear didn't hear or just didn't mind, he kept on between us and the land, drawing closer all the time to the other Eskimo. For some reason, the man appeared reluctant to shoot. The bear was almost on top of him before he finally did. And then he only wounded the animal. When it reared up to charge, we saw for the first time what a monster the bear really was.

Too far away to help, we watched, fascinated, as the man emptied his other barrel, then started to run for his life. He hadn't a chance. From where we stood it looked as if the bear just struck him a casual blow on the head, following this by one bite under the arm. Then, leaving the crumpled body where it fell, the enraged animal turned and headed for Kyooctoo and me.

Although our rifles were powerful enough to kill a bear, we daren't risk a miss and held our fire until he came within a few yards. . . . Even so, it required several carefully placed bullets to finish him.

The body of the dead Eskimo offered mute proof of the animal's strength. That one casual blow had smashed in the skull. That single bite had crushed all the ribs on his left side like an eggshell.

Later, the man's wife, aided by a number of other women, brought the body back and deposited it in the graveyard. The bear's skin they took home. But its meat they didn't use.

Whether this incident affected Kyooctoo as it did me seemed doubtful. Nevertheless, he announced that he and his family, together with Unocoluto, would leave for Wevok on Cape Lisburne as soon as the ice melted enough on the north side of the Point to get a boat along the beach. I thought this a good chance to get some things from our station, twenty-four miles beyond, so told him I'd go along.

The night of June 12 we lashed an oomiak on one of the sleds and piled it high with gear. A smaller sled, dragged behind as a trailer, held what whale-blubber and blackskin they wished to take home for summer use. An odd caravan we must have seemed, alternately sledding and paddling our way along the coast.

As we neared Cape Lisburne the second day, heavier ice made paddling impossible. So we left our boat on the beach and presently rounded the high, precipitous cape by sled alone, our talk drowned out by the screams and flapping wings of thousands of murres and gulls which nested along the cliffs in spring. Whenever I fired my gun they all flew out, casting an immense shadow over the ice. Indeed, I saw many murres fall on the ice and never get off. In order to fly, these birds must always get a good start first by flapping along in the water.

Kyooctoo made me understand by shouts and gestures that later on Eskimos would come here from all over to gather quantities of eggs, climbing down lines from the crest of the cliffs and filling their sealskin pokes.

At Wevok, where Unocoluto left us, Kyooctoo suddenly changed his mind and announced that he and his family would go on to the station with me. It was only a short trip but I was mighty glad of their company.

Woolfe was away somewhere when we sledded in six hours later. George and Black, however, met me with open arms and Baby fell all over himself. His sister Toctoo also seemed glad to welcome the white man whom she had trailed through storm and fog the fall before.

After all the novelty and excitement of Tigara, it certainly felt good to be home again, if only for a day.

My trip back to Tigara with Kyooctoo was a quick one, and a couple of days later, Woolfe, George, Baby and two other Eskimos from Corwin Bluff followed us in a whaleboat, making the whole seventy-five miles without camping once. It seemed I had inaugurated a popular shuttle service between the two points.

"And now," said Woolfe, displaying a lot of trade goods he'd brought along, "I wish you'd help me get some whalebone from these friends of yours. The old boy must think a good deal of you by now."

Whether Attungowrah did or not, when Woolfe started north a few days later with George he took a whole boatload of bone back with him, as well as my share in the three whales I had helped capture. My agreement with the Company called for shares in everything I got in Alaska.

Deepening spring painted a new and softer picture of that rugged coast. The sandspit was quite bare of snow now, all lakes and ponds free of ice and everything turning green. Farther off Point Hope plenty of solid ice still showed, but even this would be breaking up soon. And when it did, we could expect the whaling fleet direct from civilization.

Every morning I would take my shotgun and tramp up past the

graveyard north of the sandspit on the pretext of shooting ducks, actually to see if the ice barrier showed any change.

On my way back one day with a few steller eiders I had shot, two of the more popular Tigara girls came out to meet me, smiling and insisting on carrying my game. By this time I was on friendly terms with most of the young people, so thought nothing of it until their strained silence showed that something unusual was in the wind.

We had nearly reached the tents when suddenly they stopped and calmly suggested that the three of us go up into the hills for a few days.

The unexpectedness of such a proposal was a bit overwhelming. Taking my surprise for indecision, they promised as an added inducement to carry the tent and camp equipment on their own backs. I wouldn't have to do any work at all, they said. We'd have a wonderful time.

When I finally made them understand that such a thing was impossible they were very nice about it. All they asked was that I wouldn't tell anybody what they had wanted to do. I never did.

And these were two of the girls I'd seen perform so demurely in the whale-dance, never so much as lifting their eyes off the ground.

An incredible period, spring in the Arctic!

CHAPTER XI

AROUSED by Eskimo shouts early on the morning of June twenty-seventh, I crawled out, half-asleep, and looked seaward.

The sight somehow brought a lump to my throat. After swallowing hard, I did a little shouting of my own. The solid ice barrier south of Point Hope had broken at last. Already several steam whalers lay at anchor six or seven miles offshore.

Next day two of them worked in through the drift ice and lowered all their boats to try for some whales that surprised everybody by passing quite close to the beach.

We watched the boats chase whales for a day and a night without the slightest result except to draw an occasional "I told you so" grunt from the scornful Attungowrah.

Meanwhile, other steamers came in and anchored. The captain of one of them looked me over with sympathy. Then, hoping to prevent an otherwise normal white man from going entirely native, he insisted on taking me on as a member of his crew. When I explained that I was already on the Company's payroll and should even then be reporting to our station at Corwin Bluff, he seemed relieved, offered me passage there, and treated me fine.

On July second I stood at the rail of his vessel, looking long at the receding village. Good as it felt to have a ship's deck under me and be surrounded by white men again, I wouldn't have missed my several weeks' dip into the Stone Age for anything in the world. And when I compared my first ominous encounter with Attungowrah to his subsequent behavior, nerve-racking though it often was, I couldn't help feeling a certain sense of accomplishment.

For three days we broke our way north through floating ice, finally anchoring off the station at Corwin Bluff alongside a number of other Company vessels. Their captains were all ashore talking things over, and I was hardly surprised to find among them my old friend Captain Everett Smith, formerly of the "Bowhead." He was always turning up. Now, it seemed, he commanded the "Baleana."

Putting my oar into the discussion, I learned that Woolfe already had volunteered to hold the station another year, pending a final decision on the coal.

"That suit you, Charlie?" he said.

"You bet," I answered quickly. "Alaska is all right, but I'm ready to go somewhere else for a change."

So were George and Black. The question was, how were any of us to get "outside?"

Captain Smith had been doing some heavy thinking.

"If you boys want to finish the season with me," he announced somewhat doubtfully, "I'll take you south afterwards. You'll have to bunk forward, though," he added, apologetically. "We're pretty crowded for sleeping quarters aft, as it is."

I had to laugh. Compared with some of the places I'd slept in recently, a whaler's fo'castle would be a palace.

Shipping with Captain Smith, the three of us bunked forward but ate aft in style as the "Baleana" followed north along the coast towards Blossom Shoals. Here the Arctic pack was jammed hard and fast.

One day, while waiting for a northeast wind to swing the pack offshore, I caught the Captain staring gloomily over the side, but had sense enough not to ask if this was about the spot where he had lost his ship the year before. He loved the old "Bowhead."

This time he took no reckless chances of getting the "Baleana" stove in, but waited patiently with the other vessels for proper conditions before rounding the Shoals. Off Wainwright the ice held us up again and a southwest gale threatened real damage. But the main ice-pack had traveled too far north to come in on us—a great relief to the old hands, several of whom had sailed on "crowbills" a few years back.

"Aye, 'twas just north of here it catched us," one of them told me. "Betwixt here and the Sea Horse Islands. Thirty-two sail in all, we were. Nothing to do but all hands pile over the side and watch 'em sink. J'ever try walking on ice what's smashing your ship t'hell?"

I admitted, rather guiltily, that I hadn't.

"Well, I hope y' never will, son,—never."

Reflectively spraying a stream of tobacco-juice to leeward, he turned and went forward.

Although ice had nothing to do with it this time, our present fleet was not to get by without some loss, for the heavy sea kicked up by a southwest gale made bad holding ground in the shallow water. Soon every steamer had both anchors down and engines churning ahead to ease the strain. This saved the steamers. But two sailing ships with us pounded over a bar and were thrown high on the beach, to be abandoned by their crews who were distributed among the steamers later.

When the gale ended and the wind hauled northeast, we went on past the Sea Horse Islands, clear now of ice, and made for Point Barrow. South of Utkiavie the pack still formed a great ridge of ice offshore. However, by keeping lead-lines going, the "Baleana" and two others threaded slowly up the coast through an inside lead until we tied up to the ice abreast the old Government station where Captain Herendeen had wintered.

"A rotten season," he admitted. "D'y' know, we only killed *one whale*, and then couldn't save that."

"Well, if the whales weren't here—"

"The devil of it is, they *were!* Our men bungled the job. We had the best of whale-guns and everything else to work with, too. And here the natives got six big ones with nothing but old-fashioned harpoons and lances. That's what we're sore about. I don't blame the men for wanting to get away from here, but what can I do about it?"

The upshot was that most of them were given berths on the steamers. Only two agreed to stick by the station with Captain Herendeen and carry on what trading they could with the natives the coming winter.

Because each fleet-captain was anxious to end the season with a few more whales, we waved goodbye to Herendeen and his two companions, steamed around Point Barrow and cautiously headed east with the sole idea of seeing how far we could get.

Two men huddling, half-frozen, in the crow's nest and a third swinging the lead day and night kept us moving in seven fathoms until at Return Reef the ice closed in solid and brought the "Baleana" to a stop. This was about three hundred fifty miles east of Point Barrow and as far as any of the vessels could get. Since none of us had seen the slightest sign of a whale, the captains determined to go back to the top of the continent, then cruise west along the ice.

On the way back, however, the sudden sight of a number of whales off Harrison Bay sent long-idle boats splashing into the water, with eager crews at the oars. One boat, in command of our Portuguese second mate, was soon fast to a whale and for a while the crew had the ride of their lives. They killed it, though.

After three other steamers had captured a whale each, the animals vanished as mysteriously as they had appeared and we went on to Point Barrow for a few days' overhauling.

By September twentieth, all the sailing ships with the fleet had left for home, but we cruised westward along the ice for three profitable weeks during which we added seven more large whales to the "Baleana's" score for the season.

For some time now it had been getting bitterly cold over to the west, with young ice making every night and a howling wind blowing all the time. Soon everything would be too iced up to lower the boats. So, on October tenth, as though reluctantly following our secret thoughts, the "Baleana" swung her bluff bow southward and wallowed away from the ice, with San Francisco a far goal.

No one aboard was happier than George and I to pass out through Bering Strait a few days later and head for Unalaska Harbor. There we took on fresh water, and cleaned most of our whalebone preparatory to that last long stretch home.

The fact that I had been away nearly a year and a half made

San Francisco look even more like the Promised Land than before. Again I swore to stick to civilization from then on. The only possible exception might be if a chance came to move still farther south—Africa preferred.

When no other job materialized, however, and the Company offered me a temporary berth taking care of their ships in winter, I finally grabbed it—though with the definite understanding that I'd never go north again.

CHAPTER XII

DROPPING in at the office for my wages one January day, I nearly fell over when Captain Knowles asked me pointblank to go back to Point Barrow and open up a new whaling station for them.

I didn't want to seem unappreciative and stammered around a while until a perfectly safe "out" suggested itself.

"Captain," I answered, "if you'll put my chum, George Leavitt, in charge, I'll go along as his assistant."

"That's settled, then."

We shook hands solemnly and I left to look up George and have a good laugh with him over the neat way I'd got out of it.

The Captain found George first. I never learned exactly what passed between them. I only know that George's prompt acceptance left me without a leg to stand on. Having given my word, I couldn't back out.

The Company bought the old coast guard cutter "Rush" and changed her into a whaler, renamed the "Grampus." She was to be in charge of Henry Dexter, who had been mate of the "Baleana" when I came outside the Fall before. I could go north with him in March. George, traveling on the Company's tender, a big sailing ship called the "America," would meet me at Port Clarence. So, yielding to what seemed like Fate, I put lingering regrets aside and reported for duty.

My first assignment, helping receive the crew aboard the "Grampus," was enlivened by contact with an ex-convict known affectionately (?) as Sunrise Harris. While mate of the "Sunrise," this Harris had shot a man down from the yard-arm and served a prison term for it. Now he was a Special Policeman. I'm sure no man was ever better suited for the gentle art of receiving a new ship's crew, most of whom came aboard roaring drunk.

It was our job to take their liquor away. This called for teamwork. After Sunrise had backed a man up to the rail, I'd have to confiscate any liquor I found on him. Then, together we'd run him to the fo'castle scuttle, drop him down and lock the hatch.

"Receiving" with Sunrise was a liberal education, but not one to soften a man's sensibilities. I shed no tears when March ninth found the ex-convict ashore and myself steaming through the Golden Gate for whatever the North might hold this time.

The monotony of our three-weeks run to Unalaska was broken only once, when we ran into a school of spermwhales ten days out of 'Frisco. The boats had been rigged for whaling. All we need do was lower away. The third mate finally bombed one big fellow and struck another, killing it after a long chase.

All this time the ocean, except for these particular whales, might have been a vast expanse devoid of life. But the instant we began cutting up our whales a thousand sharks converged from every direction. We couldn't work without cutting them too. Attracted by blood, they were so greedy that they forced themselves on top of our whales and bit great hunks out of the carcasses.

At last we took aboard what whale the sharks left us and called it a day.

Since July sixth, the date agreed on for meeting our tender at Port Clarence, was a long way off, the "Grampus" continued north at a leisurely gait until we made the ice in Bering Sea. Then we coasted westward along the edge to within sight of Cape Naverin on the Siberian coast.

While in the pack we saw innumerable saddle-back seals, so called from a curious saddle mark on their backs. The young ones were so tame you could pick them up off the ice. But when you did, they cried softly and looked at you with eyes actually filled with tears, so that I hadn't the heart to kill any. I'll admit though that stuffed and roasted by our cook they made fine eating.

Several times we found ourselves quite close to other whalers, one of which, the steamer "Thrasher," belonged to our Company. A party of us walked six miles across the ice to visit, or "gam," as the whalemen called it, and found on arrival that she had aboard three men—Fred Hopson, Patsy Grey and Conrad Siem—who were to be with us later at Point Barrow.

Our "gamming" might have been an even greater success if the "Thrasher" people hadn't felt quite so cocky for having taken two large Bowhead whales with an estimated value in bone alone of about twenty-five thousand dollars. But theirs, we realized, was exceptional luck. Few of the other vessels encountered had bettered our own score—which, so far, stood at exactly zero.

Towards the end of May we worked out of the pack nearly abreast of Plover Bay, then for a while lay hopefully off Indian Point, where the "Baleana" had taken seven whales a couple of years before.

I went ashore here and found the Siberian Eskimos entirely different from those on the American side. The men, especially. They were stockier, with features more like the Japs. Nor could I understand a word any of them said except two old-timers who joined our crew.

One of these considered himself quite a man of the world, having shipped on whalers before. Somewhere in his wanderings he had heard a boat-steerer singing "Shoofly" and been fascinated by the song. Since he was always singing it—or trying to—his efforts promptly earned him the name Shoofly among our men and I never knew him by anything else.

Shoofly's worldliness was revealed his first day aboard when he convinced Captain Dexter that if he were loaned a shotgun and our small dinghy he'd be happy to get the ship a nice mess of ducks. Dexter agreed, giving him two full boxes of shells.

Three hours later he came back with all the shells used, but no ducks.

"I might have known you couldn't hit a barn door," barked Dexter.

Shoofly protested violently at this slur on his marksmanship. He'd shot a great many ducks, he said. The only trouble was, they all sank.

The facts came out later when his companion let it be known that instead of hunting ducks, Shoofly had rowed ashore, unloaded the shells and given the powder and shot to his wife. Then, after snapping all the primers, he had rowed back to the ship with his story.

The man was a good sailor and Dexter kept him in the crew, but we always shot our own ducks after that.

Another month remained before our rendezvous with the tender at Port Clarence, so we spent the next few weeks cruising along the western side, touching at the Diomede Islands and East Cape, finally pushing as far as Cape Serdze on the north coast of Siberia —all without seeing a spout.

In fact, the season was so bad that many of the whalers had turned to hunting walrus for the oil and ivory. Off this north Siberian coast particularly the walrus congregate in immense herds. Most of them are bulls. The cows with their young pass along the American side and join the males later on in the season.

A whaler would sail as near as possible to where one of these herds lay asleep on the ice with an old bull or two posted as sentinels. Then the small boats would go in close. Each carried an expert marksman. His job was to shoot the bulls on watch. If they could be killed instantly, the others took no notice, evidently thinking that so long as their "watchmen" stayed motionless, no danger threatened. Often an entire herd could be slaughtered in this way.

It didn't strike me as very thrilling sport though, and I was just as well content when Captain Dexter kept on looking for whales until the time approached for us to meet our tender over on the American side.

CHAPTER XIII

PORT CLARENCE presented a lively spectacle in those days, and especially at that time of year. When the "Grampus" steamed slowly into the huge land-locked bay on July 4th, 1886, I counted fifty steam and sailing vessels, and then lost track.

Our tender, the "America," was there ahead of us. Presently George sculled across and grinning broadly, clambered aboard the "Grampus." You'd have thought we hadn't seen each other for years instead of a brief four months. But those months had convinced me that I wasn't cut out for life on a whaler. Helping George run the Company's station at Point Barrow, with good chances of making our personal fortunes in a year or so—that was different. Oh, we'd show those poor superstitious natives how to whale!

Captain Herendeen's shipwreck experience had taught us not to put all our eggs in one basket, so we began at once to distribute our stuff among several of the Company's other vessels bound for Point Barrow. Then, while the "Grampus" took on her coal—one hundred twenty tons for the season—we stowed the rest of our supplies aboard her, and fumed about on deck watching some of the other whalers slip out to sea ahead of us.

But no sooner had the "Grampus" weighed anchor, after a four-day wait, than somehow the leisurely pace of the Arctic took hold of me again and I didn't give a hang how slowly the old "Grampus" nosed through shallow Bering Strait.

We stopped an hour or so at Kingegan, the Eskimo name for the settlement on the tip of Cape Prince of Wales. I had sailed past on the little "Beda" two years before without realizing what an unsavory reputation these natives had. I found out now when Captain Dexter wouldn't permit a man of us to go ashore. Our mate, Mr. Gilley, needed no warning. He wouldn't have left the "Grampus" on a bet.

77

It seemed that when he was captain of a trading and whaling schooner not long before, he had come in here to anchor for the night. That evening a lot of Eskimos paddled out and climbed aboard, bringing all their foxskins to trade for whiskey.

"Against the law? Sure it was," Gilley admitted. "But the ships used to do it when the coast guard wasn't around."

He told how the Eskimos took their whiskey ashore and raised Cain all night; how they returned in the morning, drunk and quarrelsome, a whole oomiak full of them. Sixteen men and one woman. How all but the woman came aboard demanding more booze. But since they had nothing left to trade for it, naturally he refused to give them any more. That made them uglier still.

"I had a crew of Kanakas," said Gilley, "and they're a mighty peaceable lot unless they really get mad. That's why they stood for a good deal of pushing around by the natives while all we were trying to do was up-anchor and get away. Chances were, nothing much would have happened except for my mate, a man named Finnigan, and you know what hotheads these Irish—excuse me, Mr. Leavitt, I—er—"

"Go on," grinned George. "What happened?"

"Well, one of the Eskimos finally went a little too far and the mate lost his temper and hit him. Then another drew a knife and stabbed poor Finnigan to death—and all hell bust loose.

"I'm telling you those Kanakas went crazy. They grabbed axes and spades and lit into the damned Eskimos, driving 'em forward under the fo'castle-head in no time. And that was just the beginning. Soon's they had 'em cooped up there, they'd yank 'em out with boat-hooks, one by one, and knock 'em on the head and toss 'em down into the oomiak alongside."

Considerably excited by the memory, Gilley pointed shoreward. "See that far sandspit, two—three miles from the igloos? Right there's where their boat drifted ashore with everybody in it dead except that one woman. She'd covered herself up with a piece of canvas when the row started and lay still in the bottom of the boat. Otherwise she'd have been killed too."

We shifted our gaze from the distant sandspit to the peaceful-looking village, then back to the grim smile on Gilley's face.

"No, sir, they don't like whites much around Cape Prince of Wales," he said.

The mate of the "Grampus" wasn't the only white man to avoid Cape Prince of Wales in those days, and for quite a number of years afterwards. Among the few who did risk going ashore, several were killed.

That situation has long since passed.

With the exception of Cape Prince of Wales, our other stops along the coast took on the nature of homecomings for me, revealing well-remembered settings, often familiar faces. This was especially true at Point Hope where we anchored for two days.

It was unfortunate, of course, that some of the other ships beat us in there and got the cream of the trading. But my old friends at Tigara, from Attungowrah down, seemed just as glad to see me, and just as sorry to have me go.

Later, I managed to get ashore at Point Lay where every native remembered the only white man ever to have visited them in winter. The fact that I could speak quite a bit of their language now caused Captain Dexter to commission me to do the trading for the whole ship.

On my last visit to their tents I thought Shoofly, the much-traveled Siberian native, might like to come along. Nothing would induce him to leave the ship. These Innuit, he repeated over and over, would surely kill him if they got a chance.

Why my friends here should want to injure a harmless stranger from Siberia was hard to fathom until Shoofly mentioned two boatloads of hunters from here who had been blown across to the opposite coast a few years before. Instead of feeding the castaways and giving them a chance to work their way home, he admitted that the Siberians had killed off the men and kept the women for wives.

All this, he said, was known to the people at Point Lay. Were he to go ashore with me, someone who had lost a relative would get him sure.

I didn't press the matter after that. I didn't even ask Shoofly whether he'd had any personal connection with the affair. It seemed too delicate a point.

Blossom Shoals, where we found ice extending twelve miles off-shore, meant another long wait before a lead opened up that put us beyond Wainwright. Here, too, was familiar ground, with the remains of the two sailing ships wrecked in the last year's storm still visible, their spars down, their hulls shoved farther up on the beach.

How long, I wondered, before the hulls themselves would disintegrate? In its leisurely way, the Arctic was very thorough about such things.

Again we nosed into solid ice at Point Belcher and counted the time wasted until somebody spotted a lot of old casks strewn all over the beach. Captain Dexter took a look through his glass, then ordered all the boats ashore. A little extra fuel would help eke out the precious hundred and twenty tons of coal allowed him at Port Clarence.

Those empty casks were a real find because formerly they had contained oil, and the boatloads of oilsoaked shucks we stowed aboard would drive the "Grampus" many an extra mile.

According to an old Eskimo who stood by watching us complacently, the casks had been lying there since 1871 when a number of ships had been caught in the ice. Waiting as long as they dared, their crews had finally taken to small boats and succeeded in pulling south past Blossom Shoals just before freeze-up. Near Icy Cape several vessels had picked them up and carried them to Honolulu.

Here, apparently, was one of the rare happy endings to what might well have been the usual Arctic tragedy. But his story completed, the old fellow added one ironic touch, as though to apologize for the North letting the white men off so easily. A little later that same year, he said, the ice unexpectedly cleared out. If the crews had stuck by just a few days longer they might have sailed home without the loss of a ship.

I knew how hopeless those trapped crews must have felt because it was early in August before our own ice cleared and let the

"Grampus" and other vessels get past the Sea Horse Islands. It was a tight squeeze even then, requiring constant shoving and ramming, first one ship in the lead, then another. Once through, we found ourselves way down in Peard Bay, well inshore. Only the narrowest of leads opened ahead, with ground ice piled high along an outer ridge which paralleled the coast three-quarters of a mile from the beach.

Up this miniature "inside passage" all the vessels that could come inside the ridge steamed single file. Every once in a while one would ground in the mud and have to be hauled off. The "Grampus" was lucky, due to her light draft. But I doubt if anybody in the fleet caught a wink of sleep during that final run to Utkiavie.

On a late afternoon the "Grampus" anchored off our old station just beyond the village proper. I'd never expected to see that house again. But there it stood, familiar as ever, only with this difference. I *belonged* to it now—George and I. From a transient refuge among strange natives it had become my headquarters for harvesting a whalebone fortune from the sea.

CHAPTER XIV

GEORGE went ashore at once. Almost immediately Herendeen and his two men left—seemingly delighted to get away—and an hour later we took over the station as eagerly as they had quit it. Then for the first time George and I had a chance to size up our men as a group.

Besides the cook and the three I had met while "gamming" the "Thrasher" weeks before, there was our former comrade, Ed Black. We had found Ed on another ship and arranged for him to join us again. George had also hired a New Zealander named Jack Mauri, and a couple of Finns—Gus Lief and Charlie Ice.

Ten of us in all. Enough, we thought, to man two whaleboats. If a five-man crew was smaller than customary, we had every confidence of making up for small numbers by our enthusiasm and fancied skill. Hadn't I myself learned whaling the hard way—from those natives down at Tigara?

But impatient as all hands were to get going, a lot of hard work lay ahead collecting our scattered supplies from the different vessels and transporting them to the station.

The big "Orca" was worst of all. Unable to get inside the ridge, she calmly dumped her cargo, including our two whaleboats, at an Eskimo duck-hunting camp on a narrow sandspit between ocean and lagoon a full six miles north of the house. We blew up.

"Well," George decided, cooling a little, "somebody's got to watch that stuff till there's a chance to boat it back along the shore."

Fred, Pat and I volunteered. Keeping vigil on the ice wasn't half bad, except that it cut us out of the comedy that took place in our absence. From George's description of hiring a crowd of natives to pack the rest of our outfit from the beach, it must have been quite a show.

"They were all so anxious to help," he explained, bitterly, "I figured everything was as good as under cover. But when the job started only the women did any work. The men sat on the beach, smoking and enjoying themselves. It was the grub that made me sorest, though."

"The grub?"

"When it came time to eat, naturally I gave all the women platefuls of dinner. And what did they do? Turned it right over to those loafers on the beach."

The thing had really got under George's hide—especially what followed. Thinking to protect the women next time, he had the cook call them into the house and made them eat there. That seemed to work all right until the men, seeing no food coming their way, called a strike, took their women and marched back to the village.

"They won, all right," George snorted. "They knew we had to get the stuff under cover. After that, the men ate as often as the women, but none of 'em did a lick of work."

The natives took the whole thing as a good joke, and for days kidded George by asking whether the men in his country had to wait till their women finished eating.

I believe it was partly to escape the Eskimos' kidding that he agreed to fit up our boats for a quick trip eastward along the sandspits even before we were wholly settled. The men gave a whoop. All they wanted was to begin taking whales and getting rich.

Rounding Point Barrow the first day, we met head winds and had to camp three days on the end of an island with a long lagoon between us and the mainland. I had heard one of the captains refer to this as Dead Man's Island. Now I knew why.

Parts of skeletons and human bodies in all stages of disintegration lay everywhere; and with them the usual assortment of broken sleds, tools and Eskimo handicraft, some of it probably hundreds of years old. Like a fool, I let everything strictly alone. Later, when I became more interested in collecting such relics, I found the place pretty well cleaned out, most of the articles having been sold to whaling crews by the natives themselves.

At Point Tangent, thirty miles farther east, large fields of old fresh-water ice gave the place an alluring look. Here, we told each other confidently, was just what any decent whale would love. But after a hard night and day of hopeful cruising with nothing in sight save seals, we made camp ashore and turned in, rather disappointed.

"But wait till tomorrow!"

Indeed, conditions seemed so perfect next day that it took three more long cruises to convince us that our whales, if any, must be somewhere else. So, breaking camp, we sailed east as far as Cape Simpson. Still no luck.

"But wait till *tomorrow!*"

Tomorrow brought a storm that put whaling out of the question. Rather than sit around listening to the vast number of whales we'd get farther along, Pat and I took our guns and headed inland towards a distant hill. If luck were against us for things that swam, perhaps we could catch something that ran or flew. We never dreamed that beyond that hill Nature herself had done the catching.

No sooner had we reached the top of the rise than a small lake spread out before us, its water curiously dark and ranging from a liquid center to an asphalt-like substance around the edge.

"Oil," I guessed.

Pat disagreed. He'd never heard of such a thing. Nor had I. A match touched to the "asphalt" convinced us both. It burned with intense heat and lots of greasy smoke.

Half a mile farther we came to a larger oil lake in the center of which were the carcasses of four caribou and just beyond them several spectacled eider ducks, still alive and flapping feebly. Evidently they had mistaken the oil for water and settled, only to be caught like flies on fly-paper. With their oil-soaked breasts and wings, they hadn't a chance.

We found those oil lakes in August, 1886. They have been "discovered" and "rediscovered" many times since. But I firmly believe that Patsy Grey and I were the first white men to set eyes on the phenomenon.

Back at camp on Cape Simpson provisions began to run low. Added to that, the ice threatened to come in to the beach at any moment. There seemed nothing to do but head for home. Nevertheless when we reached Point Tangent again the offshore ice looked as fine as ever and we wasted another night and day in so-called whaling.

With little left now but a canvas bag of tobacco and another of coffee, we rowed on west as far as the near end of Cooper's Island, and would have kept on if heavy fog hadn't made it necessary to camp once more—this time on empty stomachs.

Next morning, though, everybody's spirits lifted with the fog, even before we caught sight of a sailing vessel in the ice a few miles out. I think the same idea occurred to all of us at once. Now we could borrow some grub and keep on hunting a few days longer.

"Hurry up, Con!" George sang out to Conrad Siem. "Make us some coffee, man! It's your turn. Shake a leg, now, or we'll never catch that 'crowbill' out there!"

Poor Conrad, nervous at best, got badly rattled under our urging but, fumbling around, managed at last to produce the drink. There was a wild scramble. First to grab the pot, I filled my cup and gulped down two mouthfuls. Then I quit cold.

In about sixty seconds I wanted to die. But no such luck. All I could do was lie there and listen to Con's frightened explanation of how he had used the wrong bag—the one containing very black cut tobacco.

Anxious to overtake the "crowbill," the boys didn't stop to make more coffee but left me and started away as soon as they saw that I'd probably get over it in time.

The ship, however, was heading for Point Barrow and footing it far too fast to be caught. When they returned after several hours, they found me stretched out in the same place, so far recovered as actually to want to live.

Since all anybody wanted now was to get home, we rowed steadily the rest of the day and all night through a haze which made it darker than usual at that time of year.

I shall never forget the grand climax to our night's work—the realization at daybreak that somehow, miles back, we had passed through the entrance to the landlocked *lagoon* instead of skirting along outside, as we had intended. This meant going all the way back again and pulling in at the station late that evening—as disgusted a bunch of amateurs as ever tried whaling off the tip of the continent.

"But in the *spring!*"

CHAPTER XV

GEORGE vetoed any more tries at whaling that fall. There was too much to do getting ready for a long winter.

Better drinking water became an immediate problem. Ten billion wrigglers had turned each cupful of our present supply into a sort of chocolate aquarium to be downed with closed eyes and suspended imagination. We planned to remedy this by using a four-foot pond only a mile from the house where plenty of ice could be secured a little later and melted by the cook each morning during winter. Until this pond froze, probably a few more wrigglers wouldn't kill us.

Another essential was eider. We needed it badly, and great flocks of ducks were flying over the narrow sandspit, just as they still do in August and September. The Eskimos, however, didn't want their own hunting interfered with by strangers.

They had developed quite a system. Those few owning guns blazed away from far down the lagoon, killing what they could and swerving the rest directly over the sandspit where other natives could use their ancient slings, or kalumiktouns. These consisted of small ivory balls attached to three-foot lengths of braided sinew fastened together at one end. Swung once around the head, then thrown into a flock of ducks, the spreading weights curled around wings and necks and brought down many a fine bird that had escaped the shotguns.

In a way, though, we had the last laugh. Prohibited from joining either group of hunters, we ended by buying all the eider needed for less than it would have cost to shoot the birds ourselves.

As usual, it was the twenty-fifth of September when the last of the steamers left the eastern whaling grounds and crawled slowly west until only a smudge of smoke hung over the horizon. George and I knew how the men aboard her felt. A year ago we too had ex-

perienced all the thrills of quitting the Arctic—quitting it for good,
as we thought. Now we were just as glad to stay put. Thoughts of
the fortune we'd make next spring left no room for regret at seeing
the last ship disappear.

Big as Utkiavie was when we arrived, its population grew rapidly
as native hunters and trappers drifted in from the east. They came
loaded with deerskins and furs of all kinds, some caught as far away
as the Colville River. Our village and the smaller one on the tip of
the Point must have contained at least eight hundred Eskimos between them.

While the men fixed up their winter ice houses and prepared for
fall hunting, the women tanned skins and made clothing. Our station, always a popular hangout, soon resembled a sweatshop packed
with women working around the warm stove. This gave George an
idea.

"Boys," he announced one day, sizing up our tattered appearance, "we need new clothes worse than the Eskimos, and it looks
like here's our chance."

That night he bought a lot of skins and each man promptly arranged with some old woman to make him an outfit.

Dressing a deerskin was an ancient art with these old women. I
never tired of watching the one working for me. First she scraped
the skin around the edge to smooth out any places that had curled.
Then she hung it up near the stove to dry until it would crack on
the hair side. Our stove, I think, was the main reason they liked to
work at the station, for it took much longer to do the drying over a
native lamp.

Once properly dried out, the skin was wet again on the fleshy
side, folded together, rolled up and left in a cool place for half a
day. When the woman unrolled it this time it was soft and wet and
ready to be scraped all over. She usually began with a blunt flint,
scraping hard and stretching the skin until perfectly dry. Then she
substituted a *sharp* flint, finishing up with fine sandstone that removed all the remaining flesh and even some of the skin. When she
got through the hide was white and soft as chamois.

Such was the "tanning" process that produced our new outfits—two attigas apiece, extra pants, socks, and boots. I don't believe any of us was ever so lavishly equipped with clothing before or since. It helped our morale. In a way, it even compensated for the whales we hadn't caught.

Unlike Tigara, Utkiavie was ruled by two headmen instead of one. Remembering how helpful old Attungowrah had been the year before, once he had decided not to add me to his private graveyard, I made it a point to get acquainted with both Mungie and Augaroo as soon as possible. This wasn't hard because each headman had a dance house, or akuzizhe, of his own where everyone seemed welcome—including white strangers.

But I wasn't sure I'd made much progress until the day Mungie asked me to go hunting with him early in October. All I need take, he said, was white man's food. If I ate what he did I might get sick.

At the last minute Ed Black wanted to go, too. Since Mungie had no objection, Black and I loaded our sled with hard bread, tea, coffee, sugar, salt, pepper, cartridges and sleeping-bags, and showed up for a moonlight start. It was almost a family affair.

Mungie's party included his wife, Coccy, a couple of adopted sons, a brother-in-law named Appiyow with *his* wife, and one other woman to help in sledding.

That first week of travel we camped several times with other native parties who invariably begged matches of us. I never saw so much begging for matches. But it certainly was a cold job trying to make a fire with the old flint and steel on which many of them still depended. Only a few of the very oldest had ever used a fire-drill.

Their tinder was a species of thistledown gathered in the fall. This they mixed with gunpowder and kept in "water-tight" packages. When dry the stuff worked fairly well. If it happened to get wet, as was often the case, the poor devils went without fire.

I didn't begrudge them all the matches we could safely spare.

Not until we reached the Itkillik River did we stop and build a permanent camp. There was no particular reason for selecting that spot, so far as I could see, but Mungie's instinct was sound. Next morning the sight of some distant caribou—our first—got everybody excited. Mungie and Appiyow wouldn't even eat. Grabbing their rifles, they disappeared, leaving Black and me behind.

"Caribou! Turn out, Ed!" I shouted, bolting some coffee and hard bread.

He yawned.

"Aren't you coming?" I asked.

A good man in many ways, Black was an odd character. After insisting on coming along, now, it seemed, he didn't care to hunt. He'd rather help the women pack home the meat later.

Knowing Black, I didn't do any more urging but started out to try my luck alone. Well, not quite alone. Coccy made me take one of the boys along for fear I'd get lost. Although the kid had no rifle, he proved a good sleuth and I called him Pinkerton.

We hunted all day, Pinkerton and I, and saw a good many caribou, but hanged if ever I could sneak up on them near enough to shoot. On our way home I got reckless and instead of hiding, tried walking boldly towards the animals. They waited till I was within a hundred yards or so, then, to my surprise, started circling about me, coming closer all the time. I banged away with all the cartridges in my rifle and the last one killed a fawn.

As delighted as I, Pinkerton helped skin it and pack the carcass back to camp—where we got a good laugh from all the Eskimos. Whoever heard of men, or even boys, doing such work? Lugging meat was a woman's job. We should have left it there till morning when they would have sledded it in along with all the animals Mungie and Appiyow had killed that day.

I noticed, however, that my mistake didn't prevent their sailing into my fawn which the women cooked for supper. In fact, the meal put Mungie in such a mellow mood that he promised to take me with him next day and show me himself just how to hunt caribou.

He did, too. I'll give him credit for that. He showed me what I had stumbled on the day before—that if we showed ourselves the animals, instead of running away, would stop and look at us out of curiosity. It always worked. There was only one trouble. Whenever we got into good position, it was Mungie who did the killing. These particular caribou, he'd explain, were intended for Eskimos only. If a white man shot one it would have a very bad effect on the devil.

So I held my fire each time until Mungie had killed six fine animals. Devil or no devil, that was enough for any man. Before he could squeeze his trigger again I killed another fawn. Whereupon Mungie stared at me in scowling surprise, then left abruptly. As soon as he was out of sight, Pinkerton, who had been watching us for the Lord knows how long, came grinning out of his hiding place to make sure I found my way home.

I thought sure there would be murder in camp that night, the way Coccy told the world what she thought of her sullen spouse. It was just like him, she announced, her voice sharp with scorn. Mungie was always jealous if others got any game. She ended by advising me never to go hunting with him again, but to hunt alone, only letting one of the boys go along as guide.

Mungie took it all on the chin, staring stolidly at the fire as if he hadn't heard a word. I felt a little sorry for the man.

Nevertheless, I followed Coccy's advice after that and had better luck hunting alone—except, of course, for the faithful Pinkerton. I even got used to leaving my "kills" for the women to bring back to camp.

One thing puzzled me. Why did they always grease the hoofs of a carcass with a piece of blubber first?

This had to be done, they explained, because caribou were land animals and needed oil as soon as killed. Otherwise, how could the hunter expect any more good luck?

Appiyow took me out one day and was much more generous about everything than his illustrious brother-in-law. Besides insisting that I always get my full share of game, it was Appiyow who cleared up a lot of little things that had me guessing. For example, why both of them used small, heart-shaped flints instead of their regular steel knives to do the skinning. When skinning with both hands in very cold weather like this, he explained, a flint knife could be held in the mouth without freezing one's lips. Also, blood froze to a steel blade whenever one laid it down.

For nine days the caribou passed us traveling southwest. They would stop, said the Eskimos, this side of Cape Lisburne and split into smaller bands, working down through all the valleys. When the sun came back in the spring they would pass this way again, and end up just east of the Colville River in time for their fawns to be born in May.

Since we had killed sixty-four during the nine-day migration—six of them mine—we were less concerned with their future wanderings than with laying up a big house of ice cut from the river, and caching all the meat we couldn't carry home.

When the sun returned, said Mungie, viewing the finished structure with a satisfied grin, he would return and get the rest.

Except as a hunting companion, Mungie wasn't a bad sort. But with Appiyow you always knew where you stood. That, I think, was the basis of the friendship we struck up—a friendship that was to last for forty years.

CHAPTER XVI

"Don't these people ever sleep?"

We often asked ourselves that question. From early December on through the dark days the two headmen's dance houses were scenes of continuous activity. You couldn't poke your head into one without finding at least a couple of old men beating their drums for the benefit of the milling populace. It was dancing by day, story-telling day and night. I actually believe many of them never did go home.

But why should they? Every little while some woman would bring in food on a platter carved out of a driftwood root. Then what a scramble to get there first! There was no "After you" rule in their book of dark-day etiquette.

Having spent so long at Tigara as guest of old Attungowrah who held every office in the place—a regular Poobah—it seemed odd that here neither headman claimed to be a devil-doctor. That job was held by an old rascal named Owaina, ably assisted by several lesser lights.

When I alone was invited to witness the important winter devil-driving ceremony, it turned George and the others green with envy —or so they made out by their scathing remarks the night I set out for the celebration.

"What! No b'iled shirt?"

"Hey, Charlie, leave us a lock of your hair!"

I waved them an elaborate farewell, tramped over to the village, and after some formality, was admitted to Owaina's igloo where the first part of the rites would take place.

The gut window, I noticed, was carefully covered. A wolf's head hung on the wall, a dried ravenskin beside it, with the head of a seagull stuck up in one corner. This last, Owaina wanted me to understand, was his own private charm, and very powerful. More interesting was the curious red line drawn all around the house.

"What is that?"

He looked about him stealthily, then informed me that it was blood.

"What kind of blood?"

No answer.

After letting his silence sink in a minute, he said it might take some time to get the devil started and he wanted to begin work at once—*as soon as I left.*

Taking the hint, I crawled outside and joined the big crowd of Eskimos waiting around the entrance.

First, they told me, Owaina would scare up the devil and attempt to drive him from the house. If successful, then Owaina's two assistants would finish the job by running the Old Boy out of town with their spears. Thus a year's good luck for the village would be insured.

They were still discussing the chances when a couple of yips from within showed that Owaina had begun to throw the usual fit. Then he got down to business, and the racket he made would have started a dozen devils. He shouted, sang and screeched for the best part of an hour.

All at once somebody at my side declared that he'd just seen the devil come up through the entrance. Then another said *he* had, too. Each one added some vivid detail until it was hard for me to believe that I myself hadn't caught sight of the Toondrah sneaking past.

Taking their cue from the general uproar, Owaina's two assistants now started racing around the village, stabbing ferociously at the dark with their spears. Still shouting and brandishing their weapons, they finally disappeared to the south and were gone a long time. When they came back they gave an eloquent report of how they had run the devil out of town and probably killed him. If anyone needed more proof, let him examine their spears.

I did so, gingerly. . . . The stuff on them certainly was blood, but whether human or animal I couldn't say.

Since all the Eskimos seemed satisfied and ready to grant the great Owaina added prestige for freeing them of the devil, perhaps it didn't matter.

Some of our crowd celebrated the holidays that year by attending a big native dance on the Point. Fred Hopson and I thought we'd accompany one of the Eskimos on a bear hunt, instead. Result,—no bear, but a number of trapped foxes which were better than nothing. As the days commenced to lengthen after January first, I kept up my trapping and averaged two or three foxes a week.

One day I came on a particularly fine specimen just caught. Instead of killing it there, I tied its jaws with a line and carried it home on my back to show the crowd. The house was full of natives. When I set my fox down in their midst, they couldn't get outside fast enough. You'd have thought I had flung down a stick of dynamite.

"*Now* what?" said George, as the rest of us righted overturned benches and straightened things up.

Half an hour later, Nagaroo, one of Owaina's assistant devil-doctors, came hot-footing it from the village but stopped abruptly outside the door. We could see that he was a badly-shaken Eskimo.

"Come on in!" bellowed George, with appropriate gestures.

The fellow wouldn't budge.

When George went out, Nagaroo informed him that now we'd done it,—or words to that effect. Not only were the white men in for all kinds of bad luck, including no whales that spring, but it was likely the Eskimos wouldn't get any, either. Why? Because the worst possible thing one could do was to bring a fox into a house *alive*.

"Well," George replied, impressed by his earnestness, "can't we square things with the Toondrah somehow?"

Nagaroo gave the matter long consideration. In the end he thought it might do some good, perhaps, if a devil-doctor like himself took the animal outside and killed and skinned it properly.

Later, when he returned the skinned fox, its head had been severed from the body with only a piece of flesh holding it. Whenever a fox was skinned the head must be cut off at once, he volunteered, since what all foxes wanted most was a *knife*.

Although I never brought a live fox into the house again, I did keep on trapping them, and on one such trip at night fell in with a herd of caribou only a few miles from the house. That was remarkable in itself. Then, as if two perfect shots under a full moon that lighted the snowscape for miles around wasn't adventure enough for one night, a celestial display followed of such unearthly beauty that the recollection after more than fifty years still sends shivers along my spine.

To begin with, the moon became surrounded by a complete circle. This in turn was cut by five distinct but incomplete smaller circles, *with the reflection of a separate moon at each point of contact*. When I add that every circle glowed in dazzling rainbow colors, you can imagine the effect. A kaleidoscope for the gods!

Several times since then I have seen the same type of spectacle hanging, silent, in the Arctic sky. But never one so perfect, so brilliantly displayed.

It was just after the sun returned on January twenty-first—to be greeted by all the kids with songs and noise—that I joined Mungie again for a spring caribou hunt. His party consisted of the same natives as before, with two exceptions. This time he was taking along an extra Eskimo named Tootuc and his wife to help bring back the meat we had cached the fall before. The only white man in the party, I felt like an experienced hunter by now, quite incapable of silly mistakes such as the two I was to make almost at once.

Our first night out my feet got cold while cutting blocks for the snow shelter. But after a while they stopped bothering me and I went right on working. The job done and everything fixed for the night, we cleaned frost and snow from our fur clothing and peeled off our outside attigas to keep them dry.

It was while knocking the snow from my boots that suddenly I noticed my heels had no feeling. I struck a harder blow, still felt nothing. Crawling into the shelter, I hurriedly removed my boots and socks. Sure enough, both heels were frozen.

I should have known better than to wear *wool* socks beneath deerskin stockings. Traveling all day, my feet had sweat. Then, instead of drying out when we stopped, the way skin socks do, my woolen ones held the dampness which had turned to frost.

Frozen heels at the start of a hunting trip was one thing I'd never anticipated. Still, I didn't worry much, remembering how often snow had drawn out the frost when I was a boy. But Mungie wouldn't listen to any such nonsense. The thing to do, he said, was to *warm* my heels as quickly as possible.

At Mungie's insistence, and much against my better judgment, I made my second bad mistake by permitting two young women in the party each to take a foot, press it against her bare stomach and cover it with her attiga to keep the heat in. There was no pain. After a while I began to think that there might be something to Mungie's native remedy after all. Then gradually my feet began to hurt. The pain finally got so bad that I couldn't sleep at all that night. When morning revealed an enormous blister on each heel even Mungie had to admit that the hunt was over so far as I was concerned.

All he could do now was to arrange to have me ignominiously hauled back to the station on a sled, leaving the rest of the party free to continue inland. This hauling job he delegated to Tootuc and his wife—on the theory, perhaps, that since they'd only come along to haul meat, it made little difference whether the meat were alive or dead.

Reaching the station after dark, Tootuc scared all hands to death with the news that I was outside on a sled and couldn't walk. George said afterwards that every catastrophe flashed through his mind, from broken backs to gunshot wounds—everything but *frozen heels*.

He needn't have belittled frozen heels. Mine kept me in bed for a month and a half.

CHAPTER XVII

ONE day George came stomping in from the village with a grim set to his jaw and, finding me alone—I was still in bed—drew up a stool.

"Looks like something's got to be done quick."

"What's wrong now?"

"Listen, Charlie. One of the kids just told me that they've shut an old woman up in a snow house to freeze."

Both of us had heard rumors of how the old and decrepit were often disposed of in this painless manner—a fate accepted as a matter of course, perhaps even welcomed by the victims themselves. But to come up against a case firsthand gave us a nasty jolt.

"Well," I said, "we can't let her die."

"No. We can't do that. But what's the best way to handle it? Get the boys together and go over there in a mob?"

"Be trouble, sure. Better try it alone first—just quietly."

George left with a sled and I never envied anybody less. But inside of an hour he returned hauling a very wizened old Eskimo, feeble with age but quite alive after her brief exposure.

No one had objected, he said, when he broke open the snowhouse and carried her out. So here she was, and now what th' hell were we going to do with her?

This the old woman solved for us by promptly making herself at home in one corner of the house and stolidly resuming the sewing of skin clothing where she had left off when taken out by her relatives to perish.

"Granny," as we called her, kept right on sewing and patching for anyone who needed it as long as she was able. She died suddenly of pneumonia in the spring—without ever having expressed the slightest gratitude for being rescued. I honestly believe she would have preferred it the other way.

For some reason, Nagaroo, the assistant devil-driver, had taken quite a shine to me after the live fox incident, and my feet seemed to give him great concern. They did me, too. I couldn't take a step even yet. At last, yielding to Nagaroo's urging, I told him to go ahead and drive the evil spirit out of my heels, if this could be done in the village. I had no intention of turning the station into a side-show for the boys. Next day he reported that everything was all right and all I need pay him for his work was a piece of tobacco.

He really earned it a week later by bringing me two pieces of wood shaped like sandals, only cut away so as to keep my heels from touching anything. Here was the kind of devil-driving a white man could understand. To my delight Nagaroo's "sandals" worked fine. Soon I was getting around the house quite well.

Long before the Eskimos began drifting in from their caribou hunting, our crowd set to work making tents, overhauling whale-guns and bombs, grinding spades and sharpening irons—to the accompaniment of loud talk about the whales we'd take as soon as the season opened. I'm sure that at times we had at least a dozen dead whales safely on the ice—in our imaginations.

The villagers were amused at first by such early preparations, but soon began finding fault with everything we did. They objected to our hammering. Whales, they warned us, could hear a long distance. Our gear was wrong, too. And did we really intend to carry tents with us? Cooking on the ice would be even worse. But the idea of taking *extra footgear* along floored them completely. That was something absolutely "pelilak" by the devil-doctors as long back as anyone could remember. They knew for sure now that we'd never get a whale.

After a while we stopped arguing and began the long job of chipping a roadway for our boats through the rough ice to the water— or where we guessed it would be when the outer ice broke away. Not a native could be induced to help. What did they care? Their lighter oomiaks would need no roadway except in a few of the highest spots which they could cut through quickly when Mungie gave the word to go. As yet his party hadn't even returned from hunting caribou.

On March twenty-ninth, rumors of a whale sighted off Point Barrow found us ready and waiting. The Eskimos hadn't started to overhaul. Forced to pass up rough work for another week, I stayed ashore and watched the others start off sledding the boats seaward along our roadway in the ice.

Four days later all but two came back. I never saw more cockiness knocked out of men in so short a time. It took a good meal before they could describe without cussing how they had launched the boats in a nice lead, then sailed south expecting any minute to see a whale spout.

But all they found was the end of the lead. And that closed up before they could row back. So there they were, stranded far from camp with both boats and all their equipment.

"You're lucky the ice didn't pressure and crush the boats," I reminded them cheerfully.

They said that I could sit there and grin because I hadn't put in a day and night of man-killing work dragging heavy whaleboats over eight miles of ice shaped like the Rocky Mountains. As for the other two men, George had left them at the camp to keep watch. Time enough for the whole crowd to stay out there when the ice opened up for good. Maybe those Eskimos weren't so dumb, at that.

During the next two weeks pairs of us stood twenty-four-hour watches on the ice. Meanwhile, the last of the caribou hunters arrived and Mungie almost died laughing when told that we'd started whaling already. The Eskimos refused to get excited even when another report of whales on the sixteenth sent us all out again, pell-mell. I went along this time and was boat-steerer to John Shuman.

Whales were there, all right—several of them—rising in the narrow lead. But we couldn't get to them by boat because the lead was blocked by ice. Finally we took our bomb-guns to the edge, hoping for a chance to shoot. John, who had had experience with bomb-guns, stationed me near a hole and advised me to aim just back of the head so as not to strike a bone.

Hardly a half-hour passed before a whale rose right in front of me—a made-to-order shot. I took long, careful aim, pulled the trigger and executed a back somersault.

Next I knew, everyone came running to where I lay on my back, one leg badly skinned and an arm and shoulder feeling as if they'd been hit with a sledge hammer.

"You didn't hold it right," said John.

I knew that now. So, probably, did the whale. The concensus of opinion was that I'd missed it by a mile.

Shortly afterwards, the closing lead ended further attempts and we soberly went back to the watch-and-watch system.

That spring a southwest wind kept the ice shut so long that the Eskimos themselves grew anxious. Finally they commissioned Oomigaloo, a noted wind doctor, to do his stuff. Oomigaloo promised to work his most powerful charms provided all the boat-headers would pay him in bone if whales were caught, together with all the blackskin, blubber and meat he wanted. We had nothing to lose, so joined in the general agreement.

After sending us back a way, he built on the ice a tiny tent about three feet high, using willow sticks firmly lashed together for the frame and early summer deerskin for the covering. No one but his wife was allowed to help. As soon as the tent was done he sent her away too. Then, armed with his drum and a dried ravenskin, old Oomigaloo crawled inside and fastened the opening after him.

For ten hours we stood around with the natives, stamping our feet and listening to the drumming and singing issuing forth. Along towards morning there came a terrific yell, the tent seemed to explode and out from under crawled Oomigaloo clutching his drum and ravenskin. At the same instant every Eskimo was sure he saw a large black bird fly off eastward in the direction from which the new wind was to come.

I don't know to this day how the old boy managed to untie all those lashings in such a hurry. What I do know is that when the circus was over and we went out to our boats a light air actually started in from the *northeast*. By noon it was blowing strong. That evening the solid pack, immovable for days, broke off two miles beyond the end of our road and out over the ice went the oomiaks clear to the water's edge. Not a single crew stopped to help us as they passed although they didn't hesitate to use our roadway so far as it could serve them.

Chipping and chopping alone, it took us all night and most of the next morning to haul our boats to the new flaw. We got there just in time to learn that one small and three large whales had been taken by the jubilant Eskimos—but that the run was now over.

It *would* be!

CHAPTER XVIII

The season was half gone before either of our boats struck a whale. When Billy Moggs finally did, it ran under the ice, the iron drew, and Billy made a bad guess by searching to the south.

Meanwhile, in the opposite direction, a whale came up so close to Nagaroo's oomiak that they killed it quite easily, which didn't make us feel any better.

As we gathered on the ice, talking it over and watching our rivals cut up their whale and divide the bone, one of the natives came by and let slip a few words that precipitated a delicate situation.

Did we know, he asked, that Nagaroo's whale had been wounded beforehand? With his own eyes he had seen the marks of our line where it tangled when the iron drew.

Leaving that for us to mull over, the fellow casually rejoined his own crowd to help with the last of the whale.

Our boys "saw red." Most of them insisted that Nagaroo be made to hand over the bone, or a large part of it. "A whale," they argued, "belongs to the boat that strikes it first."

True enough, George admitted, but how could we be sure the man wasn't lying just to stir up trouble?

There was something to that—enough, at least, to divide the camp. But in the wrangle that followed I had sense enough for once to keep my mouth shut and "let George do it."

"If we can't keep track of our own whales," he ruled, with a look at Billy who had howled loudest, "the finders can have 'em"

Some of the boys never quite got over that, but the others soon calmed down. I felt myself that George's ruling was a wise one. Here we were, a handful of white men a long way from home. Better get along with the natives as best we could.

But I was sorry it had to be Billy again who struck the next whale. This one ran offshore in the pack. And before our boat could help, he had to let go and so lost his line as well.

"I struck him *hard*," he yelled as we came up. "Don't let him go! Come on! He can't travel far!"

Both boats hunted along the pack all afternoon without finding a trace of Billy's second whale. We might have made a night of it if the pack hadn't come in, forcing us to haul out on the flaw ice. Most of the Eskimos considered this the end of the season and took their oomiaks all the way ashore. Only a few of their younger men stayed out to prowl around the pack for anything more they might find.

Billy Moggs wasn't the only disgusted white man now. Of all the whales we'd "killed" around the cook stove, we hadn't been smart enough to save one on the ice. I think nothing showed the mental depths to which we had fallen clearer than Patsy Grey's serious,

"Maybe there's something to the heathen's silly taboos, at that."

"Don't be a bigger fool than the Lord made you, man," boomed George, with a laugh that saved the day. "Taboos be damned! We'll try once more if the ice ever opens. Let's go ashore for a rest now."

"Go ahead," I said. "I don't mind staying on lookout."

After they left, I kept awake for a while by watching some young Eskimos still scouting around out on the pack. Then I turned in.

Hours later, it seemed, one of them shook me awake to ask if I would help them. If so, I must bring along my axe because they never took theirs on the ice for fear somebody would pound or chop with it.

Half asleep, I followed him two miles out, slipping, stumbling, crawling over the jagged surface to where some of the young men had found Billy's second whale dead in the pack. Without saying a word to me, they had called the whole village out to cut it up.

I should never have known anything about this except that the whale was jammed too fast in the ice for them to roll it over, once they had the bone out on one side. To get the rest, the head must first be chopped off. What to do? No Eskimo dared break the adamant rule against pounding while on the ice.

Suddenly they remembered me. Would it do any harm, they asked the devil-doctor, if a *white* man pounded? Apparently not, for here

I was.

Their colossal nerve in asking me to help them with another whale that rightfully belonged to us made me pretty sore at first. Then it struck me funny. "Finders keepers," George had decided. All right, I'd help them keep their find.

With a hastily improvised tackle of the usual "Spanish windlass" type, they raised the whale's head enough so that I could work without getting into the water. I motioned them out of the way and grabbed my axe.

Although I never had chopped off a whale's head, the job had always seemed easy enough aboard ship. Now, it took an astonishing amount of time and hard labor. Before I got halfway through I was covered from head to foot with blood and oil.

The final shred severed at last, they gave me six slabs of bone for my work, which was more than our whole crowd had earned all season. The devil-doctor modestly accepted the same amount for his professional services, including, no doubt, the wear and tear on his conscience for having permitted even a white man to pound on ice. All the other men had five slabs each, smaller pieces going to the women.

Then came a mad stampede back to the safer flaw ice. Everybody was packing bone on his or her back. It took me three hours to get as far as our tent, for, besides my six heavy slabs, I had the axe to carry, too.

When the Eskimos got as far as my tent, where all had stopped to rest, I suggested that we have some coffee and hard bread. The men refused. But, in spite of frightened warnings from husband and brothers, one of the women finally volunteered to build a fire. Then another brought water. Soon my big coffee-pot was steaming full-blast, enveloping the exhausted natives with its tantalizing odors.

A time came when the woman who had built the fire decided that, come what might, she'd have some coffee if I would put lots of sugar in it. Such brazen flaunting of tradition caused the rest to look aghast. When she followed this by tackling a piece of hard bread and *still* nothing happened, several other women boldly followed suit, their eyes shifting furtively from side to side as they chewed.

I had a feeling that such recklessness was breeding trouble of some sort, and it was. The women were still eating when Mungie came staggering in loaded down with bone, and nearly fainted at discovering what was going on. I never saw him quite so angry. But the women of Utkiavie were different from their weaker sisters farther south. They just let Mungie blow off steam—and went right on eating and drinking until lack of breath left him glaring at them in silent rage.

I was prepared for another outburst, but hardly for his next remark.

Since nothing had happened yet, he mildly pointed out, and the whaling was finished anyhow, he thought the devil wouldn't mind if he took a little coffee himself. Whereupon, he poured down five or six cupfuls without stopping, then went for the hard bread like a wolf.

After that a few of the other men guiltily tasted the coffee. But not many dared break so ancient a whaling taboo.

Progressive as the natives of Utkiavie seemed compared with Tigara, it would be many years before the white man's point of view made much of a dent—particularly in the treatment of women. The behavior of one family was typical.

As soon as they left our camp to stumble shoreward over the flaw ice, the old man hung all his whalebone on his wife's back, first lashing the butts so that the tips of the bone stuck out six feet on either side. Although the woman took it as a matter of course, it made me groan just to see her straining under the load. Not so their two full-grown sons. Hardly had they started when the boys hung their bone on her back as well. This left them with only their rifles to carry. Soon even these were a burden, so they piled them on their mother, too.

It was a sight to remember—that loaded-down woman followed by three husky men sauntering along with their hands behind them, at peace with the universe.

CHAPTER XIX

A few days after the season closed I saw three figures coming up the coast. There was something vaguely familiar about two of them. I went outside for a better look. Then I hurried to meet them.

"Baby! *Toctoo!*"

This was like old times. The third figure proved to be Baby's wife. All had wintered at Icy Cape, but with spring whaling a flop down there, they wanted to work for us at the station.

"Sure you can," George grinned, on learning the situation. George had always got along well with Baby, and now that Toctoo was growing up he recognized her as far superior to most of the young native women.

A Company steamer arrived off the station the first of August bringing us stores, an additional man and a bit of interesting news. The Home Office, they said, was sending us a seventeen-ton sloop, the "Spy," on which we were supposed to hang our two heavy boats and try whaling off the bays to the east.

When the outer ice ridge broke through, permitting other steamers to put in briefly on their way to the whaling grounds, all eyes were glued to the little sloop which the "Orca" had in tow. She looked like a peanut.

"Hang two boats on *her?*" George exploded.

We did, though. And if our suspended whaleboats barely cleared the water on either side, so that the sloop resembled a squat dwarf borne down by two huge market baskets, what did we care? It was whales we were after—not looks. If this thing would carry us where whales were, why, more power to the "Spy."

Despite its crowded quarters, nobody was more anxious than I to try his luck aboard the tiny craft. Then in steamed the "Grampus" and upset everything, so far as I was concerned. Her mate had broken his leg and Captain Dexter, not wanting to take him farther

east, planned to set him ashore, with another member of the crew
to take care of him.

"We can't leave the station to strangers," George decided, taking
me aside. "I wish you'd stay here and look after things. Will you,
Charlie?"

That was the one time George and I came close to a row. I hated
to be left behind with nothing to do but help nurse a cripple. But in
the end I made the best of it. As a slight compensation for my personal martyrdom, however, I immediately got three old women
busy tanning skins for an outfit of new clothes that would make the
other boys' eyes stick out when they came back.

Prepared to cruise for eight or ten weeks, the "Spy" unexpectedly
returned in three. She was no deeper laden than when she left. She
hadn't taken a whale.

But poor luck, it seemed, could hardly account for the men's grim
silence, or the strained atmosphere of the station when they filed in,
dumped their dunnage and stood about, waiting. At last George
spoke.

"If anybody here is sick of his job, he can quit right now and go
out on the 'Grampus' soon as she puts in to pick up her mate."

"*I'm* quitting," growled Black.

The tension broke. Presently the men began acting more like
human beings, although Black and Jack Mauri appeared to avoid
each other as much as possible.

It came out that trouble had arisen between the two almost as
soon as the "Spy" left. Black wanted to quit then, but George had
smoothed things over.

One day, cruising off Harrison Bay, they encountered quite a
body of whales and Jack's boat, with Black in the bow, managed
to get alongside a big one worth at least five thousand dollars in
bone alone.

"At *least* that much," George repeated. "For some reason Black
didn't even try to strike, so we missed out all around."

After that fiasco Black again asked to be released, adding that
he'd never strike a whale for Mauri. But once more George talked

him out of it—or thought he had. Things went all right until a week later when Black deliberately muffed another sure strike. This was too much for George, who immediately gave orders to head for home.

What was the use, he said, of trying to whale with a damn fool in your crew?

When the "Grampus" came in to pick up her mate Black left on her, too, and I think everybody felt relieved—including Black himself.

Other changes occurred. Gus Lief and our cook went out on the "Orca" from which we got a new man, Ned Arey, in exchange; and from the "Narwahl" came a chap named Billy Star, with the longest nose I ever saw on any human. No one ever called him Billy. It was Billy the Jib. And now to take Black's place we hired an old whaleman off the "Grampus" named Joe Tuckfield, who had sailed with Captain Dexter a long time and wanted a shore-berth for the winter.

With Joe completing the reorganization, we soon had the "Spy" hauled up on the beach to lie on her bilge until spring. Then, after putting away all whaling gear, cutting ice for drinking water and making everything snug around the station, we faced the problem of how to amuse ourselves.

I hadn't seen much of Mungie in weeks and decided to join his party again for a fall caribou hunt. Mungie wasn't so bad if taken in small doses. Besides, Appiyow and his wife would be along, and I liked Appiyow very much. We ended by including Fred Hopson, too.

The caribou situation wasn't so good as the year before because an unusual number of wolves kept them stirred up and more on the alert. Of the forty-two we killed that season, two caribou stand out clearly in memory. Not only were they responsible for one of the wildest rides of my life, but it was indirectly due to them that easygoing Appiyow, who seldom offended a soul, got "in Dutch" with every woman in our outfit.

We had killed seven animals the day before, besides wounding two more that traveled a long way off before dropping. Next morning Appiyow and I left the women to haul the seven back to camp, and, taking one of the dog-teams ourselves, mushed ahead to bring in the two other "kills."

On the way back, with Appiyow sitting on the front of the loaded sled, we suddenly spotted a small herd of caribou. Our dogs did, too, and the sight of live game put the very devil into them. Almost too fagged out to drag their load one moment, the next they were taking after that fleeing herd as if our heavy sled didn't exist. We couldn't slow them down.

Yelling at me to hang on, Appiyow did likewise. There was nothing else to do, unless we wanted to lose the team. Between bumps the sled seemed scarcely to touch the ground.

When it became clear that things might go on this way indefinitely, Appiyow decided the only way to stop our runaway team would be to bring down one of the caribou. I saw him reach back for his rifle, brace himself on the careening sled—take aim . . .

My next sensation was sailing through the air, to land spread-eagle fashion in a tangle of harness, sled, meat, Eskimo and yelping canines.

Appiyow had shot our lead dog. The rest had tumbled over the body.

Since it was the women's job to raise and care for the dogs, and Appiyow had plugged the pick of the pack, he literally led a dog's life for days afterwards. I still consider his shot a lucky one.

Reaching home the end of November, I took life easy for a while and all of us spent a good deal of time in the village akuzizhes where the usual dancing, eating and story-telling whiled away the dark days. But as the time drew near for return of the sun I felt a touch of the old wanderlust.

One day early in 1888, Ounalena, headman of the village on the end of Point Barrow, asked me if Attungowrah, down at Tigara, really thought he was the strongest man in the world.

My affirmative answer displeased Ounalena who had been claiming that distinction for himself. He said he only wished

Attungowrah would meet him at Icy Cape that summer for a wrestling match. He'd show him who was the champion strong man! If I ever visited Attungowrah again would I give him the message?

My mind was made up on the spot. It would be fun to see how old Attungowrah and my other "southern" friends were getting on.

Baby, of course, was crazy to go. I never knew him to pass up a chance to visit his relatives.

By the end of January the two of us, excited as kids, were all set to start on the long trail when Toctoo announced that she wanted to go, too.

That was all right with me, though I wondered why she seemed so anxious to get away all of a sudden. She had made quite a place for herself among the natives, and both Baby and I were proud of her growing popularity.

"Of course you can come along if you want to," I answered. "Anything wrong?"

She walked off a way and waited for me to join her.

"What's wrong, Toctoo?" I repeated.

She answered in a measured speech that must have been crystallizing in her mind for a long while. The sense of it was this:

Now that she was a woman, all the Eskimos here expected her to take one of their young men for a husband. If she didn't, she'd have to belong to anybody who wanted her. I knew, didn't I, that this was the Eskimo custom?

I nodded, considerably sobered by the realization that Baby's "kid sister" had certainly grown up; more so by the thought of little Toctoo belonging to some Eskimo buck she didn't care for.

"Yes, I know the custom," I said, "but don't you like *any* of these young men?"

She seemed to be turning them over in her mind, one by one.

Then quite simply she told me that I was the only man she'd ever wanted.

CHAPTER XX

IT bowled me over.

Whatever I may have answered at the moment remains a blank to this day. Certainly Toctoo's confession seemed more a casual statement of fact than anything requiring a reply. And because she acted so simple and unaffected about it, there was no sense of embarrassment on either side.

Otherwise it would be hard to imagine the three of us starting out after that on our long trip together as if nothing had happened.

The summer before, Captain Smith of the "Baleana" had told of grub-staking a man named John W. Kelley who was wintering at our old station house near Cape Lisburne. Kelley wasn't there the night we pulled in, but showed up shortly afterwards—a bluff, level-headed prospector of middle age, with a full beard and an easy laugh.

If we waited a day, he said, he'd go on to Tigara with us—or almost that far. Had to get supplies from a fellow near there named Browne who was running a whaling and supply station just this side of Point Hope.

The news of another white man setting up so close to Attungowrah's domain surprised me. I asked how the old boy liked competition, but got little out of Kelley except that it was "quite a story."

We started early next morning and would have made Wevok, the settlement on Cape Lisburne, by early afternoon had not a sudden bending of the ice brought near disaster. It happened while crossing a frozen lagoon separated from the ocean by a low sandspit.

Baby was first to sense the danger. With a yell, he let go the handle-bars of the sled and instinctively ran off to one side, motioning us to spread out. Toctoo darted one way, I another. Kelley, glancing over his shoulder to see what was up, swung gradually in towards the beach. I can still remember how the runners of that sled looked sinking through the ice just as our floundering dogs dragged it ashore.

Luckily, salt-water ice will bend a lot before it breaks. Had this young ice been the fresh-water variety, we might have spent that night in the cold mud of the lagoon bottom instead of safe in a Wevok igloo. Then on to "Browne's place!"

Browne himself was a strange bird. Although he treated me well the three days I spent with him, I couldn't help sensing from the first something abnormal, almost fanatical about the man.

The third evening, while he and I were chatting about whaling, I happened to say that I'd be leaving next day to spend a few hours with my friends at Tigara. "A great old boy, Attungowrah," I added. "You know, when he took me whaling two years ago—"

At mention of Attungowrah, Browne had begun to swear softly, finally checking himself to ask,

"Say, do me a favor?"

"Sure, if I can. What is it?"

"Kill that big brute for me, will you?"

"Who—*Attungowrah?*"

"I want him killed! That—that—"

He couldn't pronounce the man's name without cussing, and because of his wide vocabulary, it took quite a while to catch what he was getting at. It boiled down to this:

Up to the time of Browne's arrival there never had been anybody in the Point Hope district with a stock of merchandise except the old chief himself. When Browne began cutting prices and getting the trade, Attungowrah grew very jealous. (I could well believe that.) At first, according to Browne, there was nothing but words when the two came together. Finally, however, they "hooked."

Wrenching clear, it seemed that Browne pulled a gun on the chief, but instead of shooting, hit him over the head so hard the revolver broke. Thereupon Attungowrah grabbed his rival, threw him down, and sat on him "for quite a while."

This last was what Browne, apparently, could never forgive. I gathered that it was the main reason why he wanted me to kill the chief for him.

Since I had come all the way from the top of the continent to pay Attungowrah a friendly call, the proposition was startling, to say the least. It worried me. Not knowing just what I might be up against after such talk, I decided the best thing to do would be to tell Kelley about it and perhaps get him to accompany me to the village.

He agreed, but only after a good laugh. "Why," he said, "Browne makes me the same proposition every time I come for supplies. We all think he's crazy."

Just the same, I felt easier to have Kelley along next day when I tramped once more through the familiar graveyard, then on into Tigara where, to my relief, Attungowrah and all his harem turned out to give us a great welcome.

So far as I could see, the old boy hadn't changed a bit. He was the same ugly, loud-mouthed braggart on the surface. But I knew him well enough to understand that, as usual, this was largely for local consumption. It made me feel ashamed of myself for having entertained the slightest doubts or fears.

After we had stuffed ourselves on every kind of food that his various wives could dig up, other Eskimos came crowding in to see me until the house was jammed.

We only stayed a couple of hours. But before leaving, I remembered to deliver Ounalena's challenge for a wrestling match at Icy Cape. That really started something.

Following a few sullen moments induced by the thought of *anybody* presuming to challenge his physical prowess, he turned to making fun of this upstart of a Ounalena. Then, with a shove that sent our visitors reeling back, the old boy cleared a space and proceeded to demonstrate his kicking abilities in a one-man show.

Standing in the center of the igloo, he kicked the gut window eight feet above *with both feet at once*.

This was a trick I'd never seen done before and it made me willing to believe everything else he said he could do. But as yet he had neither accepted nor rejected the challenge.

"You ought to give me something definite to carry back to Ounalena," I suggested.

Going outside, he returned bearing in one hand a boulder that an ordinary man could have lifted with difficulty. He juggled it about for a while, then let it fall with a crash that shook the house.

This, he said, was his answer. All I had to do was deliver it personally and tell Ounalena what I had seen. If the fool still wanted to wrestle him at Icy Cape, the great Attungowrah would be happy to smash every bone in his carcass.

I promised to deliver the message, anyhow. Probably he never expected me to haul that rock to Point Barrow because no further mention was made of it when he good-naturedly walked with Kelley and me as far as his private burying ground to see us off.

My last glimpse of him standing there, apelike and passive, amid the decaying corpses of those he had murdered, made a picture hard to forget.

CHAPTER XXI

REJOINING Toctoo and Baby at "Browne's place," we would have headed north early next morning except that when we went out after breakfast to harness the dogs, several were missing.

All hands combed the countryside for hours, but found nothing. I was almost reconciled to buying new dogs at Tigara, when late that afternoon Baby located the missing animals in a recently-deserted igloo three miles down the coast.

Who had taken them, or why, was a mystery for many weeks. But one day in late summer a message reached me from Kelley who wrote that he'd worked for Browne during spring whaling and thought I'd be interested in what he'd unearthed about those dogs.

Did I remember the day he and I went to Tigara? Well, in our absence it seemed that Browne had picked a row with an Eskimo hailing from Cape Prince of Wales. Had even taken a pot-shot at the fellow—but not until the Wales man had blazed away at him through the doorway of the house in which the Eskimo had then hidden *our* dogs to revenge himself on *Browne* before heading for parts unknown.

At the time, ignorant of what had gone on behind scenes, I was only too glad to get the dogs back and start the following day.

We had another Eskimo along, a chap named Arkibenna, without whom I never should have found out how simple it is to change the weather. It was while a bad storm held us in camp just south of Cape Lisburne that Arkibenna came through with his astonishing recipe. He had learned it, he said, from his father, who had been a famous wind-doctor.

All I had to do was to set fire to a grave, burning up the corpse along with the rack that held it. If there was no rack, then the dead man's broken sled might be used for fuel—or even, on a pinch,

116

ordinary driftwood.

The storm raged and time hung heavy. With nothing better to do, I crawled outside and prowled around to see if by any chance I could find a native grave such as we sometimes encountered along the coast. Luck was with me. About two hundred yards up a ravine an ancient rack loomed dimly through the storm, the body still on it.

I finally got a fire going with the help of shavings whittled from driftwood, and, feeling like a fool, managed to build up a blaze that set the rack afire. Then, calling the Eskimos, I watched their faces as they gathered around the funeral pyre. None showed the least concern.

I have found since that Eskimos care little what is done with the dead so long as their immediate family or relatives aren't tampered with. In fact, after driftwood became scarce, they were the first to break up native burial racks and drag them home for firewood.

But in those days driftwood was plentiful everywhere and the desecration of graves so rare that my Eskimos' stolid behavior interested me more than the fact that next day happened to be fair. Arkibenna, of course, laid the change in weather to his magic recipe. Kelley and I winked at each other and let it go at that.

We made Wevok, the village at Lisburne, before dark, and fortunately stayed there in a native house instead of pushing on. I say fortunately because, despite my new power over the weather, another gale blew up before morning which lasted two days and would have meant a crowded snow-shelter had it caught us in the open.

After twenty-four hours with Tatpana, our host, things got monotonous, and Kelley and I were tactless enough to start an argument with the wizened old codger about his devil. Did he really believe in all that stuff?

For a long while he tried patiently to explain matters. But the harder he tried, the more mixed up he became, until it was as good as a sideshow. And to our everlasting shame, we deliberately led the old man on.

"No," Kelley would say, "I don't think he ever had a Toondrah."

"Nor I," I'd answer with a wink. "Not one that amounted to much, anyhow."

Tatpana didn't like being made fun of. All right, he said at last, with quiet dignity, if we'd agree not to speak or make any noise whatever, he'd *show* us how powerful his devil was.

Tatpana's igloo was constructed like all the rest in that you entered the room through a hole in the floor directly above the usual entrance tunnel. The floor boards were heavy planks three inches thick and hewn from spruce logs. Here is what Tatpana did that turned our winks into blinks.

Inviting us to watch closely, he placed a piece of seal line around the first plank. Then, flanked by Kelley and me, the old man began slowly sawing back and forth. There wasn't a sound except our breathing and the almost imperceptible hiss of the soft line rubbing polished wood. But as he continued, we could see the line move along just as if a man were cutting with a saw. Farther and farther it ate its way into that plank, finally passing clear through to the next crack.

We bent down close, examined everything, rubbed our hands over the wood, looked at each other. *The plank was as solid as before.*

How he did it I never found out. Some of those old fellows were ventriloquists and not bad at sleight-of-hand. I suppose Tatpana was a hypnotist as well.

At any rate, the rest of the way up to our old station conversation between Kelley and me remained rather subdued.

Leaving Kelley there putting away his new supplies, the rest of us pushed on until we came to the Pitmagea River where we holed in with a family of strange Eskimos who hadn't been there on our southbound trip. They acted friendly enough towards Baby and Toctoo and Arkibenna, but for some reason seemed none too pleased to give me shelter. Nevertheless, I turned in as usual, leaving orders for an early start.

It seemed as if I hadn't been asleep any time when Toctoo awoke me. The sled was already packed, she said softly, and the men were

Courtesy Arnold Liebes

A PERMANENT ESKIMO IGLOO MADE OF SODS, WITH THE RIBS OF A WHALE AT
ENTRANCE

Courtesy Arnold Liebes

A PERMANENT ESKIMO IGLOO, WITH AN ENTRANCE THROUGH THE TOP

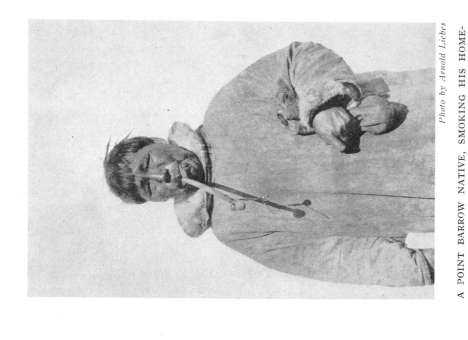

Photo by Arnold Liebes

A POINT BARROW NATIVE, SMOKING HIS HOME-
MADE PIPE

Photo by Arnold Liebes

OLD ESKIMO WOMAN ENJOYING HER CIGARETTE IN
QUIETUDE AND PEACE

waiting outside. Dragging my sleeping-skins outdoors, I saw by the stars that it was a lot earlier than we usually got away.

Arkibenna, hurriedly lashing our outfit, said we might as well start along, as Baby would soon catch up with us. Toctoo went ahead of the team. I took the rear of the sled, still half asleep. As we moved ahead I noticed Arkibenna drop back, rifle over arm, as if to wait for Baby. Suddenly he disappeared.

"Toctoo!" I called.

She kept right on. It began to dawn on me that something extraordinary was afoot.

We must have covered ten miles before she stopped the dogs and announced that here we'd wait for the other two who would be along in a few minutes. She built a fire and made some tea, but the most I could get out of her was that as soon as Baby arrived, he would explain everything—if he cared to.

After about two hours the pair showed up. We all had something to eat and were ready to start again when Baby mentioned that the family we had stayed with were from Cape Prince of Wales. Since I had forgotten that the Wales tribe held a grudge against all whites because of the Gilley affair several years before, this didn't mean much.

"Come on, Baby. Out with it!" I demanded.

Then as we traveled along, he explained how he had overheard the old man telling his son that he was going to kill me during the night when everyone slept. Baby had passed this on to the other two, and later crept cautiously outside, taking his rifle.

Armed with my own revolver, borrowed while I slept, Arkibenna stood guard inside with Toctoo who had a hunting knife. As soon as the household fell asleep, I was hustled out and started off with Toctoo, the two men staying behind to make sure nobody followed us.

I have no doubt Baby saved my life that night, as he did several other times when we were off together.

But the curious part, it seemed to me, was that neither father nor son held it against Baby and Arkibenna for their part in "kidnaping" me to safety. Instead, they ended up in a sort of love feast during which the old man admitted quite simply that one of his brothers had been killed by a white man and this had seemed a good chance to get even, that was all.

The fact that we didn't reach Point Barrow until early April was due partly to bad weather, but mostly to the many days spent hunting in the vicinity of Point Lay. Sixty-four caribou for our combined efforts!

True, that hunt might easily have turned into a headache because one of my stubborn streaks all but lost us the whole sixty-four hides.

It came about through our camping next to a couple of native families from Tigara who were on their way to Point Barrow to trade some very fine spotted skins they had brought with them.

They might better have brought their rifles instead of lazily depending on what little food they were carrying. For during several days of steady storm their grub ran out and they would have starved without our caribou meat which we gladly shared with them. But when I suggested that they take all our hides for a few of their spotted skins, they sat back and laughed.

Now, I didn't so much mind being turned down. But when they coolly added that since I couldn't take the hides along, they'd get them on the return trip anyhow, that seemed a little too much. After all, we'd been feeding the whole lot of them for days.

"All right," I said. "If you don't want to trade, you don't get the hides."

When I picked one up and cut it to pieces, they laughed all the harder, thinking I must be fooling. So I grabbed another of our hides and slashed that into *particularly* small bits. Their guffaws petered out. By the time I had ruined four caribou hides before their eyes they yelled at me to stop.

The result was that I got four good reindeer skins in exchange for our remaining sixty winter skins, and felt well satisfied. Later, the Eskimos sold these winter skins at Tigara. This made it an excellent bargain both ways.

On the whole, the trip had put me in fine feather, and as we hurried home along the last stretch of coastline, my one aim was to reach the station before spring whaling began. As far before as possible. I had been doing some heavy thinking all the way up. There was no question about it, our whaling ventures so far had been fiascoes.

Now I had a brand new plan to spring on George.

CHAPTER XXII

Iᴛ was this. If I could get a native crew together, fit out an oomiak and whale *Eskimo fashion,* it might be worth a try.

George was skeptical about my getting a native crew.

"Women go whaling," I reminded him.

"All right, Charlie," he agreed, still dubious, "go ahead and see what you can do."

I wasn't too confident of gathering an all-Eskimo crew myself, but finally found a native, Poka, whose wife's recent death barred him from whaling with the other Eskimos that spring. Even Poka's acceptance was conditional. He'd go only if I succeeded in getting a full crew of Eskimos, and if I promised to do everything the Eskimo way.

My next recruit was Toctoo. Then two more women agreed to come along. A young boy who had wandered up from Point Hope completed my crew.

Poka helped skirmish an old oomiak and furnished the necessary devil for it—a piece of obsidian chipped into the shape of a whale. He also dug up a dried ravenskin, which no native crew would think of omitting. Just before we started hauling the oomiak out over the ice an old man arrived post haste from the village to pour fresh water over the bow and recite a mumbo-jumbo.

Our own boys stood around watching the proceedings and trying to keep their faces straight. But, bolstered by the thought that we couldn't do worse than they had done last year, I finally gave the word that headed our well-charmed craft out towards the distant flaw.

The next few weeks were marked mostly by false alarms which fooled white and native crews alike. All the old men kept repeating that there must be a long point of ice somewhere to the south where the whales were touching, then going off. Finally, one of the native

122

boats did sail south and returned in a week with a whole head of long bone. This started everyone paddling and sailing south. But it was too late. The whales had disappeared.

Near the end of May a remarkable migration of small Arctic rodents called lemmings gave us something to think about besides whales. They came from the southeast, first in scattered bands, then solid masses. They *kept* coming until the whole land was black with them. You couldn't put your foot down without stepping on a lemming.

The main body, moving seaward on a ten-mile front, took four days to pass the station. Nor did they stop with the land. They kept on over the sea ice, finally leaping into the water and swimming offshore until drowned.

Cruising several miles out, our bow swished for hours through great masses of drowned lemmings, pushing them aside like small pieces of wood collected in a tide-rip. I could only wish lemmings and whales more evenly divided.

Every few years, said the Eskimos, these little animals migrated this way, though not always in the same direction, nor at the same time of year. But the older people who had seen many migrations agreed that for vastness this one beat them all. Millions must have drowned.

Yet later that summer when I happened to remark the unusual number of white owls and jaeger seen everywhere, I was told that these birds were always present *when lemmings were plentiful.* Mother Nature seemed prolific indeed—except for whales.

By the end of May most of the natives had hauled their boats ashore, considering the season ended. We decided to take the hint and quit, too. We were waiting impatiently for the dogs and sleds which were to come for us at ten that morning, when all at once the ice started moving; not much, but enough to open a small pool near-by.

As there was still some time to wait for the dogs, I had the oomiak hauled over to this hole on the off-chance of shooting a seal to take home with us. I did kill one there, too, almost as soon as we arrived, then, after pulling it out of the water, took an even slimmer chance and arranged the whale-guns handy.

"What's that for?" called George across the ice.

"You never can tell," I sang back.

This brought grins from the Eskimos and loud laughter from the others who wandered over to see if I'd gone ice-crazy or what.

"You never can tell," I repeated, foolishly, no longer conscious of the hunch that had prompted my action.

What happened then was like one of those dreams where no sooner do you *think* a thing than it materializes before your eyes.

The men had hardly returned to their boats and were still flinging back jibes when the first whale anybody had seen in days broke directly in front of the oomiak. There was only time to grab a handy whale-gun and shoot before it pitched to go under the ice.

At the report, followed by the bomb burst, back the men came on the run, thinking sure I'd had an accident. I had no idea myself of having actually killed that whale. But with everyone running around and me trying excitedly to explain, Toctoo quietly peeked over the edge of the ice and saw some enormous flukes just beneath the water. Next instant a dozen hands had grabbed irons and made them fast in the submerged carcass.

I had waited a long while to kill my first whale. Here it was. And not a bad haul for a novice! When cleaned, the bone weighed twenty-two hundred pounds and at the 1888 market price was worth about eleven thousand dollars.

Whether or not my eleventh-hour success with a bomb-gun made any deep impression on the Eskimos, the spring of 1888 marked the last season in which many of them kept to their old whaling customs. After that the younger crowd began more generally to adopt our whaling gear, tackles, guns, bombs and all. They even insisted on hard bread and tea out on the ice. Tents, however, were not to be used for many years yet; not until we began to hire Eskimos to whale regularly for the station. Then they demanded everything exactly the same as the white men.

The second steamer to arrive that summer was the "Baleana,"

Captain Everett Smith, and while Captain Smith was a good friend of ours by now, the news he brought from San Francisco didn't help his popularity at the moment.

Somebody, it seemed, had talked the Company into sending a new crowd, mostly Portuguese, up to the station. All the old hands but George and me were to be replaced.

Coming just when we felt ourselves getting the hang of this whaling business, the new orders threw the boys into an uproar.

After supper that night, George and I left them blowing off steam around the stove and went outside, both of us realizing that a serious crisis was at hand. I nodded towards the house:

"It doesn't set so well with the boys."

"I don't like it myself, Charlie, but what can I do?"

"Nothing. I guess you'll have to make the best of it."

"We've both got to."

"Not I. I'm pulling out."

He gave me a blank look. "You mean—going *home?*"

"I mean I'm quitting the Company," I said, "not the North."

Much as George and I hated to part officially, he agreed that circumstances made this a good time for me to strike out on my own hook if I were ever going to.

As for staying permanently in the Arctic, that was by no means a spur-of-the-moment decision. All the way down to Tigara and back I had been thinking it over, and had made up my mind that since I liked it up here better than any place I'd ever cast anchor, the far North was the place for me. And now, as George well knew, there was another reason why I'd never leave.

With the arrival of the first ship that summer, Toctoo and I had been married.

CHAPTER XXIII

MAD clean through at being dumped overboard without warning, there was nothing for our crowd to do except find berths on the different Company vessels and clear out. While this was going on, I called aside three of the men in whom I had learned to place great confidence.

We were an assorted lot—Conrad Siem a German, Patsy Grey an Irishman and former soldier in Arizona, Ned Arey hailing from Cape Cod, I from New Jersey. Yet we had much in common, too. We could take things as they came.

"What do you fellows want to quit for?" I began. "Why not stick it out? *I'm* staying. Let's get an outfit together and make a go of it up here."

A council of war followed. In the end we shook hands all around.

It didn't seem so crazy after we'd figured things out. I had a tent; each of us a rifle, sleeping-gear and plenty of skin clothing. That, as we explained to George, gave us a good start.

So he let us have some grub and we made our way to Berinak in order to be handy to Point Barrow where most of the steam and sailing vessels were still anchored, awaiting their chance to whale eastward. Among all these captains, we thought, it would be easy to get the rest of our outfit on credit.

Here we were over-optimistic, as I discovered after confidently tackling my friend Captain Smith, of the "Baleana."

Sure he'd stake me. All I had to do was agree to go along with the Eskimos, live with them, whale with them in the spring—then give him most of the bone in exchange for what outfit he'd advance.

The other captains, most of whom I admired personally, proved just as canny when it came to driving a bargain with anybody outside the Company.

126

I tried one ship after another, both sail and steam, but always with the same result. "Whole hog or nothing," was their motto. Finally, our grub ran low and a snorting southwest blow scattered the fleet, sending all the sailing ships around the Point hell-bent for shelter.

That gale brought our zero hour. I didn't connect it with the re-assuring "ill wind" proverb when, desperate, I paddled out to the "Baleana" two days later with Mungie and his oomiak crew for one last eloquent plea.

Captain Smith must have sighed heavily at seeing our oomiak approach, but he was polite enough when I came aboard. After leading the way to his cabin, he started talking about everything except what he knew I'd come for. The storm had wrecked three of the "crowbills." One of them, the "Fleetwing," abandoned by her crew and with her back broken on a sandbar, had torn free and drifted east of the Point. She was there yet, probably caught in an eddy. The weather had been so foul that nobody wanted to monkey with her. Too bad, too, because he understood that everything was still on her except her boats and whale-guns and a few—

"You've told me all I want to know," I cut in, already halfway out the cabin door.

That was how suddenly I became a pirate, as men were called in those days who took to the uncertain but legitimate trade of sal-vaging abandoned wrecks.

My immediate job was persuading Mungie and his crew to put me aboard the "Fleetwing" to see what could be saved. They weren't too willing, but finally consented.

The broken hulk, drifting sluggishly in rather open water some twelve miles offshore, wasn't so hard to reach as I'd expected. Once over the rail, however, we found her a mess—every rope cut and her hold full of water. There seemed no chance of getting anything out unless we could beach her. To do so meant reeving wheelropes in order to steer, then splicing the lower fore and main topsail sheets and setting them.

This took hours and called for all the skill I'd ever acquired as a sailor. But it got her moving inshore towards some of the sand-spits ten miles off Point Barrow.

All the while she was settling lower and lower. Several times I thought sure we'd have to leave her. But by splicing the jib halyards and setting that sail, too, we coaxed her along until she finally struck bottom within a half-mile of the sandspit. Continuing good weather enabled us to boat from ship to shore the sails, pieces of rope, whaling-gear, junk—everything loose that we could get at, including a barrel of black molasses winched out of the fo'castle.

Two nights and days this work went on, never stopping until, thoroughly exhausted, we lay on the sand and slept. Then, loading the oomiak with all she'd carry, we left the rest of the stuff on the beach at daybreak and paddled for Berinak.

Before the gale, the Revenue Cutter "Bear" had come north accompanied by the U.S.S. "Thetis" which was rated a man-of-war. The "Thetis" had anchored below us, almost off the station, and when we got back with our oomiak-load of junk, we found the boys ready to pay a visit to the man-of-war.

However, Con and Pat now determined to go back to the "Fleetwing" instead, and see what else might be saved. At least they could bring home all the stuff we'd left on the sandspit.

So Ned and I took care of the amenities. We fashioned some canvas into a makeshift sail, and, using an oar for a mast, sailed down to the slick and polished "Thetis." As we drew near, suddenly I became conscious of my clothes, and the fact that I hadn't shaved in a week, and for once in my life felt awed in the presence of splendor.

But a good breakfast with Captain Emory in his cabin knocked that out of my head. He was a fine man and greatly interested in what the four of us were trying to do on our own hook. When, after yarning with me a good part of the day, he ended by volunteering to let us have what he could in the way of food, I left the "Thetis" feeling like a millionaire.

Up forward, Ned had fallen among friends, too, which put us both in such high spirits that we decided to drop in on George as soon as we got ashore.

He made us stay a long time and told us over and over that he'd let some of his Portuguese go if we'd change our minds and join him again. But we felt too cocky to consider giving up our new independence.

Times came later when such an offer would have seemed tempting enough. One of them occurred at Berinak next afternoon when Con and Pat returned from the "Fleetwing" empty-handed.

It seemed that in our absence the rest of the captains had stripped the wreck of everything we'd missed. Worse, they'd stolen all the miscellaneous articles we'd so painfully accumulated on the sandspit.

"Th' dirty thieves!" roared Pat, elaborating with words and expressions that somehow fell soothingly on our ears. We all *felt* what only Pat could *say*.

Three days later another sou'wester—the pirate's friend—piled the small, flat-bottomed schooner "Ino" broadside on the shore south of Utkiavie, her masts at forty-five degrees.

We got there to find six of her crew laid out on the beach, apparently dead; others standing about aimlessly, and a number of Eskimos already rummaging the wreck. For her captain and first mate to be sitting on the ground calmly making their logbooks tally seemed a bit callous until they explained curtly that the six "casualties" were only drunk. Whereupon, they went ahead with their tallying.

After a while I asked, "What are you going to do, Captain?"

"What *can* I do?" he whined, jerking his thumb towards the marauding natives. "Them niggers come jumpin' aboard soon's we left, and they won't get off."

"Suppose we take charge of her ourselves."

"I don't give a damn what you do. All we want is to get aboard the 'Bear.' This here's my first trip to the Arctic, Mister, and I hope t'hell it's my last."

Wading and splashing out to the schooner, we climbed over the rail and told the Eskimos to put those hatches back. They refused.

After a lengthy powwow, during which I mentioned what might happen if the revenue cutter caught them stealing, they finally laid off and even brought back what they had taken ashore. They knew all about the "Bear" and her big guns.

Just as we got everything under hatches again, the "Bear" actually came steaming south and stopped abreast the schooner. Captain Healy sent Lieutenant Jarvis in with word that all wanting to come with him were to launch one of their boats and bring nothing but a barrel of sugar.

"We're all out of sugar," Jarvis explained, "and have three wrecked crews aboard us already."

The "Ino's" skipper didn't take long to decide what *he* was going to do. "But first," he said, "I want Captain Healy to condemn my schooner *proper* and *official*."

Jarvis grinned. "Don't worry. He's condemned her already— through his spyglass. Hurry up, whoever's coming!"

All but the six drunks jumped at the chance, and although the heavy surf left us soaked to the skin, we were delighted to help them launch their boat. The Arctic was no place for a spineless crowd like that. The six drunks they left behind would be bad enough to have for neighbors.

To pirate eyes the wrecked "Ino" presented a beautiful sight as each roller pounded her a few inches higher on the beach. We could hardly wait for a look inside. But first we had to get her on an even keel before too much sand should wash in around and hold her fast. The Eskimos, whose looting we had just stopped, now came around, eager to help us.

About seventy-five yards from the water's edge rose a forty-foot bluff, and on top of it we buried a great piece of driftwood. To this was fastened one end of the schooner's fifteen-fathom anchor chain. Then we swung her cutting falls from the mainmast head, hooking the lower block into the other end of the chain. By leading the running part to a block on the *foremast,* we brought it down to the windlass almost directly below.

This took until evening. But when we had our tackle rigged and all hands manning the capstan bars, it was only a matter of muscle and long hours to right the schooner, inch by inch, until morning found her on an even keel.

We were done up. Nobody thought of resting, however, before taking a hasty survey below. Then, grinning broadly, each man flopped down wherever he happened to be and slept the sleep of utter exhaustion. It was clear that except for some badly needed whale-guns nearly everything we could have wished was there.

Later, a good cleanup of her staterooms turned the "Ino" into winter quarters more snug and habitable than a pirate had any right to expect. So, taking turns as lookout, we ate and slept and loafed in luxury, well aware that we wouldn't be left undisturbed forever.

One afternoon during Con's watch, those of us below heard voices. I went up. The drunks, sobered at last, were standing around on the beach asking Con what th' hell an' blazes we were doing aboard the "Ino" and where their comrades were.

"They left on the 'Bear,' " I told them. "We own the 'Ino' now, and we aim to keep right on owning her."

The second mate, a red-eyed bruiser, came over the rail last, and, ignoring me, started telling Con what would happen if we didn't get out. I joined in again. The argument was growing hot when Ned and Pat came up.

Since Patsy Grey was the smallest of the crowd, the mate singled him out as soon as he appeared. But Pat had a tongue as nimble as the rest of him, and for quite a while the compliments flew fast both ways. Suddenly, the big mate made a lunge, Pat ducked, and the pair were all over the deck in no time.

Before any of us could pry them apart, it became clear that Pat needed no man's help. Then, with the other crowd seemingly enjoying the show as much as we, all hands let nature take its course.

When Pat finally butted his bullet head into the other's belly and followed with a lightning wallop on the chin, the winded mate went down like an empty flour sack. But only for a second. Helped up by his own boatsteerer, a Portuguese, he rewarded the fellow with curses and a blow full in the face.

That was enough for us. We gathered up the mate and heaved him over the side, telling him that if they needed anything he could send one of the men, but never again to step foot on the "Ino" himself.

"Another time," added Pat, peering down at his late adversary with a blood-streaked grin, "I might lose me temper."

Next day, leaving Pat behind for fear he'd "lose his temper," Con, Ned and I walked over to their camp and found them preparing to start for Point Hope in their boat, along with several of the "Fleetwing's" men. They had taken plenty off the "Ino" before abandoning her—far more than they could pack into the small boat. So we "inherited" what they left.

The Portuguese owned some whale-bombs and guns that he was anxious to sell me for cash, but I had no money and the deal seemed off. As an afterthought, just when they were leaving I asked whether he would accept a written order on money still due me from the Company. He agreed, but only if someone else would endorse it. One of his partners accommodated on the spot.

Weeks later, those chaps tried to reach a ship off Point Hope and that was the last heard of them. There were eleven in the little boat.

I have always been sorry that my order was never presented for payment.

CHAPTER XXIV

WE were still making things shipshape for winter when the "Thetis" came in again, this time with Governor Swineford, the second governor of Alaska, and his party aboard.

Their afternoon visit to the "Ino" was quite an event for us. On leaving, the Governor wanted to buy a fine wolfskin and several foxskins of mine, asking me to go back to the "Thetis" with him so he could pay me.

"I've got a few things to do right now," I said, "but I'll be aboard first thing tomorrow for the money."

"I'll be looking for you, Brower," he beamed, shaking hands warmly.

Next morning, the "Thetis" was gone. So were my furs.

I'm willing to put the blame on "circumstances over which he had no control," rather than any deliberate intent of the Governor of Alaska to do a gullible pirate out of valuable furs. But it was a bit disillusioning.

Better luck arrived with the "Grampus" from the eastern whaling grounds, for on her we found our old pal, Fred Hopson. Fred was as anxious to join us as we were to have him back on a share-and-share-alike basis. I had always felt sorry we hadn't included Fred in the first place.

The "Orca" anchored off the station for a few hours that same afternoon, and although she would be the last ship for another year wo didn't even board her. We were sick of haggling and were pretty well stocked up, anyhow.

But Captain Bouldry sent a boat ashore in charge of a Portuguese officer called Red Frank, from the color of his hair, and no sooner had this boat hit the beach than a familiar looking seaman made a beeline for the "Ino."

When the "Orca" put in earlier that summer, Bouldry had insisted on dumping a lot of station supplies off on the ice and one of his crew had made himself very useful to George in helping us haul the stuff ashore. We had liked him immensely at the time, and he us. His name was Tom Gordon.

Now here was Tom Gordon climbing over the "Ino's" rail to renew old acquaintance.

After we had welcomed him into the cabin, put on the coffee pot and "gammed" a while, Fred Hopson said, jokingly:

"Use another good man, couldn't we, Charlie?"

"You bet we could," I agreed, and meant it.

Tom's face showed that nothing would suit him better. But he explained that Captain Bouldry never would let him off because Red Frank would have nobody else for his bow oar. He'd better be going now, too. That damned redhead had orders not to wait too long ashore.

It was then that Pat winked all around, spit neatly into the stove and made a very practical suggestion.

Twenty minutes later Red Frank came tramping up the beach to demand what was keeping Tom.

Our innocent faces drove him furious. He ended by accusing us of hiding Tom in the hold. But when I offered to let him search the vessel, he refused, believing—not without cause—that some trick would be played on him in the dark. After hanging around a while, he flung us a few final curses and left.

We watched the "Orca" sail at daylight, after which Pat and Tom crawled out from some place well inland where, bundled in double thicknesses of skin clothing, they had spent a cold but cheerful night.

Before the heavy snows, another of our former crowd drifted in from Point Barrow. Old John Shuman said he'd just as soon stay in the Arctic as go outside broke. So we hired John as cook, promising to pay him in bone if we got any in the spring. Old John proved a somewhat uncertain quantity, but got along well enough for a while.

The other six of us worked together for three years without ever having a serious row.

One reason, perhaps, was that we made each man responsible for the job he could do best. And since whatever was needed we had either to make ourselves or buy from the Eskimos, there was always plenty to do.

As carpenter, I agreed to boss the manufacturing end. Con became "manager" in charge of all buying. Ned's specialty was gathering driftwood for fuel or building purposes. Pat and Tom were delegated to go fishing thirty miles inland, while Fred Hopson, a good man all around, made himself generally useful. It worked out fine.

First of all, I built us some sleds from pieces of hardwood found in the "Ino." Ned, meanwhile, dragged home some good driftwood logs which he and I whipsawed into frames, then put away until spring when I planned to try my hand at building a couple of oomiaks.

We all felt rather sorry for George at the station, knowing what it was costing him to stay with the Company instead of joining our crowd where he really belonged. When Christmas came around we invited him over to the "Ino" for dinner. Reminded of old John's skill as a cook—particularly for his famous duff towards which we had carefully hoarded a small bottle of brandy—poor George jumped at the chance, and nearly wept, besides.

A memorable occasion, that Christmas dinner! When all was ready, John put it on with a hearty "Help y'selves, gents! Help y'selves!" Then he went out to putter lovingly over the sauce for the duff.

John was a real cook and we cleaned up the main part of the dinner in a hurry, settling back to await the grand climax.

John finally appeared with the pudding. He started to put it on the table but drew back, scowling. After repeating this maneuver from several angles, he fixed a glassy eye on Con.

"Can't y' see there ain't room for the duff? *Take those damn lamps off the table!*"

Since Christmas was the one time of year when a man could be forgiven for pouring brandy into himself instead of the sauce, all hands got a good laugh out of it—including old John himself, later.

Early in January, two native families whom I had known at Point Hope came up the coast and on my recommendation Con shipped them all to whale with us. He also hired two Eskimo men from Utkiavie who otherwise would be out of whaling another year because of deaths in their immediate families.

With things shaping up for a busy spring, I decided I might as well get in a month's hunting with Appiyow first. Before starting, however, we found that Mungie was going inland, too, and added his party to ours.

That first night in camp I heard a wild commotion outside the shelter where the women were cooking. They all tried to pile into the hut at once, screaming and yelling as though a bear had raided the place. I grabbed a rifle and forced my way out, ready for anything, except what really had happened. A few minutes before, the moon was shining. Now it wasn't. The natives had seen total eclipses before, but still attributed them to the devil and were sure that if anyone stayed outside while the moon was gone something terrible would happen.

Luckily, the eclipse lasted only a short time, after which the women peacefully resumed their cooking in the brilliant forty-below-zero moonlight.

We hadn't gone many days inland before Mungie worked himself into his customary jealous fit, and quit camp to hunt on his own.

It was also time for Toctoo and me to head for home. I had promised the boys to be back the middle of March in order to start our oomiaks. So, on the tenth she and I set out for home with one sled-load, after promising Appiyow that we'd send all the dogs and sleds back in April to help him haul the bulk of the meat and skins.

A strange situation confronted me at home. When I went to the village to hire some of the old men to prepare whalebone lashings for the new oomiaks, they agreed readily enough but all asked for flour and molasses in exchange. Even then they failed to produce the lashings when promised. I thought it very odd. As a rule the

Eskimos were most punctilious in carrying out such contracts.

Finally it developed that the two native families from Point Hope had secretly introduced the Utkiavie people to the fine art of making hooch. Now some family always had a mash of flour and molasses tucked away in one corner of the igloo to ferment.

Their method of distilling was primitive but worked all too well. For a boiler they used a large tightly covered kettle. A twelve-gauge shotgun shell connected the top of this with the top of a smaller covered kettle. From the bottom of the small kettle a rifle-barrel, extending through a bucket of icewater, led the condensed alcohol into a cup, drop by drop.

It was these potent drops of fiery liquor that delayed my whalebone lashing until at last I found two old men who didn't want to drink.

The rest of the village presented a grave problem. Even some of our own Eskimos began to show up fighting crazy and had to be put off the schooner.

To keep them away from liquor until we needed them for whaling, the boys agreed with me that we immediately send as many as possible inland with the sleds to Appiyow. This helped a little.

"But where did these Point Hope Eskimos learn to make it?" I kept asking.

Nobody could throw light on the matter until Ned Arey recalled hearing them mention the name of some place far to the south. He hadn't understood the name, they mumbled it so. Suddenly a great light dawned.

"Was it *Browne's* place," I asked, "at Tigara?"

"That's it, Charlie! *Browne's* place."

Thus had my former host wrecked a diabolical vengeance not only on his enemy, Attungowrah, and Attungowrah's people, but on other innocent victims several hundred miles up the coast. Had I faced Browne at that moment, his earnest request that I kill a man would have met with considerable favor.

Only it wouldn't have been Attungowrah.

CHAPTER XXV

DESPITE hooch, force of habit set the whole village to overhauling its whaling gear in early April, as usual. I had an even bigger job constructing our two new oomiaks.

The Eskimos always built theirs in specially constructed snow houses over thirty feet long and a few feet wider than the boats themselves, and I decided we might as well do everything their way.

There were plenty of kinks to the job. One of the hardest things was properly to lash the stem and stern "knees" of driftwood to the keel so that all would be in a straight line.

With the "backbone" properly joined, another mighty particular job was to shape the bottom from two long boards, exactly the same length and dovetailed into the stem and stern pieces. Only then could the bottom slats be lashed in place, followed by ribs and rails, the boat shaped to the thwarts and finally the long stringer pieces lashed on. This finished the framework. Or so I thought until one of my helpers named Acarina solemnly inserted a small whale-shaped obsidian charm into the frame itself as a perpetual form of "whale insurance." If this seemed silly, I had only to remind myself of the silver coin that the white man placed beneath the foremast of a sailing ship, or the bottle of champagne solemnly smashed across the bow at any "civilized" launching.

Putting on the hide covering was a job I merely helped with now and then. Each boat required the skins from seven bearded seals. We bought these skins in the village where they had remained buried all the previous summer until rotted enough for the hair to slip off easily. They were then cleaned in the snowhouse, cut to fit the boat and sewed together with braided sinew, employing the same double seam doubtless used by Eskimo women for generations. The women took great pains with their sewing. If any bulge or

138

pocket appeared after the skins were stretched over the boat-frames, the one responsible had to rip the seam out and do it over again.

I had grown hardened to many things by now, but the smell of those skins while they were being worked on in the snowhouse nearly knocked me out. What made matters worse was the need for keeping the shelter extra warm with seal-oil lamps set in niches along the walls. I was thankful when each boat, properly covered, could at last be carried out and placed on racks in the sun to dry and bleach for future use.

George and his men, who went whaling ahead of us, damaged their wooden whaleboats severely in hauling them the five miles to the flaw even though they had chipped an ice road most of the way. We had no such trouble with our light oomiaks. Besides, experience had taught us the foolishness of hauling boatloads of stuff around. About all the camp equipment we took on the ice this time was an old oil-tin to use as a stove. It made a hot fire with blubber fuel, and we could always have tea in a hurry.

Tom, Ned and I went in one boat, and with us three Eskimo men and Toctoo. Her job was to keep our footgear in order and cook if there were any cooking to do. However, before we had been out two days, she had turned nurse, leading me ashore with so bad a case of snow-blindness that I should have been helpless without her. All we had to put in my eyes was sugar—a treatment which made them smart like blazes, but it finally did the trick.

Three days later we joined our crew just in time to help bomb the first whale of the year.

My boat killed two more in the weeks that followed; our other crew, one. All in all, the spring of 1889 was a fine season for us.

To be sure, an incident did occur, tragic enough in itself, but so unrelated to any of us personally that I always remember it with as much disgust as regret.

During the cutting of our second whale a woebegone Eskimo wandered out on the ice to where we were working, and stood about, watching hungrily. His home was far inland, he said, and this was the first time he'd come to the coast for many years.

"Help yourself," we told him, indicating the blubber.

He made a dive for a piece and gulped it down faster than I'd ever seen an Eskimo dispose of food.

Half an hour or so later, Pat exclaimed: "Will y' look at the man *now!* Faith, he'll be killing himself!"

Our guest was sitting flat on the ice with his back against the carcass, still bolting blubber and reaching for more.

When next we noticed him, his eyes were glazed, his jaws motionless. He was dead. I think he must have burst something inside.

Because fear of bad luck kept any of the natives from touching the body, there it sat for days alongside a great piece of blubber until three other strangers—relatives, no doubt—came and hauled it inland on a sled.

After the whaling was over, we pirates began to think of more permanent quarters than the "Ino." She had served us well. But what if another winter buried her under a crush of ice? To forestall such a catastrophe, it was voted to build ourselves a house on top of the hill where we'd be safe under every circumstance.

All hands spent June pulling the "Ino" apart and dragging the lumber to our new site. Then, somehow, Tom and I couldn't resist Mungie's invitation to go hunting with him and Appiyow. As a hunt it proved a flop. Even fishing gave out. And when hunger and heavy rains finally brought us home, we found that the whalers had arrived, giving to Utkiavie the appearance, comparatively speaking, of a lively metropolis.

George, however, was gone. We were told that the Company planned to send him back next year with a new crowd of men. To hold the station in the meanwhile, my old comrade Woolfe had arrived with orders to get rid of the Portuguese just as George had been forced to dismiss our old crowd the year before.

Two of the men, Antone Bettes and a Portuguese we called Joe, hadn't waited to be fired but immediately built themselves a driftwood shack at Berinak and hired out to Con as carpenters. That was why the outside of our new house was all up by the time Tom and I got back.

"And now," said Con, as I stood admiring all they'd done, "we've got to yank some more timbers out of the 'Ino' to finish up inside."

Luckily, far-off New Bedford saved us that trouble. It seemed that the winter before, some New Bedford whaling owners had pushed a bill through Washington providing for a House of Refuge at Point Barrow to harbor shipwrecked sailors. Even then carpenters from several of the ships were assembling the new building. After they had finished, considerable lumber remained and we traded foxskins for some of it to finish our house—with enough left over for me to build a separate room for Toctoo and myself. For the first time in my life I felt like a family man.

After the ships had left that fall, Toctoo and I went hunting inland with Appiyow as far as the mountains. Caribou were scarce. Still, we were having a fine time when Appiyow suddenly decided to go back to the village on the excuse of killing a few seals. It wasn't like Appiyow to give up so easily, and we wondered a little as we watched him go. Certainly I didn't suspect that in all the years to come, he and I would never go hunting together again.

Toctoo and I followed his trail in a leisurely way to where the Eshooktoo River empties into the Kooloogarua. This was a great place to fish through the ice and hunt ptarmigan, and here we encountered a young Eskimo named Takpuc who had just taken a wife. As both seemed anxious to have us stay, we camped with them for some time.

At first there was another native husband and wife there. The woman had given birth to a child just before we arrived but the baby hadn't lived. Very likely it had been put out in the cold to die. This was often done by Eskimos in those days; particularly by inland natives who were usually following the caribou and couldn't be bothered by any hindrance to their travel. Some women with whom I have talked told me that they had had as many as five babies and never saved any. It wasn't that they weren't fond of children, or that most of the mothers didn't want to keep their newly-born. But custom was too strong.

So far as we could tell, the woman at Takpuc's camp was getting along all right and needed only to rest a while longer for complete recovery. But her husband, a surly fellow, was anxious to get into the village to make hooch and insisted on her coming along.

It seemed there was a superstition among them that, after childbirth, a woman must not travel on any river. If she so much as touched ice, all fish left. Now, this fellow might easily have put his wife on a sled and taken her across country to Utkiavie. But since the going was easier for him on the river, he forced her to walk along the bank while *he* traveled comfortably on the smooth river ice.

At the end of the first day, she was all in. Next day she struggled on till noon, then had to stop. Though considerably hurt by her behavior, he thought that now perhaps he might carry her the rest of the way to Utkiavie on his sled—particularly since there were no more rivers for him to travel on.

They reached the village, but two days later the woman died. I was told that the devil-doctors held a solemn consultation and all agreed that somewhere on the trip she must have touched her foot to the ice when her man wasn't looking. Not often, they pointed out, did a woman die just from having a baby.

Luckily, Toctoo and I knew nothing of this denouement, so we continued to have a fine time, even planning to stay on until the days grew too short to hunt to any advantage. But since we were out of several things it was necessary first to take a few days for a trip to Utkiavie and back.

The village was not so nice as in other winters. Almost everyone was making hooch. What hurt me most was to discover why Appiyow had been so eager to get back. He may have done a little seal hunting, for all I knew. But when I saw him, he was far busier running a still of his own and getting rid of what wealth he had laid by for several years. Incidentally, Appiyow went on making whiskey, gradually losing all the prestige he had among his own people.

I have kept a diary for years, and many years have passed since these events. Glancing back at my entry for October 9, 1927, I am reminded that on that date we buried poor Appiyow; that he died right here in our hospital at Barrow—from the effects of a rupture acquired in the days when the hooch mills ran full blast.

Also, that at his death he was a deacon in the church.

CHAPTER XXVI

"WHAT'S that? Listen!"

Toctoo and I were mushing back to the coast after returning to Takpuc's peaceful camp for a few more weeks' fishing. Overtaken by inky blackness at the end of a short December day's travel, we had hastily thrown up a snow shelter in the dark and crawled inside.

There it came again above the howl of the west wind—a deep, ominous rumbling that seemed to shake the frozen universe.

"What is it?" I repeated.

In those days my ignorance brought many a teasing laugh from Toctoo. But now her voice sounded quite solemn as she explained that it was the ice crushing offshore.

It was my turn to laugh. We were many miles from the coast.

But Toctoo was right. On reaching Utkiavie a couple of days later the first thing we saw was a great ridge of ice piled up all along the shore, with what was left of the old "Ino" smashed and twisted and buried beneath the crush. If we hadn't built our house on a hill . . . !

Even the fifty-foot bluff on which the village stood couldn't always be depended on for safety, according to Mungie. A few years before I came among them, a strong west wind, coupled with just the right current, had forced heavy ice almost to the beach; and this in turn pushed the thinner inshore ice onto the very top of the bluff—right into the village. Several houses near the edge were crushed with everyone inside. It had all happened in the middle of the night.

Mungie scanned the Arctic horizon a moment, thoughtfully, as if recalling the vivid details. Then he added that his father had been among those killed.

Conscience got the better of me in the spring of 1890, and for

144

once I attended to repairs and outfitting instead of going off hunting. In a way, it might have been a lot better had I spent my time hunting and so added a little more meat to the small number of caribou being killed by the natives. Few even took the trouble to try. It was more fun staying home and making hooch.

Con finally got them to sell us four carcasses, but all they would accept in pay was more flour and molasses for replenishing their stills.

Whaling went no better. The ice was terrible. Although Woolfe had fitted out two whaleboats and had Portuguese Joe and our former shipmate, Charlie Ice, with him, his crews were mostly inland Eskimos who knew little about whaling. He had even shipped a good-for-nothing native woman who had run away from her last husband in Nubook and was now living with Joe.

Between hooch, inland natives and dangerous ice conditions, it was left to Pat and Fred to take the only whale killed that year.

Their boat lay on a ridge of ice which started to move, leaving holes along the edge. Suddenly, a whale broke water and lay spouting right in front of them. Pat was asleep in the bow. When shaken by Fred, he grabbed his second bomb-gun without harpoon or line and, still half asleep, darted it out as far as he could. The gun hit the water and slid along until the end of the rod touched the whale's side. Next instant the exploding bomb turned the animal belly-up.

This happened in the middle of May. Towards the end of the month the season closed on a note somberly attuned to that wretched season. It concerned Joe's woman.

She had been telling Joe for some time that soon she would have to go back to her other man at Nubook. And Joe had been urging her to. I don't think he ever cared much for her in the first place. But with a job in hand, she refused to leave until the whaling ended and Woolfe paid her off.

That was the situation at the end of May when she and Joe started to walk ashore from the boat.

Halfway in, they sat down to rest on a sled that someone had left in the ice roadway. They were sitting there talking, according to the woman, when the Eskimo came along with whom she had lived at Nubook before meeting Joe. But instead of showing anger at finding them together, he acted friendly enough, and at Joe's invitation sat down on the sled with them to talk things over.

"Sure, take her," Joe told him, "only you'd better wait 'til all the boats are in. Then she'll have a payday and you two can go back and start over again."

This seemed to suit the Eskimo fine. So pretty soon Joe got up and started for home, leaving the pair seated there together.

The woman said he hadn't gone more than fifty feet when suddenly her man hauled his rifle out of its sack and shot Joe through the small of the back. He must have died instantly. To make sure, though, the native walked up close and shot him again, this time through the head.

Leaving the body sprawled out in a pool of crimson slush, the man and woman walked on into the village where she told some of the Eskimos what had happened. Apparently, nobody laid a hand on the man. He just took his sled and two dogs and headed inland.

Our party knew nothing of all this until Mungie sent a young man out on the ice to tell us. Con then sledded the body ashore, and before long every white man in the place was making for the station.

What we had long dreaded but never discussed had come at last —an Eskimo killing a white man. Had it been Eskimo against Eskimo we could have left it to the natives to settle. This was far more serious. Nobody knew whether the Eskimos would back us up in punishing the murderer, or stand together against us.

After we had thrashed it out a while, getting nowhere fast, the need for a prompt decision of some sort was brought home to me by a glance through the window. Half of Utkiavie, it appeared, was milling around outside waiting to see what the white men would do.

"Way I look at it," I said, getting the floor at last, "this is the time for a firm hand. I don't know how they're going to take it, but I do know what they're going to think of us if we let this murderer get away with it."

There were nods all around. Woolfe summed it up:

"Aye, the man must be punished proper."

We called in Mungie and the other headman, Angaroo, and announced that we were going to arrest the Eskimo, and if he were guilty, as the woman said, he must be executed.

They showed no surprise. At the same time they refused to help, pointing out that the dead man wasn't one of their kind.

The murderer had been gone a couple of hours by now, but one of the old women said that no man could travel fast in the soft snow with only two dogs. She even hinted that he might be found not far from the village, waiting to see what would happen.

It fell to Con, Pat and me to go out for him. The trail led three miles beyond the village. And there, as the woman had said, we found our man waiting. He was standing behind his sled in a gully, rifle over arm.

At sight of us, he threw a cartridge in the chamber. When we kept on walking steadily nearer he took to covering first one then another, unable to make up his mind which of us to shoot first.

Nobody spoke. Those last twenty-five feet were the most unpleasant I ever walked.

With his rifle pointing straight at the pit of my stomach, the man made just one mistake. He waited an instant too long before shifting it to Pat who was closest to the sled. For in that split-second, Pat vaulted over, knocked the gun in the air and grabbed his man.

Con and I soon had him down and, lashing his hands behind him, we headed back to the station where the rest of our crowd were watching anxiously. Every Eskimo had left.

Believing that all the natives should be on hand for the trial, we sent word to the village. Only Mungie and Angaroo and a few of the older men showed up. However, they brought the woman along as witness and listened stolidly while she repeated what had happened on the road coming in.

She said that after the shooting she had gone with the man because he would have killed her if she hadn't. Beyond readily agreeing with everything she said, the prisoner had nothing to add except that if we let him go he would never kill another white man.

We found him guilty. The sentence was death.

It was not a popular verdict among the Eskimos, their point being that there would have been no killing except for the woman.

But at last Angaroo reminded them that had the victim been an Eskimo some other Eskimo would certainly kill the murderer and maybe his whole family. Therefore, it was right for him to die. He did think, however, that since the woman had caused it all, she also should be shot. This last, of course, we wouldn't consider.

Although all of us were hoping that the natives would at least agree to carry out the actual execution, they absolutely refused. So that, too, was left for us.

Old John loaded four rifles with ball cartridges, the others with blanks. Nobody knew which was which. Then we took the native half a mile inland and shot him. One official touch remained for Mungie. As headman, he made the woman wrap the body in deerskin and leave it where it lay.

We buried Portuguese Joe over the hill not far from the station —the first white man I every helped bury at Point Barrow. Later that summer the woman went away in one of the whalers and we didn't see her again.

When the "Bear" arrived, Woolfe handed Captain Healy a written report setting forth all the circumstances of the murder. It was a meticulous, long-worked-over document which we hoped would enable the authorities to justify our action as clearly as we did ourselves. The result was somewhat different from what we had expected.

Said Healy, severely: "I don't want your damn report, Woolfe."

"But, Captain,—it explains—"

"You men had a perfect right to shoot that fellow on sight."

And tearing up the report, Captain Healy tossed the pieces overboard.

CHAPTER XXVII

THE squirt of a grapefruit is more predictable than were the ways of the old Pacific Steam Whaling Company. I should have learned that much by the summer of 1891. But it certainly surprised me to have a new man arrive to relieve Woolfe at the station in place of George Leavitt whom we all had expected back. And when I made out the new man's identity I nearly fell over. It was John W. Kelley.

Next to George, however, I couldn't have asked for a better whaling rival than the hearty, hard-headed prospector whom I had left down at Corwin Bluff unloading his supplies after our social call on Attungowrah.

Kelley had brought several Portuguese along for boat-headers but was depending for his crews on a lot of Point Hope natives who had come north to work for him at the Company station.

Most of them I knew, and the first thing they told me, clustering excitedly about, was of a great feud at Tigara.

Trouble started, they explained, during the recent spring whaling when the wife of Ouloucharoy, one of Attungowrah's sons, broke an ancient taboo.

For many generations it had been a strict whaling custom among the Eskimos that should a woman refuse to go ashore during menstruation, she must be severely beaten. If by any chance she happened to urinate while out on the ice, her punishment was death.

This last was what Ouloucharoy's luckless wife had been seen to do as she made her way ashore from the boat. When it was reported to her husband he immediately followed her in, and with the full approval of all the devil-doctors, beat her until she died. Ordinarily, the matter would have ended there.

But the woman belonged to a warlike tribe below Cape Thompson, and when her brothers learned what had happened, they hur-

149

ried north looking for the murderer. For some time Ouloucharoy managed to avoid them. Then one day they caught him off his guard and shot him dead—and the feud was on. First one side, then the other, killed somebody every few days until the dead numbered an even dozen. Knowing Attungowrah as I did, I could visualize the old boy with the charmed life strutting about in all his glory amidst the slaughter.

But the long, insidious reach of "Browne's Place" had touched him at last. For, with the arrival of the ships he proceeded to let himself get good and drunk, and sleeping it off in an igloo with the gut window foolishly left uncovered, he, too, received a mysterious bullet which hurt him so badly that he couldn't move.

This was the moment for one of his wives to square accounts for long years of mistreatment. She had come originally from below Cape Thompson herself and so was on that side of the feud. Armed with her colura, a woman's knife fashioned from a saw-blade and shaped like an old-style chopping knife, she crept up close, paused an instant to make sure the old man was helpless, then jabbed the sharp point well into his brain.

It was hard for me to realize that Attungowrah was really dead, —Attungowrah, the most brutish human I ever met! A man who at one time would have added me to his other victims without second thought! And beneath all his bluster, a craven bully! Could anybody command *less* admiration?

Just why a mist should have come over my eyes as I learned of his grizzly end is something I have never quite reasoned out myself.

John Shuman, our cook, was getting old and quite useless. At his request we shipped him out with Captain Smith on the "Baleana" and began looking about for another cook—no easy find, eleven hundred miles from the Pole.

Last to leave that fall was the schooner "Alton." Finally her skipper, a man named Newth, admitted that he had a Dane among his crew who was a good cook but too cantankerous to live with.

"He might do better ashore," I suggested eagerly. "Would you let him go?"

Newth's laugh sounded like cracked china. "If Big George figured I *wanted* to get rid of him, he just wouldn't go,—that's the devil of it."

"But—"

"Listen! Here's an idea! Suppose you sort of coaxed him to *run away*—" He ended by winking one eye.

Pretty soon Newth arranged for Tom and me to look the fellow over in private. Big George talked all right, but was certain the captain was too mean to let him go. That was where we got in our fine work, pointing out that here was his chance to get even with the skipper by running away. Since the "Alton" was to leave early next morning, there would be no time for a search.

As the plan unfolded, Big George's eyes gleamed at the thought of so clever a revenge. He could hardly wait for darkness.

That night at nine we paddled out according to schedule, tied up at the forerigging and went aft in order to allow Big George plenty of time. After spending an hilarious hour or so helping Captain Newth and his officers celebrate getting rid of their troublesome cook, we said goodbye to all hands and strolled leisurely forward. The "runaway" was hiding in our boat and came ashore with us, glancing stealthily behind and thoroughly enjoying the thrill of putting one over on the skipper.

Somewhat to our surprise, we liked Big George fine as a cook, despite his strange allergy to shoes. He never wore them in the house, and seldom outside. His enormous feet seemed impervious to any treatment, however harsh. Their soles must have been calloused a half-inch thick.

I never think of Big George today without recalling my surprise at finding him calmly repairing the smoke-pipe while standing barefooted on the red-hot stove.

He worked for us until spring, then went with Kelley and was responsible for killing seven of the twelve whales taken by Kelley's men that season.

Kelley was setting a new fashion in whaling at Point Barrow.

Instead of hauling his boats out to the flaw light, each was heavily loaded with tent, stove, food and everything to allow its crew to live comfortably on the ice. They didn't even have to come ashore to dry their clothing. Also, the women of his outfit ran sleds out and back every day, bringing whatever else might be needed. The fact that all hands could tend constantly to business was the main reason for Kelley's twelve whales.

With a far smaller number of boats, Tom and I took five ourselves, which wasn't doing so badly. But the Eskimos, who still clung to many of their ancient whaling methods, caught only *one whale between them all.*

That demonstration, I think, did more than years of argument to bring them over to the white man's way of doing things.

After we had cleaned all our bone, Con, Fred, Patsy and Ned felt so wealthy that they thought the time ripe for a grand blowout at San Francisco, and urged Tom and me to join them.

But whether prompted by caution or greed—perhaps both— we decided to stay one more year. After that, we said—and shook hands on it—we, too, would be ready to go outside for a little fun. Finally, a friendly deal was cooked up around the stove, in which the four "playboys" sold us their entire interest in the station. No red tape was involved. We merely adjourned to the storehouse and divided our bone and furs equally, agreed on a fair value for boats and house, paid the others their share (in bone) and found ourselves with a nice little nest-egg left.

In spite of Kelley and his crowd, I can't say that Tom and I didn't feel a bit lonely after the "Bear" gave our boys passage home. But there was little time for nostalgic musing. Fate, in the form of slush ice, was already preparing our return to piracy.

Whaling had been good around the Point all summer and four of the steamers stayed later than I had ever known them. One October night, as they nosed single file through a snowstorm to anchor under Point Barrow, their course was obstructed by streaks of slush ice which called for bursts of speed to smash through.

Spotting one such patch ahead, Captain Sherman of the "William

Lewis" rang for full speed as usual, and a moment later piled his vessel high on a snow-covered sandspit that had looked exactly like slush ice in the dark. Luckily, the others stopped and backed in time. The "William Lewis," abandoned, was left to anybody who would salvage her.

By the time Tom and I got there, the Point Barrow natives had cleaned out everything easily removed. But by hiring a number of them to work for us, we saved ten casks of hard bread, one of fresh cabbage, several sacks of potatoes and onions, besides clothing from the ship's slop-chest and a lot of whaling spades.

Then we unbent her sails, and cut the rigging on the high side to get her spars for boat-building lumber. A man was stationed at the foot of each mast, axe in hand. At a signal they began chopping. Finally, down went the masts over the side, all at once. What a mess! But well worth the trouble.

That misleading patch of "slush ice" seen through a blizzard put Tom and me on Easy Street until the new year turned us from piracy to the more prosaic job of building new oomiaks for the whaling season.

While prowling around the village in search of someone sober enough to make our whalebone lashings, I came across a very old man placidly knitting himself a whalebone fishnet. He had been knitting on it for two years already. Since he planned to make the net twenty fathoms long when finished, I was sure that he'd keep right on knitting until he died. Yet I wanted that net as a curio. Would he sell it?

No. In summer, he said, it would look like grass in the water and undoubtedly catch him a lot of fish.

Without reminding him that he'd probably be dead long before those fish, I dropped the matter. Whereupon he agreed to sell me the net after all, but warned that he couldn't promise when it would be done.

Two years later, after I had forgotten the whole incident, he brought me the completed net as a matter of ordinary business procedure, having worked on it constantly ever since.

A great one to babble about the old days, he once described a whalebone bow the natives used to make for the sole purpose of assassinating an enemy. It had to be short enough to conceal under the attiga. The arrow, too, was short, and tipped with an extra sharp flint point. This kind of bone bow, he declared, could be made powerful enough to drive the arrow almost through a man's body.

I professed polite surprise, but kept my mental reservations to myself.

While breaking into an ancient, isolated icehouse only a few years ago, I was startled to find myself staring at the well-preserved body of a seated man dressed in curious loonskin clothing. How many generations he had been sitting in his Arctic tomb was any-one's guess.

All at once my old net-maker's crazy yarns came to mind. For sticking out of this corpse right above the heart was the end of a short, flint-tipped arrow that must have been driven at close quarters by a particularly powerful bow.

CHAPTER XXVIII

TOM and I had meant it. One more spring up here would satisfy us for a while. Of this we felt certain. So we approached the coming 1892 whaling with the firm determination of taking a year's vacation afterwards.

There was a time right at the start when it seemed we'd stayed too long already. Everything went against us, including the weather. Thirty-five below zero would have made whaling from open boats almost an impossibility had there been any whales to chase. Even after things started, the Eskimos got the jump on us, taking three big ones before we saw a spout.

But early in May our luck changed. By the time the short season closed, we had taken five between us, with a gross bone value of slightly over forty thousand dollars.

Spurred on by all this sudden success, Tom and I now decided that we wanted one *more* year. If that proved equally good, *then* we'd go outside for a rest, perhaps to organize a company of our own for accomplishing still bigger things. So far as we could see, there wasn't an obstacle in sight. But we didn't understand "big business."

I'm afraid our heads were just a little in the clouds when we boarded the first incoming Company ship that summer for the routine purpose of buying necessary supplies for another year. No longer beggars asking credit of canny skippers, we could now pay even the outrageous prices they were pretty sure to ask.

We came ashore from that first ship empty-handed and slightly puzzled but not at all discouraged. It just happened they were short of what we wanted, that was all. Probably the "Orca," they suggested politely, could fit us out.

We tackled the "Orca." Same result.

As the other Company ships arrived—and the Pacific Steam

Whaling Company controlled the trade in those days—I took to boarding them in succession, each time coming away more puzzled than before. Only after an eye-opening interview with one captain franker than the rest did it begin to dawn on me what we were up against in trying to keep on another year.

"Make a deal?" asked Tom, hopefully, as I came dragging in.

I answered dully: "You know what the Company has gone and done, Tom? *Black-listed* us! That's what they've done!"

Fearful that we'd cut into their own whaling under Kelley, they'd given each captain specific orders to refuse to sell us so much as a bomb. It ended our cherished plans for one more easy, profitable season.

Cooling off, I couldn't believe that Kelley himself had anything to do with it, much less that he would work actively against us. Kelley wasn't that sort. But Tom shook his head. And I will admit that the first visit Kelley paid us after the ships had left for the east went far to warrant Tom's suspicions.

His Company, said Kelley, wanted to buy us out and had authorized him to make a deal.

"What'll they pay?" I asked icily, after a pause.

Kelley cleared his throat. "Five hundred dollars."

Tom, whose home was in Scotland, hit the ceiling. I laughed myself. Even Kelley grinned. But on leaving, he added, significantly, that he wanted to do us a good turn if he could.

"A hell of a good turn *that* is!" roared Tom, when we were alone. "Five hundred dollars!"

When Kelley returned next morning and raised his offer to a thousand, Tom's brows went up a notch but we both refused. The following day he dropped in again. Fifteen hundred this time.

We sat tight with an effort. Except for the valuable bone which would still belong to us, we didn't have seven hundred dollars' worth of stuff in the place.

Kelley's calls continued for several days more, each bringing a raise of five hundred dollars. It was a ridiculous performance. When his price touched thirty-five hundred, Tom and I both yelled our acceptance before he could possibly back out.

Reassurance of my faith in Kelley's friendship was nearly as heartening as the draft on the Company that he handed Tom and me before Captain Healy of the "Bear" took us south.

Many days later the familiar contour of San Francisco loomed up through the early morning mist. We piled ashore and made for the office of the Pacific Steam Whaling Company to present Kelley's draft and try to sell them our bone, as well. Thanks to careful drying, it hadn't shrunk the usual ten percent during the long passage south and so should be a fine buy.

Our draft they cashed promptly but sale of the bone was something else. Unfortunately, Captain Knowles, head of the firm, had gone to New York and Ned Griffith who was in charge refused to commit himself.

The uncertainty kept us fuming around 'Frisco until Knowles got back and agreed to take all our bone at near the market price.

Flush for the first time in our lives, and with no immediate problems ahead, the sale left us with a let-down feeling hard to describe. Life would have flattened out completely except that each was busy planning a long visit home before again tackling the thrills and uncertainties of the Far North.

And so a few days after pocketing our cash we headed east. I had written my family to get the fatted calf ready, but Tom, with a continent and an ocean to cross, preferred to surprise his folks.

That trip back home was something I have never regretted. My father wasn't in very good circumstances or health, and although still working as station agent for the railroad, expected soon to be replaced by a younger man. On top of this worry he was trying to sell a new house, hardly finished, so that he and mother could live in a smaller place.

I couldn't have shown up at a more critical moment. And what fun I had paying all he owed on the new house, furnishing a smaller, cozier one to suit them and moving them in! Then I paid off a bothersome mortgage on some other property he owned. This, with his Civil War pension and what he could make as Justice of the

Peace, would give him enough to live on comfortably the rest of his life.

A far cry, indeed, from the bleak ice-pack off Point Barrow to the comforts of a snug house in New Jersey!

But the fact that one had made the other possible seemed somehow to justify my return to the top of the world where Toctoo would be waiting.

CHAPTER XXIX

On the tenth of June, 1893, the little schooner "Jennie Wand" tacked out through the Golden Gate and squared away towards the northwest horizon. The fact that she had been leased by the newly formed Cape Smythe Whaling and Trading Company, so named from the promontory on which Utkiavie stood, requires a word of explanation.

When I joined Tom Gordon in California after his return from his surprise visit to Scotland, we tried hard to get the old Pacific Whaling outfit to back us in a new whaling venture. Perhaps it was as well the deal fell through for want of an adequate guarantee because we made a far better tie-up with H. Liebes and Company, the largest furriers on the coast.

At first, Mr. Liebes, as cautious as he was generous, hesitated to go in with Tom and me. But when he discovered that, unlike most promoters, we actually wanted to put in *our own* money along with his, he hit the desk a sledge-hammer blow and exploded:

"Done! Charter a schooner, boys, and get up there soon's you can."

That was the way I liked to do business.

So here we were, Tom and I, aboard our own schooner properly outfitted for once, with Mr. Liebes in 'Frisco to dispose of what we shipped out—and at our side Conrad Siem who, wandering about the waterfront, had jumped at the chance to come along and work for the new company.

In time the "Jennie Wand" anchored off Utkiavie where everybody was glad to see us again. All hands landed our stuff on the ice, later helping erect first our important storehouse, then the main building containing living quarters, store, workshop and kitchen. For the new station we had chosen a handy spot a half-mile north of Kelley's.

One of the few things we still lacked was a team of dogs. Con, who loved trading, thought he could buy six good ones from some inland Eskimos then at Utkiavie. Only he said we must let him take his time if we wanted a bargain. He took so much time that Tom and I got worried.

"Lots of time, Charlie," he insisted. "Just leave it to me."

One day we heard that the natives were leaving that same night for up the rivers, so at last Con sent word for them to bring over any good dogs they wanted to sell.

One fellow arrived with a fine looking animal. Con bought it, and giving the Eskimo a chain told him to tie the dog to some lumber. Other natives followed suit. Presently we had six dogs tied, and Con came beaming.

"That's the way to get a bargain. If I'd gone at 'em sooner they'd have held me up, see? I know natives."

Yes, we admitted, Con was a shrewd trader. They seemed excellent dogs, all six of them.

After the inland people had left, Tom and I thought we'd look the team over and walked across to the lumber pile.

There were six dogs, all right—and not one worth the price of a bullet to kill it. We yelled for Con.

When our expert trader saw that the Eskimos had skillfully switched dogs on him just before leaving, his face was worth more than what the deal cost the Cape Smythe Whaling and Trading Company.

With all the good-natured kidding, we made a merry crew. I should have felt supremely happy except for the absence of Toc-too, who had been staying inland with one of her younger brothers. When word finally reached her of my arrival and she came hurrying down the river to join me, bringing our baby and a boatload of dried fish, my home-coming was complete.

Why she had gone inland instead of remaining with Baby and his family at Utkiavie wasn't quite clear at first. Then I was told that, like many of the villagers, even Baby was full now whenever he could get hold of hooch. This was just as long as the trading schooners were here and the "Bear" somewhere else. Apparently hooch had a firmer-than-ever grip on Utkiavie. Three Eskimos had been murdered the year before, all on account of liquor.

It was partly to have a long talk with Baby that I took him to Wainwright in November to buy skins for the six boats that Tom and I planned to run in the spring. Loyal and lovable as ever, he seemed to appreciate my arguments and promised never to touch hooch again.

Halfway to Wainwright we met a team coming from Port Clarence. Though strangers to me, Baby made a great fuss over them, explaining that they were friends of his father's. I was glad to know that they were to be at Utkiavie. Perhaps, with their help, I could keep Baby straight.

We got back shortly before Christmas. Two days later he beat up a couple of village Eskimos so badly that they couldn't see. This was followed by another drunken spree in which he was joined by one of his father's good friends from Port Clarence. It ended during the night with Baby nearly killing the fellow.

But Baby's number was up. When he left, the Port Clarence man silently trailed him, rifle in hand. Just as they reached the last house in the village he shot Baby through both legs and hurried away, leaving him lying helpless on the path. Then, one of the pair that Baby had thrashed a while before came running up. After stabbing Baby through the heart, he tied a rope around his neck and dragged him some distance off the path.

I knew nothing of all this until somebody reported finding Baby's body just after daylight. An hour later his family silently sledded their dead son and brother over to our station, where all stood about with expressions that boded no good for anyone concerned. Baby's youngest brother swore to kill the Port Clarence man who had done the shooting.

When the old fellow heard that this young man was out to get him, he sent word that if the boy ever made a move he'd kill him on sight. It looked as if we were in for a feud like the one at Tigara —something I determined to prevent if humanly possible. Finally,

I got hold of the kid brother and backed him into a corner.

"Now, listen," I soothed, "Baby was a good friend of mine, too. His sister is my wife. Just the same, he brought this on himself. What good will any more killings do?"

Leaving the boy smoldering, I hunted up the Port Clarence man and read the riot act to him until he finally promised to pay Baby's mother what he considered a fair compensation for his part in the trouble. More important, he also agreed to quit Utkiavie before the youngster could do him harm. I was ashamed to carry the man's offer back to Baby's mother—astonished when she accepted it promptly. *One new sled and four dogs!* But it was the best I could do.

Not until we came to bury Baby a half-mile back from the station did I realize the full extent of his popularity along the coast. All of Kelley's natives, as well as those working for us, showed up to help. The proper ceremony, they insisted, would be to leave the coffined body on the ground beneath an immense pile of laboriously gathered driftwood.

So that was the end of Baby—a mighty fine fellow when sober, a loyal friend to me at all times.

Luckily, the Port Clarence man had cleared out as promised. I never saw him again, for the next summer he and his two sons were killed somewhere to the south. The identity of their assassin was to remain a mystery for two more years. Then one of our own villagers, a distant relative of Baby's, became blind, and in that condition suddenly confessed that it was he who had polished off the trio.

Because of his lifelong "weakness" for relatives, however distant, could anything have pleased Baby more?

I was glad when the holidays were over and a new sun began to turn the Eskimos from hooch to early preparations for spring whaling. Hard work seemed their only salvation.

We at the station set an example by nearly killing ourselves building oomiaks and overhauling equipment. I myself worked so constantly making lashings that by February I hated to look a piece of whalebone in the eye. Since we were out of fish, I seized on that as an excuse for a short fishing excursion all by myself.

The camp was only about forty miles inland and clear moonlight and long hours of mushing brought me there in a day and a half. Presently, I started back with all the fish the sled would load.

The weather was fine that morning, with just enough breeze to make one hustle to keep warm. Afternoon brought a freshening of the wind. By dark it was blowing a gale, and with the temperature dropping fast, I knew I couldn't reach home that night. Still, I was warmly clad in skin clothing, so decided to push on as long as possible. To help the straining dogs I even harnessed myself alongside the sled.

The forty-below-zero weather offered a challenge and I was glorying in the rough going when all at once I slipped and went down awkwardly. But my laughter was cut short by a draft of icy air that made me feel like one of the little tomcods which curled and froze stiff the instant the women fished them up through the ice.

Investigation showed that in falling I had split the inside leg-seam of my skin pants from knee to crotch. This called for major repairs in a hurry.

Shaking from the icy up-draft, I managed to build a tiny snow shelter and feed the dogs without actually freezing to death. Then, crawling inside, I lit my native stone lamp, feeding it with seal oil and using chopped moss mixed with oil for a wick. It gave little heat and hardly any light—just enough to let me find my sewing kit. I always kept this vital item in a certain part of my pack, so knew exactly where to look. But the kit wasn't there.

Really alarmed now, I wound my snow shirt around the exposed leg and began pawing through the whole pack. Still no kit.

For the first time in my life while traveling, I'd left my sewing kit behind!

Well, I had to sew those pants up *somehow,* or freeze.

After much rummaging I found an empty 45/70 cartridge shell

and made a small hole in it for an eye. Then I whittled away at the thing until something emerged that might pass for a needle. Thread was easier,—the ravelings out of my sled cover furnishing the raw material.

I have often laughed at the picture I must have presented that night: a lone, shivering white man with no pants on, seated tailor-fashion in a snow hut eleven hundred miles from the Pole, sewing for dear life by the faint gleam of a seal-oil lamp. It was no joke at the time.

I was thankful enough to wriggle into my pants once more, and eat a couple of frozen fish, gratefully washing them down with a small bucket of tea for dessert.

Next morning the weather turned fine again and that night I reached home with my patchwork still holding. I shall never forget Toctoo's face when she looked at those pants. She didn't know whether to laugh or cry. In the end she gave me some advice about leaving sewing kits behind when traveling in the Arctic.

Good, sound advice—but needless.

CHAPTER XXX

As far back as George Leavitt's day, I had seen the beginning of a change in the Eskimo attitude towards white man's whaling methods. By the spring of 1894, those few natives who still preferred running boats of their own to hiring out to us met little success. Somehow, their forefathers' charms no longer worked—regrettable as this seemed from a sentimental point of view.

But neither native nor white had time for sentiment where whaling was concerned. Which leads me to make a confession. I've never felt particularly proud of the incident, and yet—well, here goes.

The first season of the Cape Smythe Whaling and Trading Company had been a big success. Nine whales! It was while cruising far off the coast in search of a tenth that my crew spotted a flock of seagulls feeding on what we found to be a dead whale, almost fresh. We towed the carcass to a small piece of ice for easier handling.

Suddenly one of the men gave a surprised grunt and pointed excitedly. Our whale had an iron in its body. By rights it belonged to someone else.

You may remember how several years before, when we hadn't killed a whale all season, the Eskimos had robbed us of one that we had struck and lost; and how we'd let them get away with it for fear of trouble. I had thought that our wisest course, but the injustice had always rankled.

Now the sight of this tell-tale iron brought it all back.

"Swing around so I can see whose iron that is," I ordered.

They swung our stern until I managed to cut out the protruding metal. But nobody ever examined it. Somehow, the iron slipped right through my fingers and fell overboard.

Still kidding me because of my "awkwardness," the boys headed for home with the extra bone which closed our season.

165

No, I've never felt exactly *proud* of the performance. Yet the squaring of that old account, almost forgotten these fifty-odd years, gives me a glow of righteous satisfaction even today.

Another source of satisfaction about then was the addition of my old friend, Fred Hopson, to our Company payroll again. Everyone liked Fred. Besides, his joining the station left me freer to spend the summer as I wished.

In those days Harrison Bay, 150 miles to the east, was a great place for boat-lumber; and since we wanted to run eight oomiaks next season, including three new ones to be built, I decided on a leisurely trek eastward, hunting, fishing and exploring, with Harrison Bay and its lumber my nominal objective. One of the Point Barrow natives named Attooktua, who knew the country and was an excellent boat-builder, agreed to go along.

Taking our whaling oomiak on its sled, with another frame sled and four dogs, we finally got away late in June—Attooktua and his wife, Toctoo with our baby, and I—traveling by easy stages until we came to a party of Eskimo hunters camped near the mouth of the Chipp River back of Point Tangent.

Some of them hailed from far-off Kotzebue Sound, having left there the previous summer. When we saw how loaded down they were with furs of beaver, land otter, marten and mink, I suddenly remembered that ours was a trading as well as whaling company.

"When you get around Point Barrow," I told them, "take all your stuff to my man, Con. He'll pay you more than the ships will."

There was a powwow. Finally most of them said they would, although several made it clear that they wanted their pay in "tonga," or whiskey. I have no doubt they got their "tonga,"—but not from the Cape Smythe Whaling and Trading Company.

Then, striking inland for some days, we paddled, hauled and shoved through a tortuous region of rivers and ponds until we reached huge Tashicpuk Lake. Attooktua assured me it had a bad reputation. Very bad, indeed.

The Eskimos used to come here to spear ducks from their small kayaks, he said. Now they were all afraid, since several had been attacked by ferocious fish larger than a kayak. A pleasant tale to fall asleep on just before setting out on a two-day paddle down that same waterway!

I kept a sharp lookout the whole time, hoping to catch sight of one of these fish, but nothing bothered us. Shortly after landing at the eastern end, Attooktua came running with bulging eyes and pointed in triumph to the ancient bones of some large animal which he insisted formed part of the backbone of one of the man-eating fish.

This was the only "proof" I ever found of their existence. However, the legend undoubtedly had its source in something besides Attooktua's lively imagination. Long afterwards an old man told me of having escaped death from these terrible fish only by being in a big oomiak with others, instead of in his flimsy kayak alone. At the time, they were using paddles stained bright red. The great fish, he said, came alongside their oomiak, snapping viciously at the blades which they probably took for raw meat.

We were in no hurry to come out on Harrison Bay for our oomiak lumber. With caribou all about us and fish so numerous that sometimes we could catch a week's supply in a single hour, it was a great life.

Attooktua seemed quite familiar with the whole region and one of our camping spots reminded him that right here was where some Nubook natives had lost two of their children to an oogroognoon not so long ago.

"That's a new one," I observed. "What's an oogroognoon?"

Attooktua pictured the animal minutely. It was the size of a small bear and lived in a den under the banks of the lake, coming out only when hungry. He described how its fur, fine like a beaver's, glistened under water when the sun shone on it.

"Well, what about these two children?"

Attooktua shrugged. They had gone over the hill to play and never had been seen since. So undoubtedly the oogroognoon had carried them to its den and devoured them.

I tried to suggest that wolves might have been responsible, but he looked so hurt that I didn't press the matter. In fact, it passed out of my mind entirely until he came back to camp one day lugging a curious skull. Perhaps now I would believe what he had told me. See! Here was the skull of an oogroognoon—no doubt the very one that had dragged the children to its under-water den.

I examined the skull and, with a solemn nod, handed back to him the skull of a *prehistoric horse!*

Just east of us was a river widened to a lake. Here we visited some native hunters engaged in spearing caribou from their kayaks. Attooktua showed me two rows of sod piled a couple of feet high and covered with pillars of black moss. The rows were about three miles long, I judged, and a mile apart at the far end, but narrowed to a point of land which led into the lake.

Whenever a herd entered the wide-open section, all the women and children circled about, gradually driving the animals into this converging runway where they mistook the moss-covered pillars for more human enemies. It was amazing the way they sheared from side to side as they got in deeper, too frightened to leap the low ridges which alone separated them from freedom.

Finally, driven out on the point, they would take to the water to escape. The waiting hunters, lying under the bank in kayaks, now forced their craft right in among the swimming caribou, spearing them from both sides. Sometimes they killed as many as a hundred in one drive.

Just for the experience, and much against Attooktua's advice, I took my place in one of their kayaks and listened as a great antlered herd came plunging across the soft tundra right into the water where we lay hidden.

As Attooktua well knew, I was no expert with a ticklish kayak and had my hands full keeping rightside up, let alone using a spear. The result was that several animals had been lanced before I got anywhere near. But after a while I managed to maneuver into proper position and killed two. That was enough for me. It seemed like slaughter.

Before the hunters broke camp I bought one of their kayaks. Attooktua bought another, thinking it would give him a better chance to rescue me when I turned turtle.

Then for several weeks we hunted by ourselves, and in our own orthodox way. It was grand sport except for mosquitoes. We wondered, sometimes, who was the hunter, who the hunted. That was when they grew so fierce that we could do nothing but seal ourselves in the tent and wait for a breeze.

The caribou fared worse. They would plunge madly into any handy lake or river and stand there all day with only their noses out. Otherwise, they tried to escape the torment by just running.

By the middle of August, with over one hundred caribou to our credit, we finally pitched camp at Harrison Bay, loaded down with bales of dried meat and skins. Then began the job of selecting lumber for next year's oomiaks.

Attooktua and I were busy roughing out some frames one evening when the women cried that there was a whaleboat coming from the east.

CHAPTER XXXI

PRESENTLY, a second boat appeared. Spotting our camp, both headed in.

As they drew nearer I could make out a lot of cussing mixed with their loud talk, and gathered that to them we were just one more lousy bunch of natives.

I didn't mind in the least being taken for an Eskimo, but the language coming across the water would have 'roused a saint. I was all set to bellow back in kind. On second thought, I waited until the first boat hit the beach, then, bowing low, cut short their leader's foul abuse with a clipped and really elegant,

"Good evening, gentlemen! Please consider us at your service."

Sixteen jaws dropped. The second boat grounded in silence. At last somebody laughed and I haw-hawed back. Next moment they had turned into human beings, so far as possible for a type like that.

It seemed they belonged to the bark "Reindeer," recently forced ashore by the ice at Cross Island. Their captain had transferred to another ship. The rest of the crew would be along later in a third whaleboat. All were bound for the Refuge Station at Utkiavie; and now, they inquired quite humbly, what th' hell could I give 'em to eat?

Several kettlesful of boiled meat put them in an almost skittish frame of mind. It wasn't long before somebody noticed our two kayaks and several of the men immediately wanted to test them out. Both Attooktua and I tried to prevent this.

"Aw,—let th' damn fools drown if they want to," their leader put in.

The first fellow had hardly pushed off from the beach before he wobbled a few times and capsized. So we hauled him out and put him in bed while Toctoo and Attooktua's wife dried his clothes.

Nobody else wanted to try.

My sole regret over the incident was that it confirmed Attook-tua's poor opinion of any white man fooling around with a kayak. Whenever I took mine out he still cackled like an old hen over a duckling in a pond.

After sending our shipwrecked mariners west next morning with ample fresh meat in their whaleboat and a good wind behind, we stayed at Harrison Bay a couple of days longer, then packed up and sailed after them, our two kayaks towing lightly behind.

It was while held up by several days of bad weather at the mouth of a river half way to Cape Halkett that we watched the third whaleboat from the "Reindeer" wallowing by well offshore. We could see that they knew nothing about sailing. They even had their sail hoisted upside down. How they got this far without coming to grief seemed a miracle.

Attooktua's worry over me and my kayak came to a head shortly after. It happened that a Utkiavie-bound party of natives came ashore and camped near us on a lagoon, beyond which was some excellent hunting. Since these chaps used their kayaks for getting across and bringing back their meat, I insisted that we do the same. But poor Attooktua was so afraid I'd drown that our new neighbors thought it a good joke. Finally, one of them grew careless and actually tipped over himself—fortunately in shallow water, since none of the natives could swim a stroke. After that, poor Attooktua's well-meant warnings really got on my nerves. I didn't like being coddled—before strangers, anyhow—and decided to end this kayak foolishness, once for all.

The day was unusually warm. While our two parties were lying in the sun swapping news, I quietly pushed off in my kayak and sounded the river from bank to bank, finding good, deep water the whole seventy or eighty feet.

Sneaking into our empty tent unnoticed, I peeled off every stitch of clothing. Then with a yell I burst out, galloped full-speed to the bank and took a header in the river.

Coming up on the opposite side and looking back, it seemed as if all hands had gone crazy. Men, women and children ran around shouting and screaming. A small rescue group led by Attooktua was shoving one of the big oomiaks into the water. They never had seen a person dive before and thought I was drowning. When they noticed me swimming leisurely towards them, a great silence fell.

But afterwards, Attooktua said plenty, and for quite a while was very angry with me for scaring him to death. His real grievance, I think, was that he couldn't worry over me in a kayak any more. In fact, he never referred to my kayak again except once.

We were halfway across shallow, treacherous Smith Bay when a squall hit us. Soon our deeply laden oomiak was shipping water dangerously. With the nearest land five or six miles off, and two women and a baby aboard, we were in a bad way. Then in rapid gutturals Attooktua explained how my kayak might save us.

"Worth trying," I yelled back.

After hauling the wildly yawning craft alongside, we tied a raincoat over the "manhole" cockpit to make it tight. His scheme was then to lash to the kayak, forward and aft, some of those boat-frames we were taking home, fastening their other ends to our oomiak. This gave us a makeshift catamaran with a kayak "outrigger" to keep us steady. Our whole party now shifted to the lee side to prevent the kayak from lifting out of the water at every roll.

When all was ready, we cautiously raised a reefed sail, prepared to yank it down again at the first sign of trouble. She took it beautifully. So, giving her full sail, we came tearing over to Cape Simpson in a cloud of spray and presently landed behind a sandy point, thoroughly soaked, but otherwise unharmed.

A few days later saw our party safely home with one hundred thirty-seven skins, many bales of dried meat, and all the woodwork for three new oomiaks.

That was my idea of a summer vacation!

One thing bothered me, though. "Anybody seen the crew of the 'Reindeer'?" I asked, as soon as we landed.

"Don't worry," said Fred, with a disgusted laugh, "they're over at the Rescue Station. You can't drown drunks or fools, Charlie."

When we didn't arrive as early as expected, Fred had gathered an Eskimo crew and started down the coast to investigate. Forced to camp near Point Tangent by the same bad weather that was delaying us farther east, his introduction to the "Reindeer's" men consisted in helping the crew of the third whaleboat to get ashore from their badly stove craft.

"I *figured* they were greenhorns from the way they had their sail set," Fred observed. "And I *knew* it soon's we got 'em on the beach. That blacksmith— O Lord—!"

Fred doubled up with laughter so that others had to describe how the blacksmith, considering himself an officer of sorts, had strapped on a 45/70 revolver and threatened to shoot anybody who didn't do as he ordered.

After getting the men ashore, Fred's first job had been to take the fellow's gun away. His second, to try and prevent their setting out next morning in weather that would have finished any new boat, not to mention a hastily repaired one.

But when the blacksmith insisted on trying it, all Fred could do was hand him back his revolver and wait until they'd stove another hole in their boat—which fortunately happened close enough to the beach for Fred and his men to haul them out, as before. Only this time they lost everything they owned.

"Yes, sir," Fred resumed, "takes more than one ducking to knock sense into imbeciles. But it sure made me hot," he added, apologetically, "having to lug them back here to the Rescue Station instead of going on to look for you."

We were all quite satisfied later when long-suffering Captain Healy of the "Bear" gave the "Reindeer" men passage south where they belonged.

CHAPTER XXXII

THE Point Barrow of those days was the world's northernmost "gambling den."

With the ice pack our table, bomb-guns for cards and whales the stake, we handful of whites played against the Arctic through good luck and bad, too busy dodging thrashing flukes to realize that the industry as a whole was beginning to slip even then.

Ice and storm took their annual toll. Many of the sailing ships were lost each season, never to be replaced. When a new steam whaler went into service now it was only to make up for another crushed and abandoned. But to us, one profitable season meant another sure to follow. If it didn't, we cheerfully chanted our old refrain— "But wait till *next* spring!"

Only a God-given optimism could have kept us grinning after so disappointing a season as the spring of 1895, with two lone whales taken by our eight boats. It helped, of course, to know that Kelley, with all his twenty crews, had killed only *one*. We were very human.

But if bone was scarce, excitement wasn't. It started right in before the season had fairly opened when a heavy northeast gale caught all Kelley's boats and most of ours many miles south of the road. Soon neither Attooktua nor I nor anybody else in our boat could see fifty feet inshore. That was all right. We were used to it. No one thought for a minute that the ice we were on could possibly break.

So all hands felt reasonably secure until I glanced seaward and grabbed Attooktua's arm. Then he, too, saw the great outer pack drifting towards us *directly against the gale*. Here, it seemed, was something new under the sun. The laws of nature in reverse!

Attooktua caught the truth quicker than I—that instead of the pack coming to us, we were floating towards the pack. Adrift and miles from help, it seemed an age that we stood huddled together on that drifting floe before a narrow, crooked lead opened up almost at our feet.

Into this we launched our oomiak and clambered aboard. Then, sailing and paddling a zigzag course, with the lead threatening to close any second, we finally hit a fifteen-foot ridge of ice with a jar that threw us in a heap. We had hardly hauled out on a small ledge and hacked a path for our boat through the ridge when the lead closed behind us with the deafening crash of a freight-train collision. Another minute and we should have been pulverized "exceeding fine."

Kelley's boats had a bad time of it, too. One of them under a chap named Nelson was stove in and lost. When an Eskimo led him stumblingly to my camp late the next afternoon, this Nelson was as badly rattled as I ever hope to see a white man. Just why he had abandoned his *clothes* during his mad scramble over the ice I never quite understood.

In thinking back to 1895, that is the picture which always stands out—Nelson coming over the ice in only an undershirt, with a woman who worked in his boat following at a discreet distance loaded down with all the duds he'd thrown away.

If the ceremonial whale dance was less elaborate than usual that year, both natives and whites made up for it by cutting loose in the popular football game which followed.

As played by the Eskimos, football was a game of endurance, not skill. Every moonlit night, spring and fall, the whole village turned out for the sport, and since Kelley's arrival we'd all been joining in. The ball used was about eight inches in diameter and covered with tanned deerskin, each side kicking it along the hard snow. Since there were no goals nor any limit to the playing field, a game might end five or six miles from the start.

The great game of 1895 was certainly the longest and best that had taken place. It ended as usual far out on the sea ice amid holes already melted large enough for setting seal nets. We had been getting the better of it when Kelley's crowd suddenly grabbed two of our fastest runners and ducked them through a handy hole. Our boys then singled out their best-dressed pair and ducked *them*. That finished the night's football and everybody came ashore to wrestle.

That is, everybody except one of my Eskimo boys who, in kicking at the ball, had ripped his foot from the front end of the big toe almost to the instep.

I got him over to the station and started gingerly sewing him up. Soon, however, I discarded my gentle touch. The skin on the sole of his foot was so thick that it took muscle and a pair of pliers to force the needle through.

And because he sat there watching the operation with the dead-pan face of a bored spectator, I was thankful he felt no pain. Later, I wasn't sure whether it had hurt him or not because of what happened when I tackled a real emergency the following spring.

This was caused by some boys fooling around with a rifle that "wasn't loaded." The old story. So here they came bringing Arni-vigger, one of our best whalemen, with a .44 bullet lodged somewhere in his hip.

I probed around a while, found nothing and hesitated to start in on all the butchery that would be necessary to get the darned thing out. It was apparent that this was no plain sewing job on an Eskimo's calloused sole, but one for a surgeon equipped with anaesthetics and something more than an old razor and a pair of forceps used for pulling teeth.

"Does it hurt when you move?" I asked Arnivigger.

He sat up on the kitchen table, swinging his legs over the side. Then he took a few cautious steps.

No. It didn't hurt him. He was all right.

"But that bullet ought to come out, you know," was my half-hearted reply. "Otherwise—"

No, it would heal, he insisted. Better leave it alone. Besides, he couldn't afford to miss the whaling.

"Well," I answered, against my better judgment, "I'll bandage it the best I can, and we'll see."

As whaling approached, I examined Arnivigger's hip every few days and each time drew a longer breath of relief. It did seem to be healing fine.

By the time we hauled our boats out to the flaw the last of April, Arnivigger was on the job as usual and went through all the hard work of a second poor season. Not a whale was taken by our crowd until the very end of May. Then we killed five in succession, but all so small that the bone wasn't worth much.

Except for a lucky accumulation of one hundred twenty-five bearskins, most of which had been dried on a big driftwood rack behind the house, the Cape Smythe Whaling and Trading Company would have been "busted."

On top of this situation, Arnivigger came limping into the station one day with what I thought was probably a twisted ankle. But no such luck.

The trouble, he explained apologetically, was that three hard substances hurt him—*here*.

When he pointed to that long-healed bullet wound in his hip I must have groaned, but he assured me that it was very simple. All I need do was cut the hard substances out and he would be well.

Finally, I promised to do what I could, but explained bluntly that it would hurt and that we would have to tie him to the big table in the front room to prevent his moving.

No, he said. It wasn't the pain he minded. It was being tied up. Besides, that wasn't necessary because he wouldn't stir a muscle.

The only other thing he insisted on was being allowed to remove his labrete, the stone lip ornaments then worn by every native man and boy over fourteen. Just why he was so particular about this unimportant detail I never discovered.

After getting him to strip and lie face-down on the table, I called in four of our men and showed them how to hold his arms and legs. Then I got out the old razor and forceps, gritted my teeth and started in.

At the first incision I hit something hard that refused to budge without more cutting around the edge. But at last the forceps brought this away—a piece of bone over an inch and a half across.

I wiped my face and stopped to regard the situation. As Arnivigger hadn't moved, I thought I'd better go through with the rest of it.

At the next try I must have cut a large vein from the way the blood flowed. It scared me. But after keeping my finger pressed on the spot for about a minute, the blood stopped and I removed the .44 bullet with one end smashed that had caused all the trouble.

Once I thought sure Arnivigger had fainted. Nothing of the kind. He was just lying there like a piece of driftwood waiting for me to go ahead.

Then I went after the last of the "hard substances," which came away quite easily and turned out to be an inch off the end of his backbone.

I don't know how much longer we could have kept up this sort of thing had there been need. I was beginning to feel like an archaeologist and my patient showed no feeling at all. But it was a relief to be able finally to clean the wounds, bring them together with adhesive tape and call it a day.

I last heard of Arnivigger years later, in 1927. He was trapping along the Colville River and making a good living at it, too.

But if I felt some pride in what I'd done for him thirty-one years earlier, I also remembered that his prompt recovery had not been an unmixed blessing at the time. For after that, cutting became a fad at Point Barrow, and I was in constant demand by the natives. Whenever one of them had a pain he couldn't account for, he wanted me to *cut* it. My refusal only sent them to their own devil-doctors who now added plain and fancy cutting to their more ancient rites, keeping small flint knives for the special purpose of "cutting pains."

Even today a knife is the first thing those Eskimos think of if they feel so much as a headache.

CHAPTER XXXIII

My life in the far North has always been marked by periods when nothing much happened and Time itself offered the quaint illusion of having congealed along with the elements. Then all at once events would pile up as if trying frantically to restore the balance.

News brought by the ships in 1896 was a case in point. Refuge Station abandoned by Government—building bought by Captain Knowles for a new whaling station—Knowles' death soon afterwards—his company's decision to quit whaling at Utkiavie.

All this was upsetting. I hated particularly to see Kelley and his crowd go. Nor did it help to have Con and our cook leave with them. But there was a cheerier side. The fact that H. Liebes was sending up the schooner "Bonanza" to act as tender meant that our company was to keep on whaling in a field now practically our own.

In the midst of all these important changes came the incident of John to furnish a note of comic relief. It happened this way:

Fred and I had started out to visit the Herschel Island fleet's tender "Jennie" which had tied up for a day to an ice ridge just north of the house. I was rowing and so couldn't see ahead. But I wondered what Fred was staring at so popeyed. At last I turned around and, resting on my oars, stared popeyed too.

A slab of floating ice ahead of us bore an old leather trunk on which sat a man whose long mittened hands fairly *drooped* dejection. It was something straight out of a comic opera!

Half believing ourselves victims of an optical illusion, we pulled alongside to be greeted by a disillusioning blast of salty oaths. They were directed not at us, as we first thought, but at Captain Mason, of the nearby "Jennie." Between outbursts, the castaway said his name was John, that he was bound for Herschel Island and had shipped on the "Jennie" at Port Clarence.

It seemed he and Mason had had words about something that morning and the skipper had ordered him ashore as fast as he could "git." Not satisfied with the speed shown, Mason then threw John's trunk overboard and John after it. By some work of the devil the ice broke adrift at that moment, leaving John yelling for help "and that God-damned skipper yelling back that I could drift to hell for all he cared."

Fred and I reconsigned the man to a larger slab of ice farther in, with the promise that if nobody came along meanwhile we'd take him back to the beach when we returned.

We did, too—although Mason assured us that the fellow was a lazy lubber whom he'd had to dump overboard because the "Jennie" needed no more "dead ballast."

John—I never did learn his last name—stayed with me for several years and proved a handy man, despite a childlike tendency to "lift" whatever caught his fancy. He never took anything that amounted to much, and when caught not only acknowledged the theft but always insisted on paying for it.

He was one of the oddest of many queer specimens to cross my path. Not even Mr. Stevenson, our missionary and school teacher, ever quite understood him.

Which is saying a good deal because Mr. Stevenson had a rare understanding of human nature, both native and white. After visiting the Point Barrow district a couple of years before he had been forced to go outside again for a year and had only recently returned. This time he brought a lot of lumber for a new schoolhouse and mission which he got the Eskimos to help him erect.

I have known numerous men and women sent to these parts to teach the natives. For some I had no use. Others I admired. Stevenson, a Christian gentleman with his feet on the ground, was one of the most successful of them all when you consider that every devil-doctor in Utkiavie worked against him at the start. He had a special knack with all the kids and made some headway teaching school as well as giving them their first inkling of what we call morality. I hoped some time to send my two oldest daughters outside so that they might go to school in Ohio. When Stevenson agreed to take them out as soon as circumstances permitted, there wasn't a man I'd have trusted them to any quicker.

His work at Utkiavie was helped a little, perhaps, by the fact that just now, after hundreds of years, a spirit of change was in the air. White men had shown the Eskimos better whaling methods. Maybe the white man wasn't such a fool after all.

Mind, I don't say the spirit of change was responsible for the unheard-of rebellion of Taha's wife. Probably the combination of Taha's puny stature and Ocpullu's Amazonian proportions had more to do with that.

The little runt of a devil-doctor had taken this strapping female from Nubook for his second wife—something he should never have risked since she had already buried two husbands since I had known her.

Taha's next mistake was in treating her like a slave. After this had gone on a while, the huge woman up and quit him. Whereupon the little devil-doctor, feeling his manhood at stake, caught up with her and attempted to give her the sort of thrashing that he and the rest of the village felt she deserved. That was his third—and nearly fatal—blunder.

Before she was through with poor Taha he had been clawed and scratched and pommelled and finally laid out cold. Ocpullu came quietly back to their igloo, leaving her "lord and master" to recover at the place where she had knocked him out.

It was several days before Taha could walk. Then he came home, too. But now she would have nothing to do with him whatsoever and Taha lost face with everyone. This was a perfectly awful thing to happen from an Eskimo point of view. So the whole village got together officially and shipped the woman back to Nubook, where she belonged.

Although she finally married a white man and moved with him to Point Hope, "Ocpullu's Rebellion" was long discussed around the household hooch stills.

Unfortunately, the hooch problem was one thing that had undergone no change—at least, none for the better. We were the only whites there now, so that I knew that all the flour and molasses being used must come from the Eskimos at our own station. After a couple of Christmas murders had brought matters to a peak, I went over to the village one day to see what a little talk would do.

"Why don't you people quit making this stuff?" I asked. "It's killed some of your best men already. Do you want the people of Utkiavie to *die out?*"

Mungie acknowledged that what I said was true and many agreed with him. A lot of the older ones, however, declared stoutly that they would make the stuff so long as they could get anything to make it of.

"Then I'll smash your stills as fast as I find 'em," I said, and walked off amid laughter.

I'd tackled the problem at the wrong end.

Reaching home, I told our Eskimos that if any of them ever gave or sold his ration of flour and molasses to the villagers I'd stop issuing it to all, guilty or not.

They saw I meant it and promised that no more flour and molasses would reach the village through them.

I don't think it did very often. In fact, I heard of only two cases after that in which hooch was being made in Utkiavie. John and I took direct action against these by walking in and smashing the stills à la Carrie Nation, only we used pick-handles. Nobody made the slightest attempt to hinder us. It merely saddened them to see so much good liquor go to waste.

In spite of the current poor run of whales, word reached me in 1897 that our Company intended establishing a branch station down at Icy Cape. This meant that material would probably arrive with the first steamers to get through the ice that summer. I decided to meet them at Icy Cape.

Leaving early in July with one boat and an Eskimo crew, it took nearly three weeks to reach the Cape. Luckily, my men were young and husky and not afraid of tough going. They got plenty that trip.

Associated Press Photo

TYPICAL ESKIMO CAMP IN THE SUMMER

SUMMER AT BARROW, SHOWING MR. BROWER'S STATION AND WAREHOUSES

We had to sled the outfit, boat and all, the whole distance. But we had a chance to kill two polar bears along the coast, besides twenty-three seals later at Blossom Shoals during a week's wait. Then the first ship arrived from the south. She was the "Navarch."

I went aboard at once to get the latest news from her skipper, Captain Whitesides, and for the first time met the man whose extraordinary behavior was to go down through the years as an ugly blot on my memories of the sea.

Nothing of this was apparent at the time, although his news was disappointing. Our Company, he said, had changed its mind and finally decided not to start a branch there, after all. Too bad I'd made the hard trip for nothing. He'd be delighted to give me passage back to Point Barrow where he planned to stop anyhow on his way to the eastern whaling grounds.

"Afraid I've got too many men with me, Captain," I reluctantly explained.

"Then send 'em back along the coast and come with me yourself. Easier than sledding a boat over the ice, eh?"

It certainly was. I arranged for the boys to carry the sealskins back along the coast, first transferring our bearskins to the "Navarch." Then I gratefully took up quarters aboard her. The Captain introduced me to his wife and the evening passed pleasantly until I mentioned the steamer "Karluk," under Captain McGregor, which had come in that same afternoon and now lay anchored close at hand.

It seemed McGregor's wife was with him this trip, too, and I soon gathered that the two women had a grudge of long standing.

Said Mrs. Whitesides at last: "If that woman steps a foot on this boat—"

Her husband evidently knew what was coming for he got up abruptly and left the cabin.

Presently, the "Navarch" weighed anchor, rounded the icy Shoals and anchored again on the north side—a rather unwise thing to do with the wind west. But it turned out that Whitesides had chosen what to him appeared the lesser of two evils. He was grimly apologetic when I joined him on deck later.

"Better keep 'em away from each other—the women."

How ironical it seems now, many years afterwards, that so great a tragedy could have come out of a silly backyard scrap!

CHAPTER XXXIV

THE "Navarch" lay at anchor reasonably secure until the morning of the twenty-eighth when, coming on deck, I noticed that the ice had closed in around us considerably over night.

I had seen the insidious, creeping action of ice too often not to call Captain Whitesides' attention to the danger. But instead of steaming south of the Shoals again he seemed to think it safe to tie up to a large floe, apparently grounded. So here we stayed, while drifting ice gradually packed in solid on all sides.

More concerned with keeping two quarreling women apart than with the safety of his ship, he never woke up to our peril until the huge floe to which we were anchored broke loose without warning and drifted out, carrying the "Navarch" with it.

This seemed to paralyze the man's ability to act. Vital hours passed during which he might still have smashed his way out of the gathering trap. When he did try to work loose there wasn't a chance.

Forced farther and farther into the offshore pack, the "Navarch" finally reached a point from which ice stretched in every direction —miles of it. The whole world had turned into drifting ice.

Far to the southwest we could still see the "Karluk" safely anchored behind the distant Shoals. Finally, her hull disappeared. By mid-afternoon even her masts had dropped below the icy horizon. The "Navarch" continued her northeast drift, helpless as a fly glued to a sheet of floating flypaper.

We had traveled perhaps thirty or forty miles when the wind, hauling northeast, moved the pack farther offshore where it caught the full effect of the current sweeping north at three miles an hour. The piece we were tied to now began milling around, so that we were heading in every direction. Several times during those first days we listed dangerously to port or starboard as the ice crushed

185

in around us, first on one side, then the other.

The second of August, when we were somewhere north of the Sea Horse Islands with little chance of ever working free, Captain Whitesides talked things over with his officers and reluctantly decided to abandon ship.

His plan was to haul three whaleboats over the ice to the edge of the pack, then try to make the nearest land. He turned to me:

"You've traveled on ice, Brower. Any suggestions that will help?"

I explained how we always put a deep hardwood keel on wooden boats to raise them off the ice and keep the bottom boards from getting stove.

"How deep a keel?"

"Three inches. Four would be better."

He shook his head. *One* inch, he said, was plenty. As for taking along a bolt or two of heavy canvas to patch with, didn't I understand that we must haul as little weight as possible? There was no arguing with him.

That night we left the "Navarch," after first putting a couple of hogs overboard on the ice and shooting them.

With the crew divided into three sections, all but two of the men harnessed themselves to the boats and strained forward. This pair, too old to pull, just tagged along in my care. I was to look after Mrs. Whitesides, too. All this time the Captain was adding to the general confusion by running around excitedly and issuing needless orders.

We hauled all night in a southeasterly direction, hoping to head south and at the same time in towards land. By morning all hands were fagged out and had to rest. But if anybody slept I didn't know it. One thing surprised me. Mrs. Whitesides never made the slightest fuss over what was happening. She was game.

Another long haul brought us to ice so rough that the slowest progress was a man-killing job. What I had feared now began happening to the boats. Without keels deep enough to raise them above the jagged ice, two were soon worthless, with bottom boards ripped away and no canvas to patch them. One we abandoned that night.

"Smash it up for a fire," bellowed Whitesides, stamping about. "We'll boil coffee, anyhow."

Feeling some better for the hot coffee, we pushed on until nearly morning when a wide stretch of loose, milling ice stopped us dead. It was a time to keep one's head, but the "old man" lost his entirely. He seemed to think that the edge of the pack, and open water lay just beyond.

"Wait a while, Captain," I urged. "It may quiet down. I've seen ice like this before."

Whatever I said, he took the contrary view. Now he was for getting across at all hazards, and gave orders to start ahead.

We started. But in trying to get from one piece to another we stove both our remaining boats so badly that there was no use saving them even if we could. All hands had hard enough work saving themselves. When the last man was dragged back to solid footing, the Captain broke down and cried. To him that milling ice meant the end.

And yet he had one resource left that I didn't know about. A bottle. After taking repeated drinks, he fished a handful of gold from his pocket and shook it in our faces.

"Listen," he croaked, "I'd give all this—*all*, mind you—to be ashore right now."

So would the rest of us, but there was no use bawling about it. The only thing to do now was get back to the ship, the masts of which were still visible on the horizon. So back we turned, the stronger ones helping those who were all in.

We had hardly started when the skipper suddenly ordered: "Every man for himself!" and lit out for the "Navarch," leaving his wife to shift for herself.

Since losing our last two boats Mr. Belaine, the mate, had been helping me with Mrs. Whitesides, who could hardly walk now. This made our progress almost inch by inch. Once we saw the smoke of two steamers on their way along the coast to Point Barrow, but so many miles inside us that there was no possible chance of our being seen.

We managed to keep together—Mrs. Whitesides, Belaine and I —up to within ten miles of the "Navarch." At least we could just make out her black hull. But right here we came to a new break where the ice was crushing badly, pressure causing the edges to grind together and pile twenty feet high like a jagged mountain range.

"Now what!" muttered Belaine through tight lips.

Mrs. Whitesides said nothing, although she must have known that carrying her across would be next to impossible. It was all a man could do to get over by himself; and, once started, he daren't stop for fear of being crushed under. However, if the ice on the far side were as solid as it looked from where we stood there might be some sense in *trying* to get the woman across.

Leaving Belaine with Mrs. Whitesides, I managed to get over myself with nothing worse than bruises, and after a quick survey signaled them that the ice was fine. Then, before I could get back to help with her the pressure let go, leaving a wide lead of water where the ridge had been.

I waited several hours, hoping the lead would close. Finally, Belaine and the woman started along the edge, eventually finding a far way around. I then headed for the ship. When I got there, two polar bears were feasting on the hogs killed when we left.

Whitesides himself had long since come aboard and turned in. So had a number of the crew. They were completely done up. All at once my head grew too heavy to hold up and the last I remember was slowly sliding off a bench. When I awoke, Mrs. Whitesides and Belaine had arrived. The two bears, having finished their feast, were gone.

The Captain's first remark when we met was to accuse me of abandoning his wife.

"What were *you* doing all the time?" I asked.

He turned away without a word.

Other members of the crew wandered back during the day so

that by night we had the satisfaction of being all together once more, even if our position was infinitely worse.

The "Navarch," wedged tighter than ever into the pack, had been drifting steadily north. Soon we'd pass the latitude of Point Barrow, beyond which only one ship, the "Young Phoenix," had ever drifted and returned. Another attempt to reach shore was imperative.

In the little time remaining, all hands worked feverishly building a small, hickory-framed boat, copper-riveted and covered with oiled canvas to make it watertight. She was light enough for two to lift over any kind of ice, yet capable—we hoped—of ferrying as many as ten people at a time across otherwise impassable leads. Then, if we got to the edge of the ice before passing Point Barrow, there would be some chance yet of making shore.

The "Navarch" must have been somewhere off Cape Smythe when we got ready to abandon her the second time. The Captain asked me to go ahead with most of the crew and pick out the best route.

"I'll relieve you of Mrs. Whitesides this time," he said, icily. "We'll follow with the boat and enough men to haul in two shifts. I've got a compass too," he added, "if a fog comes on and I have to go back to the ship for anything."

"How about grub?" I inquired.

"Don't worry. We'll be along with all supplies."

I insisted on one thing, though. Digging out my polar bearskins, I lashed them, fur side down, under the bottom of the little boat to protect the canvas and make her slip along easier.

And so we quit our comfortable quarters at three on the morning of August tenth, my crowd taking the lead to search out the best route for the Captain's party who would follow with the boat.

Unhampered except for light poles which a few of the men had brought to help over the roughest spots, we picked our way along for hours without making much progress. Occasionally I'd climb a high hummock and look back. Although the men were soon strung out a mile or so over the ice, all appeared to be traveling steadily.

The Captain's party I assumed to be somewhere at the tail end, making sure no one was left behind.

Sometime in the afternoon we had a diversion up front. An old she-bear with two cubs came quite close and followed us along a couple of miles before she decided that we weren't worth eating and lumbered off in disgust. I had the rifle but didn't shoot that family.

Around five o'clock our vanguard reached the edge of the main pack. The ice ahead was all broken, with a thousand leads running every which way. Here was where our boat would be worth its weight in gold; our little boat with all our supplies which would soon be coming along with the Captain's party.

The hungry men straggled in at long intervals. Most of them had eaten what little food they'd brought along. Now they flopped down on the wet ice, thankful to rest, eagerly anticipating the "old man's" arrival and a square meal.

"Seen anything of the skipper?" I'd ask.

"Skipper? Why, no, Charlie. He must be coming back there somewhere."

Always the same answer. Nobody had seen Captain Whitesides' party—"but they must be coming along."

The last of our crowd to join us at the edge of the pack was John Egan, the second mate. When he appeared, with no one visible behind him, I knew something was wrong. Egan's story only deepened the mystery.

He reported that he'd been with the Captain at first, but after traveling two or three miles from the "Navarch" the skipper had suddenly ordered his own group back to the ship.

"Back to the ship?" I repeated.

"I figured he'd probably left something behind."

"Even so, he'd be coming along by this time. He'll have to. Why, *he's got our food!*"

The others crowded around, worn and gaunt. Whatever the explanation, we were in a fix.

CHAPTER XXXV

IT WASN'T food alone—or even the boat. We lacked everything. Advised by the Captain to travel light until he caught up with us, not more than two besides myself had even brought spare boots.

Some time during the night fog closed in, and later the ice we were on separated slightly from the rest. This left us practically marooned.

What worried me most, though, was knowing that north of Point Barrow in summer the main pack always splits, one part drifting west away from all land, the other taking a northeasterly course so that at least there's a coastline somewhere to the south.

Scratching a diagram in the ice with my knife, I explained that we were probably near the latitude of Point Barrow by now, and that when the pack split I for one intended to be on the east side.

"A man carried west on the old pack would—well, you see—" I jabbed the knife-point into what represented the open Arctic.

They saw, all right. But we couldn't make a break for it until the fog cleared.

When it did, morning showed that we had traveled a long way north of Point Barrow already, and water-clouds ahead of us reflected open water where the pack was beginning to split in two.

It was high time we moved.

I don't know yet just how we scrambled back to the solid floe. I only remember that after the last man had been hauled, dripping, out of the icy maelstrom that lay between, the ice we had been on drifted off to the northwest. Then we had to hurry away from the churning edge and on to heavier ice, brown and dirty with age.

Whiting, the steward, who had taken a gloomy view from the start, was the worst off.

"I can't go any farther," he kept repeating.

I tried to show him that at least we had reached the safe side of the split, so wouldn't be carried west. If we just kept going south we'd reach the edge of the pack sometime, with the chance of being picked up by a ship.

This wishful thinking seemed to put new life into him. He got up off the ice and paced around as if trying to get warm. He's all right, I thought, and turned away.

Next I knew, Whiting had wandered off into some rough ice and shot himself.

This was bad for everyone. Leaving the body where it lay, we started south as fast as we could travel.

On quitting the ship I had stuffed a dozen pieces of hard bread into the top of one of my spare boots and these kept us going the rest of the day—these and all the water we wanted to drink.

Throughout the pack we came on little fresh water ponds above sea level. They were formed by the higher ice peaks melting in the sun and precipitating their salt. So when it rained hard that night and nobody minded, it wasn't that we needed drinking water, but merely because we were so generally miserable that a little thing like rain didn't matter. We were never dry after that.

On August twelfth we lost two more men. They just gave up, asking to be shot. They said they didn't mind dying at all. It would be a relief from traveling any more over ice.

Since carrying them was impossible, we finally had to leave them behind, still hoping they'd follow along when they understood we couldn't stop. . . . We never saw them again.

Next morning our chief engineer, Sands, went crazy, wandering off by himself if no one were watching. All day he appeared to be flickering out, mentally and physically. Along towards evening he died.

It seemed enough death for one day. Yet no sooner had Sands passed away than two firemen made that a welcome excuse to stay behind "to rest."

Although low fog hung over us much of the time, we held our course by occasional glimpses of the sun. I had managed to keep my watch dry and going, and knowing that the sun bore south at noon and north at twelve midnight, I could figure our position at different hours of the day. This was a big help.

Otherwise, clear weather brought nothing but discouragement, for then the water clouds were visible far south of us. And since these never came any closer, it became increasingly evident that we were making no headway towards the open water that lay between us and land. In other words, the pack was drifting north as fast as we were traveling south.

It was about then that Egan, the second mate, went snow-blind. Aside from that he was in fair shape. To guide him I gave him the end of a line I carried around my waist. This worked all right except in crossing channels that had thawed partly through. Then I'd tell him how wide the place was, and he'd jump. Sometimes he made it. More often I'd have to haul him out by the line. It has always given me peculiar satisfaction to remember that Egan was with those of us left alive at the end.

The men's clothing now began to wear out rapidly. It was mostly fawnskin which grew so heavy when watersoaked that it cut through the linen stitches and literally fell apart.

In a different way, clothing was largely responsible for the death of another man, a young Portuguese, strong and able when we left the ship. The trouble was he refused to leave his good clothes behind and came away wearing three brand new suits, the weight of which, when wet, simply wore him down. Then when he finally began discarding them he was all in. A day later we left him behind.

This chap was one of six Portuguese, or South Americans, who died during the terrible fifth and sixth days. It was heart-rending to see those fellows drop back one by one, hear their cries fade out in the distance. Hardest for me to bear was the fact that they always called,

"Charlie! Charlie! Don't leave me—Charlie!"

Their voices rang through my head for years. It almost got me at the time. I had never deserted a man in my life, but there was nothing we could do—we who were in almost the same condition. Unless we reached the edge of the ice in a day or so it would be the end for all of us.

The next man to go was the blacksmith. I don't remember his name, only that he hailed from Minnesota. He hung on until the soles of his boots wore through, leaving him to stumble barefoot over the cinder-sharp ice. Soon his feet were cut to pieces. Then he started falling, tearing his fawnskin pants until his knees looked like raw meat. Yet all the while I never once heard him complain. When we finally had to leave him, he called after us an almost cheery—

"Goodbye, boys. I hope you get out."

That blacksmith from Minnesota was the gamest man I ever saw. I wish I knew his name.

Remarkable how deceptive the top of high ice, when viewed above low-hanging fog.

"Land! Look, over this way!"

With fresh hope, the men would turn and hurry off towards what they mistook for a distant coastline. This happened many times during the seventh and eighth days. If longer experience in the Arctic hadn't taught me what it was, I, too, would have worn myself out in these senseless stampedes. It was hard enough to round the crowd up again and get them headed south. Such false alarms were tough on morale.

Presently some of the men suffered hallucinations. As the eighth day wore on, they grew so confused as to what was real, what false, that when we actually came out on the south edge of the pack that evening they wouldn't believe what they saw.

Stripped from the main floe by a northeast wind, cakes of all sizes were breaking off and drifting south on an endless ice-strewn sea. A thousand rafts to ferry us to land, if—

The "if" was a big one—so big that some of the men wanted to stay right where we were. The ships, they argued, would certainly be looking for us.

"Most of the ships," I insisted, "are whaling to the east. Besides, when the wind changes and blows this loose ice back again we'd be so far from the edge that they couldn't see us even if we lived that long."

One huge slab of ice near-by seemed ready to break loose any moment. It looked fifty or sixty feet long and nearly as wide. With one end rising to a miniature peak to be melted by the sun, we'd have drinking water, if nothing else.

"Here's our raft," I said. "Come on."

Convinced now that my idea was right, two of the men nevertheless resolved to take smaller cakes themselves. Before we could prevent, one of them, a colored fellow from Martinique, jumped on a piece far too small and pushed off from the pack. He hadn't drifted far when over it rolled and that was the end of him. The other man went under, too, and didn't reappear. Frankly, I can't say exactly why or how this last happened because of what was taking place farther along the ice.

For Scanlon, the second engineer, had walked away from the group to a high place on the pack, probably with the intention of searching for a better "raft" than I had chosen. No one realized—least of all Scanlon—that he'd ventured onto a piece already adrift. When he tried to jump back again he fell short by inches and was too weak to keep afloat until somebody could get there.

Scanlon was the last man we lost. Sixteen out of thirty-two! The rest were willing now to quit that cursed pack, no matter what lay ahead.

At last our piece was released by the ice outside. We started drifting southwest before the wind, slowly at first, then gaining speed the farther we got from the main floe.

It was curious how we passed other floating ice traveling in the same direction. We would head for a cake, almost smack against it, then suddenly veer off and pass it several yards away. There must have been a powerful counter-current sweeping east.

Out here we sighted seals for the first time. One came close to us that night and I shot it, hoping we might reach it with one of our light poles. But it sank like lead.

Gradually the ice became more scattered until by morning our piece was drifting in comparatively open water.

Then suddenly we found ourselves in the midst of one of the greatest schools of whales I have ever seen in my life. They stayed with us through the day. There were literally hundreds, all bound west. But what excited us far more was a two-masted steamer which hove into view that afternoon far to the south. We lashed three of our poles together and tried frantically to signal her with a shirt. Nothing happened.

Later, we were to learn why. The steamer was the "Karluk," and from comparing notes with Captain McGregor, it seemed that at that particular time the "Karluk" was abreast Smith's Bay *at least thirty miles away*. What we had signaled was only a mirage.

Except for shooting and losing two more seals next day, we just lay about dully on the ice until evening, when suddenly all hands were galvanized into action by another prospect of rescue—sure fire this time.

Laughing weakly, we pointed out to one another the schooner which was coming from the east on a course that would have to bring her not more than three miles inside us. Three miles! We were as good as saved.

"The signal!"

"What for? They can't help seeing—"

"Gimme that shirt!"

Up went the signal, just to be sure.

On she came, booms well out, heeling gracefully to the northeast wind—a sight for the gods!

So we stood on our cake and waved and watched, expecting her to head our way. When she was fairly abreast we began yelling. She *must* see us. She couldn't help it.

The yelling died off, but we kept our signal going until long after the schooner had passed us by.

This was too much for one of the men, a boatheader named Enos, who went insane. It was amazing the trouble he gave us—a man hardly able to keep his feet—trying to throw himself into the sea.

Then, exhausted, he sat down on the ice and stayed there in a stupor the rest of the time.

Several of the others seemed nearly gone. We had been eleven days without food, all the while doing the hardest kind of work. Only three besides myself were in any kind of shape—a boat-steerer named Hanson and two seamen, one of them a former German soldier. I remember him in particular because he never shared any of his tobacco, though most of the men would have given their souls for a chew.

Sometimes it's a little thing like that that sinks into one's memory of life's curios among the so-called human race.

Tobacco or not, we all got through that night somehow, and about eleven in the morning sighted what some thought was land. By early afternoon I was certain of it. A few hours later I recognized Cape Halkett, and figuring our present bearing and drift and the direction of the wind, had great hopes for a while that we would drift inside the point.

But the current from the west was too strong and our ice cake passed the tip of Halkett fully two miles out. Even so I scanned the distant Cape until my eyes blurred. This had always been quite a camping place for Eskimos on their way from the Colville River. But not a tent was visible as we continued our offshore swing along the barren coast.

Even our approach to Cape Halkett had caused no great stir among the men. They had been disappointed too often to care much what happened. I was beginning to understand how they felt when, late in the afternoon, the smoke of a steamer coming east brought a last flare-up of hope and dread. When she hove in sight over the horizon, gradually it dawned on all but poor Enos, who never shifted his fixed stare, that her course between the bulge of Cape Halkett on one side and the ice pack on the other must necessarily bring her near.

An increasing stir of excitement went through us. Too weak now to rig any signal, we could only sit there on the ice and watch her approach. Suddenly one of the men's outstretched arms with pointing finger announced eloquently that she was heading our way. . . .

The steamer was the old "Thrasher" of the Pacific Steam Whaling Company, with Captain Barney Coogan in command. I learned later how narrowly we escaped being seen, after all. A Siberian Eskimo had been in the crow's nest at the time and reported a herd of walrus off the starboard bow. Since walrus seldom go east of Point Barrow, one of the officers turned curious glasses on where we were huddled together on the ice.

That was why the "Thrasher" was soon easing alongside and lifting aboard what remained of our original crowd of thirty-two.

"Twelve days? My God!" exclaimed Captain Coogan.

He wouldn't give us much to eat at first. Coogan was too wise for that. All I wanted, anyhow, was sleep. The steward, Felix Terry, was a colored fellow with whom I'd been shipmates on the "Grampus." Felix had a tub of hot water ready for me in no time. So I took a bath, and in the process dropped asleep.

When I woke up ages later I was in a bunk, with the "Thrasher" anchored at Point Barrow and Tom and Fred aboard to take me home.

CHAPTER XXXVI

It had been nearly two months since I started south along the coast for Icy Cape, only to drift north around Point Barrow on the pack and end by coming in from the east aboard the "Thrasher."

Many ships had arrived and departed. Four still lay at anchor, among them our Company tender, the "Bonanza." Captain Sam Smith had stubbornly refused to quit the North without learning definitely whether I was alive or dead.

Tom, who planned to close the station if I didn't show up soon, had kept all the Eskimo crews hunting for us, sometimes staying out days at a time. Until recently, the "Bear," too, had been constantly searching. She was under Captain Tuttle this year, with Lieutenant Jarvis second in command, and for days they had been cruising along the ice east of Point Barrow, returning to the Point each night to anchor.

One of my first questions, of course, was "What about Captain Whitesides? Did his crowd ever get ashore?"

"Him?" Tom exploded. "Why, that—that—" He gave it up and turned to Fred. "Tell him what happened."

Then for the first time I found out that Fred had been on the "Bear" himself, volunteering to help stand "masthead." One afternoon as they were heading in towards Cooper's Island with Fred in the crow's nest he spotted a tent on shore. Thinking it barely possible that whoever was camped there might have news of us, Captain Tuttle sent a boat in to investigate. When the boat came back it brought Whitesides, his wife and several members of the "Navarch" crew, all in excellent condition.

Captain Whitesides had left his ship the day after abandoning us and, properly equipped with the light boat and plenty of food and other supplies, had come in over the ice to the edge of the pack. From there it took them only a day to row to Cooper's Island. Had

199

Whitesides followed us with the boat as he promised, my whole crowd of thirty-two might easily have been saved.

Why hadn't he? That was what I wanted to know.

"When Tuttle asked him about you folks," Fred went on, "he said you'd been gone four days and must be dead. He was so certain that Tuttle finally agreed there wasn't a chance. That's why the 'Bear' quit looking nearly a week ago. My God, Charlie! If anyone had thought—"

"I don't blame Captain Tuttle," I said. "There *wasn't* a chance. Just one more question. Did anybody find out why Whitesides went back to the 'Navarch' that day without letting us know?"

"Tuttle asked him about that."

"What did he say?"

Fred gave a harsh laugh. "Nothing. He just turned away."

I found out later that Whitesides had left six men behind on the drifting "Navarch"—three of the older, more helpless ones and three who refused to take any more chances with such a skipper. So far as anyone knew they were still aboard.

The fifteen who had come in with me were distributed among the four ships at the Point. The crazy one, Enos, was put aboard the "Bonanza" to be taken out, but died on the passage south. Holmes shipped on the "Thrasher." He was killed that same fall while helping cut a whale. Four of the other men had their feet amputated. The others just disappeared, as sailors do everywhere.

More personal sorrows faced Toctoo and me. Our youngest daughter was sick when I arrived home, and Mr. Stevenson, having given me up for lost, was making arrangements to take the two older girls out to the States as he had promised. They were all packed and ready to sail on the "Bonanza" when I appeared.

For a while I didn't know whether to let them go or not. But since Stevenson was leaving anyhow, it seemed like the one opportunity I'd have to send them out safely in care of someone in whom I had the utmost trust. So they left on the "Bonanza."

That same day our youngest died.

CHAPTER XXXVII

THE blow was a hard one—particularly for Toctoo. Unexpected demands left me less time for private sorrow.

The fleet which had wintered at Herschel Island had hardly started west when the schooner "Rosario" stuck fast in the ice off the Point. Next came a report that the steamers "Orca," "Belvedere" and "Jessie Freeman," after smashing their way to the vicinity of the Sea Horse Islands, were hopelessly jammed, the "Jessie Freeman" already abandoned and her people taken aboard the other two. Since none of these ships had more than enough food left to get home on, it looked as if we'd have to quarter all their officers and men for the winter.

Meantime, an Eskimo brought word that the steamers "Newport" and "Fearless" had been caught seventy miles *east* of the Point, the Herschel Island tender "Jennie" more than a hundred, and their skippers wanted to know if we could help them in case they had to winter there.

For once the ice pack did me a friendly turn by bringing heavy responsibilities when needed most.

What, then, could we offer in the way of help and housing? I could rely on Dr. Marsh and his wife who had arrived to take Mr. Stevenson's place as teacher and missionary. The Refuge Station had been rented to E. A. McIllhenny of Avery Island, Louisiana. With two assistants, he was here to collect birds and mammals How, I wondered, would he take to collecting shipwrecked sailors? I needn't have worried.

All these people immediately volunteered to aid in any way possible, McIllhenny himself promising to use his big stove for "mass" cooking. There was also Kelley's empty station which could be turned into a bunkhouse.

After assuring the crews stranded to the south that we'd take

201

care of them, I fitted out Tom and MacIlhenny to go east as far as the "Newport" and "Fearless" to let their anxious skippers know that at least they wouldn't starve.

Tom and Mac came back from their hurried one-hundred-forty-mile round trip with a fantastic tale. They doubted if the third ship they had seen thirty miles beyond was the "Jennie."

"Charlie, maybe I'm plumb crazy," said Tom, solemnly, "but if she ain't the '*Navarch*' may I never strike another whale!"

That name turned my thoughts to the six men Captain Whitesides had left aboard, and from them to the flour and other provisions I knew she carried in her hold. If only she *were* the "Navarch"!

But first we had to arrange for the crews coming up from the south on sleds already dispatched to bring them. The captains could bunk with us—officers in the Rescue Station—most of the men in Kelley's old place—double rows of makeshift bunks—a wood stove in the center—no end of details.

A couple of days' lively work did the trick. But when the main crowd arrived I wasn't sorry to hear that a few had chosen to stick by their ships. We had enough confusion already. The captains didn't even try to manage their men, seeming only too glad to shift responsibility on us. To bring some sort of order out of the mess, I arranged for MacIlhenny to be given a week's rations for each man. He was to cook it for them as needed. Then I explained to the mob that this would be the week-by-week routine so long as they were with us.

Satisfied that things were going as well as could be expected, I left Tom and Fred in charge and started east over the ice with some natives at four o'clock one morning, nominally to make arrangements about feeding the crews of the "Fearless" and "Newport," actually to get a look at that mysterious craft stuck in the ice far beyond. We made the seventy miles in twelve hours.

My first act, after greeting the skipper of the "Newport," was to borrow his glasses and climb into the crow's nest. . . .

She was the "Navarch." I'd never forget her.

Calling together some of my Eskimos, I sent them back with word for Tom and Fred to let me have all the sleds and men they could get hold of in a hurry.

While they were gone, John Thomas, mate of the "Newport," made a hurried trip out to the "Navarch" to see in what condition the men were and tell them our plans.

"They're all in pretty good shape," Thomas reported, "only it looks like we're in for a mite of a row if we touch anything in the hold."

"Did you tell 'em we had to divide the grub among all these other crews?"

"Sure. But they figure the 'Navarch' and everything on her belongs to them. They say they're going to salvage the ship."

I had to laugh. They'd be lucky to salvage themselves. Just the same there was a chance for trouble, at least at first, and Thomas and I made our plans accordingly.

Within three days seventeen sleds arrived, with more on the way. When our first teams reached the "Navarch" the six men on her refused to let any of us aboard, but finally agreed to talk things over with Thomas and me alone. Once on deck, I congratulated them on being alive and for a while we had quite a sociable chat. They said that at one time the "Navarch" drifted almost free; that if they had known how to start her engines they might have reached the Point long ago. But the ice had closed in again worse than ever. So here they were, growled one of the men whom I'd marked for a trouble-maker before, and the ship belonged to them and what were we going to do about it?

I explained how we had suddenly been called on to feed several crews during the winter, and said we couldn't let them go hungry when the "Navarch" had so much food in her hold.

Most of the men grew reasonable and all but the trouble-maker seemed anxious enough to come ashore. He claimed now that he owned the ship himself. What was more, he'd kill anybody who took a thing off her. He was going on at a great rate when I nodded to Thomas, and before the fellow finished telling all he'd do to us we had him in irons.

There was no further trouble.

The first teams took the men part way to the "Newport," leaving them on the ice in charge of two Eskimos for fear they'd wander off and get lost. Then back came these teams to the "Navarch." By now we had the other sleds loaded with provisions ready to start a systematic shuttle service for salvaging all the provisions possible before the wind shifted.

All but two of the men we had left on the ice arrived at the "Newport" in good shape that first night. The others got in later, and considerably the worse for wear. One was the elderly Chinese cook, the other, an old Norwegian named Pete, well over seventy and utterly unable to travel.

Luckily for Pete, he had been placed in charge of one of my most reliable natives, Long John Ungertegera. Long John stuck to Pete like a brother. Finally he peeled off his deerskin parka to wrap around the shivering old man and spent the rest of the night running around in a cotton undershirt to keep from freezing himself. They staggered in about dawn—the Eskimo carrying old Pete on his back.

During the next few days and nights our men, reinforced now by several more teams, ran six round trips to the "Navarch." They made quite a sight. Twenty-six sleds strung out across the ice!

After the last pound of provisions had been removed, we looked longingly at all the coal in her hold. Eighty tons of it, and not a chance of getting it ashore.

However, the "Navarch" still had stuff aboard that could be used for trade. So, after talking it over, Thomas and I called all the Eskimos together. They'd done such a good job, we told them, that anything else they could get from the "Navarch" would be theirs.

For two more days and nights they worked like mad. It was amazing the variety of things they managed to get out. On their final trip some of them even brought a huge oak sideboard that had adorned the "Navarch's" after cabin, painfully lugging it over the ice lashed on two sleds. On learning that they intended to take it the remaining seventy miles to Utkiavie, I thought them very foolish indeed—until I discovered that they intended it to be a personal present for me.

It stands in my home here today. I have only to glance at it as I write to be reminded afresh of the "Navarch" and those sixteen shipmates lost during our terrible trek over the ice.

The Eskimos were lucky to get that sideboard out when they did, for a few hours later the wind changed and blew the "Navarch" away. Still solid in the pack, apparently intact, she seemed good for some time yet. But watching her drift away I was thankful to be on the "Fearless."

Here I stayed until all the able-bodied men, including a few members of the "Fearless" and "Newport" crews, had left. Then, wrapping the Chinaman and old Pete in the heaviest deerskins I could find, I put them on the one remaining dog sled and we, too, headed for the Station seventy miles away. I counted on three days of necessarily slow travel. We made it in two, but not without our troubles.

Everything went fine until we were paralleling the beach within a few miles of the Station. Then we ran onto a snowdrift in the dark —and there was the devil to pay. It was only about a foot high, but it started at a point and spread out like a wedge. When we took it with the dogs on the run, the hard edges forced our runners apart, snapping off the stanchions and depositing old Pete and the Chinaman in a heap on the ice.

A case for major repairs, it meant searching the beach in the dark for small pieces of wood, fitting the stanchions back into the mortise-holes along the bed of the sled, then lashing my wood to each broken piece like a splint. All this was done to the accompaniment of comments in Norwegian and Chinese, as my cargo of old men hopped around on the ice to keep warm.

Sometime during the night we arrived at the Station where Tom and Fred were thoughtful enough to let me go to sleep in blissful ignorance of brewing trouble.

It came next morning, with a delegation from the bunkhouse.

"It's this 'ere MacIlhenny, what's doing the cooking," their spokesman announced. "He's holding out on us. So help me he is, Charlie."

I looked the men over—a hard-bitten, ill-clad bunch—and reminded them that not every shipwrecked crew had regular food, let alone somebody to cook it for them. But since they thought they had a grievance I promised to look into matters.

Mac, of course, hadn't deliberately held out on anyone. What he had done was to give the men only as much as he thought they needed at one time.

After that it was arranged for each man to get his entire week's rations direct and turn over to Mac only the amount he wanted cooked. Then if he was short at the end of the week it was his own fault.

The food question settled, those of us in charge turned to more important problems.

Talking things over with the captains and MacIlhenny, we decided to send two messengers overland in different directions to let the outside world know that the crews were safe. We finally chose a man named Charles Walker for one, and for the other George Tilton, second mate of the "Belvedere."

Walker made Herschel Island, then pushed southeast to Fort McPherson, thereafter being passed from post to post by the Hudson's Bay Company until he finally reached Edmonton.

For Tilton I built a special sled and hired an Eskimo to take him as far as Point Hope. Somehow he got from there to Kotzebue Sound; then, working through the mountains by way of the Buckland River, to Norton Sound. After resting a while in the Army Post at St. Michaels he crossed to the Yukon, then the Kuskoquim and on over the divide to Katmal. Here he found an old dory and in this fragile craft crossed wide Skellikoff Strait to Kodiak Island, where at last he caught a small steamer to Vancouver Island.

Both men reached civilization in April within a few days of each other.

Nowadays, such journeys in winter would be considered almost unbelievable sagas of the North. They were all in the day's work then.

CHAPTER XXXVIII

As WINTER deepened fuel became our big worry. We had barely enough coal to cook with, and there was very little driftwood left along the beaches.

Matters took a grotesque turn when Baby's old mother, who often camped at her son's grave on moonlit nights, complained that somebody had stolen the great heap of driftwood which had covered the coffin ever since Baby's funeral.

Shortly afterwards, one of the natives who worked for us died. As usual, we furnished a coffin and all new clothing for the burial. A few days later the man's wife declared that the mittens left on her dead husband had just been sold in the village. The white men, she said, had stolen them.

"What makes you think they're the same mittens?" I asked.

Because their pattern was unusual. She'd made them herself and would know them anywhere.

Just to satisfy her we went out to the graveyard and examined the corpse. She was right. Not only were the mittens gone but the clothing as well. All I could do was furnish a complete new outfit and have her and her family dress the body again, with orders to nail the box securely.

Two days later she came back in despair. They'd done it again. Only this time they'd rolled the naked body out in the snow and even taken the coffin, probably for firewood.

I said a few things under my breath, then walked over to the bunkhouse and repeated them aloud. Of course the men denied everything, and while I knew they were lying, I had no proof. After that the whole graveyard was gradually denuded of burial racks, broken sleds—anything made of wood.

And there was little I could do about it. The men were a tough lot, to begin with. Their clothing, too thin and worn for hard outdoor work in winter, furnished a fine excuse for loafing, and it would be some time before the old women of the village could make up enough new skin outfits to go around. Even blankets were lacking. The best we could do was try and keep all hands as busy as possible.

One thing that helped was the inauguration of "quilting parties" at the old Refuge Station. Mac had brought north plenty of cotton batting for fixing his bird specimens. I had bolts of print calico. Using the cotton for stuffing, the men finally turned out enough quilts so that everyone could at least sleep warm.

Things went better then until the day when the men, crowding in for their tobacco ration, managed to steal a lot of other things off the shelves. Next "tobacco day" only one man was admitted at a time, given his tobacco and shoved out again. I checked the names off on my book, while just inside the door stood Fred and another man, each armed with a pick handle.

"Anybody showing up before his name is called will get a busted head. All right, now,—who's first?"

It worked.

Along in January one of the Eskimos reported that from the high land at Skull Bluff forty miles south he had made out a ship in the ice far to the southwest. I told him he must be "seeing things." But a couple of days later the mysterious vessel was only twelve miles south of us and slowly drifting along up the coast.

My first look convinced me that it was I who was "seeing things."

We immediately sent some of our men out to her. When they got back next day, with their sleds badly smashed by the ice, it seemed that my *eyesight* wasn't so bad but that the North must be doing things to my *reason*. The last I'd seen of that ship she was a hundred miles or so *east* of the Point—yet here she came up from the *south*, and only a mile or so out.

What followed was still more incredible. On a Saturday, when she had reached a point directly abreast the Station, suddenly the pack surged inshore, crushed her sides, cutting her bottom almost in two, and finally shoving what was left of the old "Navarch" high on the beach, as if to say,

"Here's your coal."

We got her two whaleboats off the davits and ashore late that afternoon, then spent the evening organizing our Eskimos so as to start hauling coal early Monday morning. Providence had delivered that coal at our front door. We'd take no chance of losing it now. Because the bunkhouse crowd weren't properly clad for such work, we didn't even ask them to help. I turned in that night easier in mind than for weeks. The fuel problem was solved.

Sometime before midnight there came a tremendous pounding, and shouts of "Fire! Fire!"

Out we tumbled, half asleep. The Station seemed all right. But down on the beach an ominous glow brightened and flared into licking crimson tongues. Before we could get any sort of fire brigade working, the flaming "Navarch" was doomed. So we just stood around and watched her go—coal and all.

It appeared that two sailors from the bunkhouse had walked out to the ship earlier in the evening and built a fire in her blubber room, using bits of wood and straw from the fo'castle mattresses for fuel.

When I questioned the two idiots next day, their excuse was that they were trying to find some rope to make pads for their worn-out boots and had built the fire solely to furnish light.

This sounded pretty thin. But it was hard to conceive of any of our "guests" *deliberately* setting the vessel afire. Why should they? We wanted that coal for them. They had nothing to gain by destroying their own winter comfort.

I finally concluded that the pair were merely plain garden-variety fools, and from all the advice showered on me by their comrades, I think the others agreed. Suggested punishment ranged from flogging to hanging. But since none of those things could replace the fuel, in the end I did nothing at all, merely announcing to the angry crowd:

"Whenever you fellows feel chilly, you can warm up by giving 'em a licking."

So far as I know they never "took it out" on the guilty pair.

February brought the three coldest days of the year—also a sled bearing an enormous wooden box weighing one hundred fifty pounds, and a colored man too fat to waddle.

Dragging this strange load up the coast came the mate of the "Belvedere," Jim Wing, whose long nose was so badly frozen when he arrived that eventually he lost a quarter-inch off the end. The negro, he explained, through chattering teeth, was the "Orca's" cook.

After thawing the men out and giving first aid to Jim's nose, we were naturally curious to learn what was in the big box that he'd taken such pains about.

Jim was as curious as we. He had no idea what it contained. Somebody on the "Orca" had just asked him to take it along, he said, telling him that it would probably be well worth his while.

With much grunting and cussing we finally got it into the Station. Then all hands crowded around close while Jim eagerly pried open his unknown treasure.

When he discovered what he'd lugged clear from the Sea Horse Islands at fifty-six below zero, to purify the Station atmosphere would have taken more than that box of Bibles put aboard at San Francisco by the Salvation Army.

The next few weeks were busy ones for all but the bunkhouse crew. The rest of us were up to our necks in boat building and taking care of the meat which Eskimo hunters began hauling in. Teams arrived every day now bringing from ten to twenty caribou at a time—some from a distance of fifty miles. We never had so much meat. Every icehouse was full, and what we didn't need had to be sledded seventy miles east to the other crews stuck in the ice.

About this time my old friend Mungie arrived after a long sojourn at Herschel Island, and with him came another Utkiavie native named Pisa who said he had stopped off at Flaxman Island till the food ran out.

We all knew Pisa as a good whaleman. He had worked in our boats before. Now, however, we regarded him suspiciously, not knowing whether or not to believe ugly tales that had come to us earlier that winter. He was said to have been flogged and run out of Herschel by the crews of the ships there on account of getting drunk and beating to death a little girl he had adopted.

Just the same, Tom was anxious to hire him again for spring whaling. If the rumors were false, he argued, we'd be losing a good man all for nothing; if true, it wasn't entirely Pisa's fault. The crews had no business selling him liquor to get crazy on. In the end, we decided to take Pisa on again, let him live in one of our small houses as usual, but watch him like a hawk.

That was the situation when Lieutenant Jarvis and Dr. Call of the cutter "Bear" came mushing up the coast. My first thought was that they had been wrecked and were coming for aid. As a matter of fact, it was the other way around. They were there to help *us*.

According to Jarvis, one of the whalers which got back to 'Frisco the fall before had reported various vessels caught in the ice. The ship owners, not knowing that we were taking care of the crews, persuaded the Government to send out a relief expedition, President McKinley finally calling for volunteers from the Revenue Service. Jarvis was practically drafted to lead the expedition. Lieutenant Berthof and Dr. Call volunteered.

Fitted out with provisions for twelve months, the "Bear" left San Francisco for Cape Vancouver, where Jarvis and the others bought a sled and dog team and struck out north for distant Point Barrow, meeting our messenger, George Tilton, somewhere in Norton Sound.

From Tilton they learned that the crews were safe but doubtless facing slow starvation. That was enough to keep Jarvis headed north. Reaching Cape Nome (there was no settlement there yet), he induced an Eskimo named Charlie Antisarlook, who owned reindeer, to come along with his herd. At Port Clarence they added Mr. Lopp to the party, along with a lot of deer *he* owned. Still more animals were picked up at Cape Prince of Wales.

Jarvis now dispatched Lieutenant Berthof to Point Hope to take

care of any of our men he might want to send back along the coast.
Then, with Lopp in charge of all the deer, they drove across Kotzebue Sound to Cape Krusenstern and over a pass in the mountains
to just below Point Lay. Jarvis and Dr. Call here left the others
and pushed ahead to let us know that meat was on the way. Lopp
and Charlie arrived with their deer two days later.

This whole expedition, from the fitting out of the "Bear" to the
final delivery of the deer to us, upheld the finest traditions of
Arctic rescue work. But perhaps it was just as well that Lopp
started back to Wales with the dog team almost at once, making
the seven-hundred-fifty-mile trip in twenty-one days. Had he
stayed around longer he might have realized that he'd really been
driving "coals to Newcastle," so to speak, because of all the fresh
meat our Eskimos had been bringing in for weeks.

Jarvis knew, though. That was one reason he refused to let
Charlie Antisarlook kill more than the first two or three. The other
reason was that they proved to be nothing but skin and bones after
their long trip, so couldn't be used for food.

"Too bad Jarvis has to kill the whole herd," observed Mac, putting on a long face.

"Why should he?" I asked, innocently.

"Otherwise, how's he going to report that he got 'em here just
in time to keep us from starving?"

I thought this a pretty good one, and passed it on to Jarvis.

It was the first time I ever saw that fine but literal-minded officer
really mad.

CHAPTER XXXIX

NOT that it lasted long. In fact, after a thorough canvas of the situation, Jarvis asked me to stay in charge of everything.

I appreciated his trust, of course, but felt that as the official representative of the Government, he was the logical one to take over. What I didn't say was that I was sick of all the wrangling and needed a rest. Still he insisted. And after he had promised to use his official position in any way I wished, there seemed nothing left but to carry on.

One thing I had wanted to do for a long time was get the men out of their filthy bunkhouse where they lived packed together like animals. Only a kind Providence had kept contagion away so far. I had suggested to Mac and Marsh several times that they rearrange their own spare space so as to take some of the crowd. The others could be moved into an empty warehouse. But somehow these hints never "took" until Jarvis backed me up.

Next, with his help I organized ball teams and for the first time all hands took regular exercise. We made them. If the weather was too bad, they had to take walks. The United States Government—through Charlie Brower—so ordered.

Since most of the men still lacked adequate clothing, Jarvis now suggested that the Eskimos might be persuaded to make a "tarpaulin muster," each native throwing in whatever clothing he could spare.

I didn't know how the Eskimos would take to the idea of helping white men who had stooped so low as to rob their very graveyard. But I did my best—and was fairly overwhelmed by their generous response. Even Pisa contributed his part. I was careful to take down the names of all donors, however, and when the "Bear" came later, we saw that each native was well rewarded. They never forgot that.

Our own crowd had fairly good whaling that spring. We even outfitted one boat for some of our wrecked men and the single small whale they managed by some miracle to catch pleased them as much as though they'd made a fortune in bone.

Before I realized it, spring was over, summer slipping by. And presently, here lay the "Bear" off the Station. We had intended to get the men aboard her at once, but suddenly the wind changed and the ice came piling in to cause a two-week delay. The "Bear's" crew even unloaded all their supplies on the ice, fully expecting her to be crushed before their eyes. That, I think, was the closest shave the old cutter ever had.

But after buckling her engine-room floor, the pressure eased off, the pack broke up and floated offshore, and next day I found myself headed for home in a ship so crowded that there wasn't room for all to sleep.

The reason I had to go out with the crowd was that I had kept all the accounts and now none of the men would settle with anybody else. But I didn't mind going outside for a rest. The Station would be in safe hands with Tom Gordon in charge. Fred would be there, too. And for good measure I had hired a couple of new men, Jack Hadley and John Greubin, to stay with them for a year.

However disagreeable the slow voyage south on a cutter badly overloaded with fault-finding men, that trip was to give me a ringside seat for a bit of history in the making.

The love of gold may be the root of all evil, but from what I witnessed when the "Bear" called at Kotzebue Sound, the *rumor* of gold is worse. It showed itself in a mushroom growth of tents and galvanized houses scattered over the beaches, with hundreds of homesick men and women milling about aimlessly.

And all because of fake rumors of gold that had reached them during the summer. A ship had hauled up nuggets on her anchor flukes. The Eskimos at Kotzebue were using lumps of gold for bullets. Gold lay around everywhere. All you had to do was pick it up—according to rumor.

With visions of another great strike—far to the east the Klondike rush was then in full swing—excited men and women, old and young, had sacrificed everything they had and flocked to bleak Kotzebue—and bleaker disillusionment. I talked with one helpless old couple who had sold their home in Pennsylvania and come all this way expecting to pick up enough gold in a day to make them rich.

It was a crime!

But later we touched at Cape Nome to land Charlie Antisarlook, the Eskimo deer-herder, and here I saw a cheerier side to history in the making.

Shortly before our arrival a man at near by Anvil Creek *had* struck gold. Actual gold! Already six other whites were on the job, all too busy even to come aboard the "Bear."

Pretty soon I was as excited as they. But Captain Tuttle and Lieutenant Jarvis finally talked me out of accepting Charlie Antisarlook's invitation to spend the winter with him and his wife, so that was that. At any rate, we carried first news of this bona fide gold strike to St. Michaels and so were instrumental in starting the historic rush to Anvil Creek.

But when the "Bear" headed for 'Frisco, I'm sure that not even the most imaginative among us dreamed that a brand new town called Nome would shortly sprout on what was then barren tundra.

All the way down there had been trouble with the shipwrecked men. At first the officers had decided that, since lack of space prevented all from sleeping at one time, they would divide them into watches, like any regular crew. It didn't work. Those with a chance to sleep refused to turn out, at which the others raised all kinds of Cain.

When matters reached a point little short of mutiny, Captain Tuttle had the crowd lined up on deck.

"Everybody willing to obey my orders stand one side," he barked.

Only six moved.

"All right, men."

Before they knew what was happening the rest were chained

along the rail, to stay there until they "saw the light." A few hours of this brought most to their senses, but some we carried clear to Seattle in irons.

I wasn't sorry to see the last of them. A hard lot! But no worse than the average whaling crew on whom the gentler half of civilization used to depend for corset stays.

After talking everything over at our office at San Francisco, it was finally decided that I should go to Washington that winter and see what the Government would do to compensate us for having taken care of the men before Jarvis and his "relief expedition" arrived. From then on it was Uncle Sam's headache, anyhow.

But first I went home to New Jersey, stopping in Ohio to visit Mr. Stevenson and my two daughters. Mother and father were quite upset when I arrived without the girls.

"We want them with us," they said.

So my sister brought them on and they stayed with their grandparents until I came north again. Then she took them herself and raised them in West Orange, a happy arrangement all around. Eventually, one married. The other became a teacher.

In some respects my work in Washington proved harder than hunting whales off the pack. All winter and spring Jarvis and I labored in the offices of the Revenue Service, adjusting prices, preparing claims, and hoping the Government would see fit to reimburse the Cape Smythe Whaling and Trading Company. At last the Government did—and in addition awarded me three thousand dollars "for extraordinary services."

This last took me completely by surprise. I had only done what most men would have done under the circumstances. Just the same, I accepted the gift, finished up one other important piece of Washington business, and by the middle of May was sailing out of San Francisco for the Arctic.

Our tender, the schooner "Bonanza," also had a newly married couple aboard, Mr. and Mrs. Spriggs, who were going to Point Barrow as missionaries. I don't think they enjoyed the first few days of their honeymoon. If there's anything hard on romance it's seasickness. But the Spriggs weren't the only ones under the weather.

I hadn't been feeling well before we sailed, but thought it nothing serious until the third day out. Then I knew I was in for something. So did everyone else.

There was no end of doctors aboard the "Bonanza." The skipper had his book of rules and dosed me from the ship's medicine chest whenever I felt too weak to resist. Mr. O'Brien, the mate, had his homeopathic sugar pills which he secretly fed me to counteract the skipper's medicine. Unfortunately, Mr. Spriggs had taken a short course in some kind of doctoring and now and then got in *his* work. The only point on which all of us agreed was the nature of my illness. I had seen too many cases of typhoid fever to be mistaken.

What bothered me most as I lay in my bunk through that darkly remembered period was the important appointment I had secured just before quitting Washington. For with the 1900 census just around the corner, I had been given the job of census taker for the northern part of Alaska and the threat of having to give that up did more to keep me going than all the medicine put together.

By the time the "Bonanza" had crawled into Port Clarence and anchored among the whalers, I was able to lie bundled up on deck and enjoy the astonishment of several old friends, none of whom recognized me at first.

All the time, however, I was gaining strength that would be needed if I were to do anything with the census. Some days later, on reaching Point Hope where my territory was to begin, I felt well enough to make a try at it.

A Dr. Driggs was in charge of the mission just north of the Point, and there I made my headquarters for several days, the doctor often accompanying me as I worked around the immediate vicinity. All went smoothly until I tried to interview a drunken white man known as Wild Jim, who answered question number one by leaping to his feet and offering to fight the whole Government.

Side-stepping his first rush, I was trying to recall the official rules for handling such a case when Dr. Driggs demonstrated the best Arctic method. An ex-athlete, the doctor had his man down in no time and, *holding* him down, made him tell me every last thing I had to know. At the end, Jim got up and brushed himself off and we all parted the best of friends.

Before finishing in the Point Hope vicinity, I hired some Eskimos to paddle me eight miles south to the end of a lagoon where some Portuguese were living with their Eskimo wives. The settlement was known among ship captains as "Jabbertown." Here I found my old friend Antone Bettes who had worked for us at Point Barrow three years before. And above the noise of all hands jabbering at once, Antone introduced me as "Mister De Charles, coming to take the centuries."

It wasn't hard to elicit vital statistics from "Jabbertown" except in one case. Tom George, a colored fellow from the West Indies, wouldn't answer anything. Finally, I got him off a way from the babble.

"You needn't tell me anything," I said, folding up the sheet and putting it in my pocket, "but a smart man like you must have some good reason for keeping still. I'd like to find out what it is, that's all."

Then he opened up. And the reason he gave seemed to me pretty sound at the time, and does still. Several years before, he had been at Herschel Island. When his time was up he naturally wanted to go back to San Francisco on the tender, along with some of the other crew members. But he was a good boat-steerer and the captain asked him to stay. He refused. He was sick of whaling. The captain then fired a lot of questions at him, just as I had, and finally showed him where to make his mark on a piece of paper.

So he made his mark, and it turned out to be the worst thing he ever did in his life. It forced him to stay on that ship *two years more*. He'd never made marks or answered white man's questions since.

I explained that "the centuries" had nothing to do with signing ship's articles, and besides, he didn't have to make his mark for Mr. De Charles or anyone else.

With the mark eliminated, he readily gave me all the routine information I wanted.

The "Bonanza" weighed anchor early next morning and worked her way slowly up the coast, putting in at Wevok and Icy Cape where I listed the people. There were several settlements farther along, but I decided they could be visited that winter just as well. So, from Icy Cape we never stopped until safely anchored off our Station.

I couldn't blame Tom and Fred for wanting to take their year outside as soon as the "Bear" arrived, and when she showed up a few days later, now in charge of *Captain* Jarvis, it tickled me all the gifts he handed out to the natives as extra pay for having helped us with the wrecked men.

That done, Jarvis came ashore to pay the Station a visit. I met him on the beach and we walked up together. As we neared several small houses occupied by some of our Eskimos, I saw Tom come racing full-speed over the sandspit towards us.

Now, Tom had always liked Jarvis well enough but it seemed a bit strange that he should suddenly break his neck to say "Hello." Then when he came up, he made some inane excuse to steer us *around* one of the small houses instead of past it on our way to the Station.

If Jarvis noticed anything peculiar in this he gave no sign but remained at the Station an hour or so, smoking and "gamming" as usual. When he left, Tom stood in the doorway watching until he had passed the last of the little houses.

"Now," I exploded, "maybe you'll tell me what in Sam Hill this is all about!"

The answer came reluctantly, in one word,—

"Pisa."

CHAPTER XL

SUDDENLY I remembered Jarvis remarking about a fine rifle he'd brought for "that Pisa chap of yours. Where is he, anyhow?" and Tom turning it aside with something about Pisa being sick.

What had happened in my absence, as Tom told me now, was this. When Pisa came back from Flaxman Island after being run out of Herschel by the ships' crews, it wasn't lack of food that had prevented his staying longer at Flaxman. He'd lied about that.

According to the half-blind woman he brought with him, she was the sole survivor of two Nubook families that had been camping on Flaxman Island when he stopped there. Pisa, she said, quarreled with them over meat, and a few nights later shot both families while they slept—eight people in all, including three children—then forced her to accompany him back to Utkiavie.

For a long while the woman had feared Pisa would kill her if she ever told, so nothing was known of the wholesale slaughter until a few weeks ago. It must have been while I was down with typhoid that she got away from Pisa and made a clean breast of everything in the village.

"Do they believe her?" I asked.

Tom shrugged. "Some of the relatives of those two families have gone to Flaxman Island to see if it's true."

"Then he's safe enough until they get back, anyhow."

"Maybe. But the others are watching him all the time and he knows it. When he saw you and Jarvis today he thought sure the Law was coming to get him."

"So *that* was why you—!"

"Sure. He was waiting in the doorway with his rifle. A boy told me he heard him say he'd kill you both if you tried anything, see? That's why I sort of steered you *around* his place."

"And Jarvis doesn't know?" I asked, after a pause.

221

"Well," Tom replied, "I figured why bother Jarvis? This is an Eskimo affair. You know how the natives are about these things, Charlie."

I knew, all right. But when Tom and Fred left on the "Bear" early next morning, I only hoped the rest of us wouldn't be drawn into the mess. A clean-cut Eskimo feud was a racial institution, but a crazed killer was everybody's affair.

The last doubt of Pisa's guilt was swept away after the ice made that fall and the investigating committee got back from Flaxman Island with their report.

They had found the eight bodies, just as the woman said.

The thing to be decided now was not whether Pisa should die, but who was the proper one to kill him. The whole village held a big consultation. It was finally decided that, since both families were practically wiped out, the brother of the first man slain would be the logical executioner. The fact that his name, Elebrah, was the same as one of the murdered men undoubtedly helped justify the choice.

All this time Pisa was living in one of our small Company houses and threatening to shoot anybody who came near. The woman who had told on him was there too. That was something I never could fathom. Perhaps he didn't know she'd told. Or possibly he was too muddle-headed to comprehend. I think it more likely that he used some strange hold over her in order to insure a necessary food and water supply.

At any rate, she carried him all he needed, and when he slept, if he ever did, she kept watch outside the door. Most of the time, however, he sat there on a bunk, day and night, with his loaded rifle and a hunting knife at his side.

A situation like this, of course, couldn't go on forever. The whole village grew jittery. No one knew whom he'd try to kill next.

Things came to a showdown one November afternoon when a lot of Eskimos stopped at the Station to inform me that they were going to get Pisa and take him away for Elebrah to execute.

"Go ahead, boys," I agreed, thankful it was their job, not mine.

They hung around the rest of the afternoon, talking big but doing little. Finally I lost patience and calling Jack Hadley told him that if anything happened to me he was to take charge.

"What are you going to do, Charlie?"

"Somebody's got to get that crazy killer away from here."

He saw that I meant it, and kept still. That was lucky. It wouldn't have taken much argument on Jack's part to make me think twice—which was the one thing I couldn't afford to do.

Having firmly decided that if Pisa made a move towards his gun I'd kill him first, I got my revolver and started for the little house.

It was worse than the time Con, Pat and I had gone out to get the Eskimo who had murdered poor Portuguese Joe. Then we could keep our man in sight, watch every move he made as we drew near.

This was different. The little house, ominously quiet, brought to mind everything I'd ever heard about the diabolical cunning of demented killers. A dozen times I would have sneaked away except for the Eskimos watching from well back. There was no easing of the strain even after I gained the comparative shelter of the side wall, for just around the corner was the door. And back of that door—

For a moment or two I crouched under a window sill, somewhat astonished that nothing had happened. Then came the steadying thought—what a fool I'd look, hunched over this way, with a cocked revolver, if the place turned out to be empty. Why not? How else account for the dead silence? Pisa could have picked me off a dozen times if he were there.

Holding firm to this vastly reassuring idea, I walked around front, pushed the door open and jumped sideways. Not a sound came out of the blackness. Certain now that Pisa had escaped, I was about to step inside when someone landed squarely on my shoulders, pulling me over backwards, then jumped through the doorway and leapt like a cat on Pisa. In one motion, it seemed, he yanked the man out of his bunk to the floor. Then he sat on him until other Eskimos came running to help.

The one who had jumped me was a kid of seventeen. Hearing in the village that the Eskimos were letting me go for Pisa, he had run all the way, arriving just in time to prevent the white man from mixing in a strictly native feud.

They tied Pisa hand and foot and I followed the crowd as he was carried across the lagoon lashed to a sled. At first he kept yelling at me to stop them. When I took no notice, he quieted down and only spoke once more. It was while Elebrah was taking careful aim that Pisa flung them his final defiance—product, no doubt, of a distorted brain.

He was a hunter, he growled. A *hunter*. They'd never kill him with *one bullet*.

They didn't, either. Elebrah shot the bound man like a mad dog —but it took a second bullet to finish the job.

CHAPTER XLI

Tom and Fred came back on the "Bonanza" the next summer, and when the schooner turned south again she was carrying out not only Jack Hadley and John Greubin but a cargo of bone and furs which represented the best season the Cape Smythe Whaling and Trading Company had enjoyed.

Thirty-five thousand pounds of bone alone! All hands were jubilant. And with the villagers still under the festive influence of their greatest whale dance in years, it seemed to whites and natives alike that life in the Arctic was very kind indeed.

No whale dance I had witnessed could compare in magnitude and hospitality with the one just given. The whaling had hardly ended when messengers set out carrying dance invitations to the farthest inland tribes.

It was on July twentieth that our guests from "the sticks" arrived all at one time in about fifty oomiaks. They landed at Berinak where there was good fishing in the lagoon, and set up camp. Only a small group of us, including Mungie, was on hand to act as a welcoming committee.

"Where are those messengers of ours?" I asked. "Weren't they supposed to come back with the crowd?"

Mungie explained that we mustn't ask about them.

"Why?"

Because the messengers were supposed to be smuggled into the dance house without being seen.

"Why?" I persisted.

Mungie eyed me in amazement, but all he could say was that this had always been the custom. It was bad form for us even to look the strangers over too closely.

I did, anyhow. Some I recognized as regular summer visitors, but most had come from so far up the rivers that their young people had never seen a white man before. I couldn't get anywhere near the children, and quit trying after the first kid let out a screech and ran for its life.

A foot race took place a couple of days later, our two best runners going to Berinak for the start. The rest of the village waited at the dance house for a good view of the finish. It wasn't much of a race from our point of view. The visitors won hands down, their first man coming in a mile ahead of their second, and both as fresh as if they'd just started. After an embarrassing wait, our pair finally trailed in with tongues hanging out.

The main body of visitors followed, two hundred or more stretching out in a long line. Some bore mysterious packages on their backs, others dragged sleds piled high with skins. Everyone was dressed in his worst. I never saw a more disreputable looking crowd —nor one whose tatters covered more suppressed excitement.

Just above the Station they were met by a picked group of village men naked to the waist. Each wore a loonskin on his head and carried a few arrows and a bow. Suddenly they gave a yell and started shooting over the heads of the strangers. Their arrows gone, they then retreated to the dance house where the rest of our crowd was congregated, still a bit put out over the result of the foot race.

All this time our messengers, who had supposedly returned with the guests, were nowhere to be seen. They'd have a hard job sneaking into the dance house now, I thought, unless they, too, had dressed in old clothes, hoping to mingle with the guests and escape detection.

I was scanning the crowd with this in mind when a riot broke out around the doorway. A group of visitors, laden with rolls of deerskins, were demanding entrance, the guards steadfastly refusing to let them through. Higher and higher rose angry voices until, with final protesting shrieks, the guests were forced to unroll their deerskins—and there inside lay our messengers nearly smothered by heat and stifled laughter.

Mungie came by grinning broadly. An old trick, he said. These inland people must have thought we'd never heard of it.

Our "home folks" furnished the music that first day, visitors doing the dancing. A man and woman would enter and dance, then loudly announce what they had brought for the one who had invited them. After which the recipient joined in and all three danced together.

Later, the women disappeared to make ready the feast—mostly whale meat and seal. Many of the inland people, unfamiliar with such delicacies, couldn't get the stuff down. Lucky for me that I'd learned to take my muctuc like any coast native, for this enabled me to join the crowd in making fun of our visitors. Their only comeback was to hint broadly at what they expected in return for their presents.

Since it was a matter of tribal pride that visitors be satisfied or else given back their own presents—a most humiliating procedure —our people went to ridiculous lengths to meet the demands. Many sold their whalebone to provide needed funds. A few of the poorest even asked for additional credit at the Station. Anything to uphold the reputation of Utkiavie! It was silly—and a little touching.

I hadn't yet seen our visitors at their best, for all this time they had been wearing their most ragged clothing. But when they took over the drums the second day while our crowd danced it was like the transformation of cocoons into butterflies. Decked out in all the finery they had brought in bundles, they certainly were a fine looking lot of people. Many of the men were six feet tall. Even their women seemed larger and better looking than average Eskimos.

The third and last day was given over to the actual exchange of presents. I say "exchange." In reality, it turned into one grand bargain-driving spree. If a gift fell below expectations, the donor kept adding to it until he had nothing more to offer. And when *this* failed to satisfy, the other party demanded his present back even though he often sold it later for whatever it would bring.

The swapping and wrangling over, our guests seemed in no great hurry to leave. One couldn't blame them after all the distance they'd traveled to get here. Besides, fishing was excellent in the lagoon. So they stayed on at Berinak until the arrival of the ships— among them our tender "Bonanza" with Tom and Fred aboard.

Then came the inevitable. Amid general jubilation over the fine season we'd had, the inland people began trading what furs they had left to the whalers' crews for whiskey. In the light of what followed, however, I have never begrudged them the good time they had on that bad whiskey.

For the ships stayed just long enough to give the Eskimos a germ of some sort—probably a kind of flu. A number of our own employees caught it, too, as well as half Utkiavie. Fearful of a sweeping epidemic, we spent the next days and nights looking after the sick villagers. Nobody had time to worry about the crowd at Berinak.

"They're a strong healthy bunch," said Mac. "I doubt if it's hit 'em hard."

But when we had a chance to go over there and see how they were making out we found whole families down with the sickness. It had taken a far more virulent form than anything we'd seen in the village. Too sick to move, nevertheless they were being urged by their devil-doctors to pack up and leave for home. The coast, it seemed, wasn't good for them. Once they started back they would soon be well. So said the devil-doctors.

And because they still held great power over the simple inland folk, nothing a white man could say had the slightest effect. It was pitiful to see all those fine men and women grown so weak that only their devil-doctors' ranting, coupled with their own will power, enabled them to crawl about trying to load their oomiaks for the interminable voyage up the rivers and home.

We had to stand there helpless on the littered beach and watch them go—the whole fifty boatloads.

Two or three of our own sick died later from pneumonia, but when the rest recovered rapidly, we thought maybe we'd been too pessimistic about those inland natives. They had seemed a husky lot. And, as Tom put it, "Maybe their damned devil-doctors knew what they were doing, after all. Kept telling 'em they'd soon be well, didn't they? Y'know, Charlie, some of these devil-doctors do funny things."

I nodded. "Once I saw an old duffer named Tatpana cut through a three-inch spruce plank with a seal line."

Not long after this, an Eskimo from the village who had been far inland and so hadn't heard of any sickness, burst into the Station to tell us of a lot of dead people scattered all along the banks of a river where he'd been hunting.

We left for Berinak at once.

Following the homeward course of the stricken people we came to the first evidence of disaster not ten miles away—a woman with a young baby. She had died on the bank of the lagoon. The child had lived a while longer. Its body lay quite a way off.

The farther we went, the greater grew the tragedy. It was clear that from the day they set out for home in their oomiaks they had been dying all along the coast and up the rivers. From the postures of the bodies, we could almost visualize it happening—the stronger members dragging the weaker on to the banks to die, then paddling a little farther until it came their turn to be abandoned.

I never shall forget one camp we came to, with its three empty boats and a dozen bodies sprawled around on the bank. Men, women, children—all as cold as the ashes of the fire they'd tried hard to build. And off at one side a string of turquoise beads that would have brought a fortune a few years before.

From there we turned back, realizing that what we had seen was only a sample of what lay farther back along the remote inland waterways.

All that fall and the next summer we kept getting reports from hunters of bodies discovered along far river banks, sometimes alone, sometimes with a few belongings scattered around.

It is my opinion that of those two hundred or more husky inland Eskimos who so light-heartedly danced with us at Utkiavie, not one was left alive.

CHAPTER XLII

THE tragedy left its imprint on the village. Every Eskimo saw that those devil-doctors of the stricken inland people had made a mess of it. Could it be that their *own* devil-doctors weren't anywhere near so powerful as they pretended?

I don't say that this tragedy marked a sudden break in the people's old-time faith. Minor doubts had been arising ever since we white men broke all their whaling rules and still managed to kill whales.

Then too, there had been puzzling incidents like "Ocpullu's Rebellion." If devil-doctors were all-powerful, how was it that little Taha, mean as he was, had been beaten up by a mere woman, thus losing face with everybody? And what about Mr. Stevenson and his strange new religion that had nothing to do with orthodox devil-doctoring?

Which was right, which wrong? It was all very confusing.

But while no one event could take away the power of their devil-doctors over night, the tragedy of the inland people cracked it so wide open that the "profession" had to take a new tack. Several of our local devil-doctors suddenly hinted at a wonderful new religion far better for Eskimos than the white man's, and the fact that each soon had quite a following was a great worry to good Dr. Marsh who had done his best to carry on where Mr. Stevenson left off.

"Let the devil fellows stick to their own hocus-pocus. They're running that into the ground already," he said, "but when they tell the people about seeing God and talking with Him—well—that's going too far, Charlie. It's *dangerous*."

"They'll hang themselves by their own rope soon enough," I answered.

They certainly made a good start when one of them told his followers that God had taken him to a new heaven where all the differ-

Photo by Arnold Liebes

WINTER AT BARROW, SHOWING MR. BROWER'S STATION

CHURCH AT BARROW. FARTHEST NORTH CHURCH IN AMERICA

Courtesy Alfred M. Bailey

TESSIE GEORGE, A BARROW ESKIMO SCHOOLTEACHER

ent animals were so tame that you could walk right up and kill one whenever food was needed.

That was enough for the more skeptical. Who ever heard of being able to kill meat without even hunting for it!

But what finished this particular devil-doctor was his further insistence that God had given him the job of baptizing them.

About fifty agreed to be "saved." The great event took place on Sunday afternoon in an outlying igloo. Accessories: a small tub of water, and a very dirty rag with which he bathed one and all from waist to neck. For some reason his efforts didn't "take" well. But everything else did. . . . It required a year, off and on, for me to cure the sores they contracted by that ceremony.

The last devil-doctor to lose out in Utkiavie was an unmarried woman. How she got her reputation for devil-driving I never quite understood, unless it was because of her strong personality coupled with a flare for the dramatic. The fact that she would soon have a baby presented no obstacle to her teachings. Quite the reverse. She capitalized her condition by pounding in the story of the Immaculate Conception until only the actual birth of the baby was needed to set her up as a second favored Virgin.

Day by day the whole village eagerly awaited this final infallible proof of her divinity. Had all gone well, it might have restored to the devil-doctors their former prestige for another decade.

One day Dr. Marsh, who had been particularly upset by the sacrilegious angle, came bolting into the Station, beaming all over:

"She's done it this time, Charlie!"

"Done what? Who?"

"That woman devil-doctor. Her baby's come, and now everybody knows she's a fake."

"I thought the baby was supposed to prove that she's another Madonna."

"So it was. But, Charlie," his smile broadened, "they can't see any Madonna having a *girl!*"

That was the end of devil-doctors at Utkiavie.

But I couldn't always agree with the missionaries, either. For example, they were urging the natives to live in frame houses like white people. This meant heating by stoves, and as driftwood continued scarce as hens' teeth, the result was that the wooden shacks were usually cold and drafty, with much pneumonia ensuing. They weren't half so practical as the old-style native igloos which generations of trial and error had developed for just such conditions, and in which an even day-and-night temperature could be maintained by stone lamps. The new houses certainly were harder to keep clean, and soon each contained as many Eskimos as ever packed into a single igloo.

One of the biggest mistakes, I think, was in tearing down the dance houses for fuel. While this put an end to young people freely congregating there at night and sometimes, no doubt, doing things they shouldn't, it didn't improve matters to take away this common family rendezvous. They simply went off somewhere else and continued committing just as many indiscretions.

About the only thing to benefit from the "new order" were the consciences of the well-meaning missionaries themselves. Perhaps it's always this way when "reforms" are forced on people faster than conditions warrant.

Early in September, 1902, one of the Pacific Steam Whaling Company's steamers, westward bound from Herschel Island, came in to land a sick Eskimo woman.

If the skipper knew what ailed her he was mighty careful not to tell anybody. He just dumped her on the beach and sailed away. The people around the Station put up a tent for the woman, doing all they could to make her comfortable, but she died within two days.

It wasn't long before the Eskimos began getting sick. I couldn't diagnose their fever for some time. But when they started breaking out all over with red blotches, Dr. Marsh and I felt pretty sure it was measles. One after another came down. Then it spread to the people farther out on the Point. There came a period when all the Eskimos both in our village and at Nubook were sick at the same time.

Neither Marsh nor I had any medicine, and since the natives made no effort to help each other, we were busy day and night, hurrying from one stricken family to the next, doing what we could for them without medicine.

Food was a problem. All had to be fed. I made somebody go the rounds every morning to find out how they were fixed for food. Where the whole household was too sick to cook, we arranged for an outsider to do it for them. Had nobody been on hand to see that this was done, I believe they'd have lain there and starved.

Our hardest and least successful job was making the sick ones stay indoors *after* the rash came out and they began feeling better. That was the critical time. They paid no attention to my orders and used no sense of their own. Feeling a bit better, they insisted on going outdoors where they lay around and caught cold and got pneumonia—and that was the end of them. Sometimes entire families would die in the night.

I had better control of those near the Station, but here my chief worry was Toctoo. Hard as I tried to keep my family quarantined, for once I couldn't do a thing with Toctoo. She saw the need and insisted on helping. Her tireless efforts undoubtedly saved several lives.

Not one of the whites took the disease. Thanks to his elaborate personal precautions, like always fumigating himself before entering his house, Marsh managed to keep even his children from catching measles.

So many of the natives died, however, that we had to organize a burial system. Ned Bosqui and Charlie Graber, two prospectors camping at the Point, became coffin makers; Fred and Tom, undertakers. As soon as a new death was reported, they put the body in one of the rough new coffins and carried it out of the village, leaving it on the tundra to be buried later when we had a chance.

Most of the deaths occurred in October and November, few after the first of December. But I buried one hundred twenty-six people before the epidemic ran its course.

An air of desolation shrouded the Station as Christmas approached that year. There was no holiday spirit in Tom or me; no spirit of any sort. Tom had lost his wife and child, and Toctoo, too, finally contracted the disease, her death preceding that of our young baby by a day.

CHAPTER XLIII

In 1905 my son Jim, who is now a major in the United States Army, was, to put it mildly, a handful. Had I realized the scrapes a "handful" could get into aboard ship, I might have thought twice before taking him outside with me on the "Bear" that summer.

What with an overindulgent crew, a mischievous boy and a tobacco-eating goat that doubled as ship's mascot and devil incarnate, I remember our chaotic run to Nome as a continuous three-ring circus.

For fear of permanently ruining the discipline of the Revenue Cutter Service, I decided we'd go the rest of the way to Seattle on the passenger steamer "Victoria."

During our wait at Nome I was delighted to meet Conrad Siem. It seemed he had skippered the "Albion" in shortly after gold was discovered and had stayed on ever since. We walked the streets talking over old times, and at one point stopped to let a dray pass. When I turned around Jim was nowhere in sight. I was badly scared. Conrad and I looked every place, finally starting a systematic search of the near by buildings. Far back in the rear of a store we found Jim. He was shaking all over. Those dray horses had been too much for him.

That little incident made me realize what the familiar "outside" world could mean to a small American boy brought up on the shores of the Arctic. But any hope that the "elegance" of a passenger steamer like the "Victoria" might awe such a boy into behaving himself was shattered at dinner the first night out.

At the end of our table sat a "dowager" of about fifty. Next to her came Jim, then myself. The rest included several women from up river and a number of miners. Instead of eating his soup, Jim seemed hypnotized by a fly buzzing around. Suddenly he came out with a shrill:

"Dad! What kind of bird is that?"

All but the "dowager" sniggered.

"You know you've seen plenty of flies, Jim," I answered indulgently, as if it were some private joke between us.

Still he kept his eye on that fly until it settled alongside, when with a sudden swipe he missed the fly but piled the "dowager's" soup plate into her lap.

I offered to pay for the dress and followed this up with every apology I knew. But she left the table without a word and didn't show up again the whole trip. The rest of the folks howled and, of course, made friends with Jim at once. That didn't help much, either, for whenever he was missing after that I could be sure he was up to something his new friends had put him on to.

Jim's world widened fast. His first train trip, Seattle to San Francisco, was followed by the longer one east. I was as excited as he. It seemed good to visit my folks, and mother, getting old, was mighty glad to see her lost son again. The climax came Christmas with a big reunion which included all my brothers and their families as well as my daughters. The girls were in high school now, Elizabeth seventeen, Flora fifteen. It was the last time our whole family got together.

Around Easter I took the girls to Washington for a little sightseeing. While we were there a banker friend of mine arranged a private meeting for us with President Theodore Roosevelt. It turned out to be anything but the ordeal I had envisioned, for, noticing my Masonic charm, the President immediately put me at ease by a hearty "Brother!" He complimented my girls on their good looks, telling them they were the first Alaskan-American citizens he had ever met. Then, giving each a double carnation, he had an attendant show them through the White House while he and I swapped hunting yarns. Presently he was drawing me out on one whaling adventure after another until the girls' return ended our visit.

"Did you tell him a lot of things?" my daughters asked as soon as we got away.

"I'm afraid I bored him," I admitted, thoughtfully.

"No you didn't, Daddy," Elizabeth put in. "I could tell from his eyes."

I think perhaps she was right about Mr. Roosevelt's interest. At any rate, I used the occasion to point out to the girls how easily they, too, could be charming just by showing a real interest in others —whether important folk or rough whalemen.

Not wishing to shoulder my sister with the care of all the kids, I planned to take a reluctant Jim back to Alaska with me. Our tickets bought direct to San Francisco, we were all set to leave when on April eighteenth word of the earthquake and fire brought consternation to everyone in the country—save Jim. Now I *had* to leave him. He wasn't a bit sorry.

When I reached what was left of 'Frisco five nights later, one of our office men conducted me to Mr. Liebes' house on Pacific Avenue, the big ballroom of which now served as temporary quarters for the Company.

I didn't see much of the destruction that night. But next morning—what a sight! Nothing downtown but desolation, with here and there a building standing. I almost cried. After breakfast, which the Jap servant got for me on a stove in the street, I walked all the way to the ferry just to have a look at what had been the city I loved.

The schooner "Vine" had been chartered to go north as our tender this year, and although she lay safe at Oakland there was nothing to load her with until I had picked up an outfit in other cities to be shipped back to Oakland. This trip took me only ten days, but by the time I returned, wooden buildings were shooting up like magic, new stores already being opened.

Somewhere I had heard it said that a city is more than brick and mortar. Now I knew what that meant. The real San Francisco—my San Francisco—was still alive and kicking.

The "Vine," loaded at last, sailed for the north one day in June with me standing on her deck torn between two desires. I was eager enough to get back to the peace of the Arctic again, yet reluctant to leave behind what seemed to me a miracle in the making.

For once we had fine weather nearly all the way up to Point Barrow. The boys seemed as glad to see me as I felt to get back and resume the calm routine of Arctic existence where no epoch-making events ever took place.

I was still checking supplies unloaded from the "Vine" when an Eskimo from Berinak reported a strange looking vessel creeping along outside the sandspits. Taking my glasses, I got hold of Fred and started for the Point. . . . We got there in time to meet her coming in from the east.

I'd never seen just such a sloop in these waters before. Neither had the Eskimos, a small group of whom stood watching silently as she came about in the sluggish breeze, lost headway, drifted slightly astern, then dropped her anchor.

Viewed broadside, she seemed about seventy feet long. Certainly she looked the worse for wear, as if her home port—wherever that might be—were a long way off.

I can't say what first suggested it—perhaps several slightly foreign-looking details that caught my eye—but suddenly I *knew*.

I should have guessed sooner. Hadn't I seen the newspapers last winter when word had first been flashed out of the wilderness to an astonished world?

No matter. Here she was before my eyes. The "Gjoa"—the little sloop which in three forgotten years had painfully accomplished what navigators had been attempting for centuries.

Strange that I should come so long a way to dodge the turmoil of historic events, only to be the first to congratulate Roald Amundsen as he completed his epoch-making Northwest Passage right here at Point Barrow!

CHAPTER XLIV

FOR some time the Bureau of Education had been putting up better schoolhouses along the coast, thus booming the Three R's at Wales, Tigara, Wainwright and now Utkiavie.

With us at least, this "higher education" was a mixed blessing. Encouraged in school to follow the white man's eccentricities as closely as possible, the older boys now turned their New Year's celebration into a general rough-house, on the theory that if a little whoopee was good, a riot must be infinitely better.

No longer were they satisfied with making a harmless racket. They had to barge into our locked houses with their oil cans, horns and drums and smash things up.

"Boys, that's something you can't do around here any more," I told a grinning bunch, trying to sound tough. "If somebody asks you in, all right. But mind you don't try it otherwise. Especially on *me*."

They laughed heartily, saying that I was only an old man (I was forty-three) and they were many. So what could I do if they wanted to come in?

There was nothing spiteful in this. It was just that they hadn't learned when to stop. And since that subject didn't seem to be in their schoolbooks, I decided to teach it to them myself.

It was fifty-two below zero that New Year's Eve—just the right temperature for lively devilment. But I was ready for them behind locked doors.

In due time I heard the boys break into the ten-foot snow-porch, or entrance, attached to my house. I waited until all had had time to crowd into this narrow space. Then, jerking the inner door open, I threw four pails of icewater over them in quick succession.

The place was cleared in no time and nature did the rest. Their clothing froze almost instantly. Some of the boys who couldn't
239

bend their knees to run or walk had to be lugged home on sleds.

The rest of the winter passed so quietly, without even the dance houses to furnish needed exercise, that active preparations for spring whaling came as a great relief. Perhaps that was why we had such a good year. It seemed, however, that hardly a season could pass without at least one accident of some sort. This time it happened near the very end.

The pack had closed in, leaving a chain of holes all up and down the flaw. Although I had our boat in a favorable spot, we lost a couple of small whales by not getting irons into them quickly enough. When a third came along, my crew put the boat right up on its back and I had that fellow harpooned before he could possibly dive. It was still a trick to get him alongside. With all hands shouting and hauling, nobody paid any attention to a lot of yelling from the boat above us until an Eskimo came on the run.

He was too excited to make us understand his jibberish, but gestured towards his crowd and started back. Following him across the ice to his own boat, I was met by the sight of a hideously bloody smear where a man's face should have been, and off to one side a couple of natives struggling with a third, the boat-steerer, who acted crazy.

The story came out while I gingerly mopped the blood off the wounded man to see what remained of his face, if anything.

It seemed they had guessed by our yells that we'd caught something big, and thinking we might need another gun to finish off the whale, Cicriccowra, the injured man, had tried to get one for us out of the bow of their boat; but in his hurry he ran his face against the rod which sets off the charge. The bomb had ploughed clean through his cheek, taking off the end of his nose and driving powder into everything. A nasty job to tackle anywhere! And we were miles from home!

I sent a man ashore for a sled, anyhow, and turned again to see what could be done before the sled arrived. When closer examination showed that the Eskimo wasn't likely to die, I straightened up:

"*This* man is going to be all right," I said, "but what's the matter over *there?*"

At my words, the hysterical native stopped struggling with those holding him and finally calmed down enough to admit that he had been trying to kill himself. It was all his fault, he chattered. He had left the gun without fixing its firing pin.

I had Cicriccowra temporarily patched up before the poor boat-steerer could be convinced that he wasn't a murderer.

The patching job was a crude one. It meant sewing up the great star-shaped hole, split four ways, where the bomb had gone through his cheek. But before attempting any sewing, I must somehow get the powder out. That had me stumped until one of the others volunteered to suck it out.

While he was doing this I heated a skin needle over the camp stove and bent it into a sort of hook. For thread I got the cook to yank several coarse hairs out of her head and braid them the way she braided sinew for sewing. Then, with two of the men to help me, I closed Cicriccowra's cheek by six stitches. Not much could be done to his nose except cut off the fag ends with my knife and bandage him up with the cleanest snowshirt in the crowd.

Since the sled wouldn't be along for quite a while yet, there was nothing better to do than go back and cut up our whale, with Cicriccowra sitting on the sidelines an interested spectator.

I had fully intended to accompany him ashore but presently the ice opened up and we decided to try for another whale. Everything save death had to be put aside when whales were running. The season was short.

I knew, of course, that the whaling industry had been undergoing certain changes as reflected in lower prices for bone and the fact that more and more ships were being laid up. Such things were straws in the wind—or should have been. But the full blow didn't hit Point Barrow until the summer of 1908 when the "Herman" came in with word that bone was practically *unsaleable*.

Now what to do?

The "Bear" had left. But I went out on the first available craft —a schooner—and after endless head-winds and calms, reached

Port Townsend and hurried south to the Company's new quarters in a rebuilt San Francisco.

There the grim truth was forced upon me that ladies' corsets, our chief market for years, were on their way out. Those still being made no longer used whalebone for stiffening. They had substitutes. That was the worst of it. For even if corsets came back, what chance was there of bone being used again?

Other factors, too, had conspired to knock the bottom out of whaling; things so far apart as whips and automobiles. Where formerly a good whip with a bone heart had been a smart adjunct to any moon-lit buggy ride, young men now chugged their girls around in new-fangled horseless buggies.

But before giving up entirely, I went East to look into the whole matter myself, as well as to visit the family.

It was good to find Elizabeth teaching school, Flo attending State Normal, and the boys both doing well in their studies. Then I spent a few days at home with mother and father before going on to New Bedford which had always been the home of the whale-bone market.

My old friends there gave me little encouragement. "Too many substitutes, Charlie. Get out while you can."

"Where are they using some of these substitutes?" I inquired.

The nearest factory was at Butler, New Jersey. So to Butler I went. The plant manager was interested at once in the piece of whalebone I took from my pocket, examining it as one might a relic of some bygone age. In return, he showed me how thin steel, covered with rubber, vulcanized and polished, worked as well as the real thing.

That night I wrote San Francisco that bone was done for so far as we were concerned. Completely fed up now with ladies' corsets and perhaps wishing to get as far away from them as possible, I took a trip to the Hawaiian Islands, then, on an impulse I've never regretted, came back to the eastern seaboard for another brief visit home. It was the last time I saw my parents. Both died not long afterwards while I was again in the North.

For some reason Isaac Liebes still thought the market for bone might be revived, and insisted on our staying in the game. So I stayed—and before long was broke. Even Isaac Liebes had to agree that bone was done for.

Perhaps it needed something like this to jolt the Company into trying out a new plan which I had urged for some time. With my associates' full backing, I returned to Point Barrow, called all our Eskimos together and announced that we were quitting whaling.

Blank surprise.

"We're going in for *furs*," I explained, "and instead of wages, you'll each have your share of what the furs sell for. If you work hard I think you'll all make more than you ever did before."

From the broad grins that greeted this last it was evident that the new order of the day might pan out quite well.

Meanwhile, I could keep some of the men profitably busy in another way. My interest in collecting had grown steadily, and I had been hiring more and more of the natives to help excavate the old mounds in this vicinity. Each had a place where he dug if and when the spirit moved, scratching away with a small adz or even a piece of metal lashed to a handle.

It was slow work but brought to light engraved implements of ivory or musk-ox horns, lance-heads made from light gray flint, whalebone buckets, ancient fire-drills, round stones blackened in the cooking of many a prehistoric meal.

I had some particularly choice relics; for example, a pair of eye-protectors made of musk-ox horns, beautifully polished and etched all over with elaborate designs. Among my most cherished jade treasures was a woman's knife fashioned out of one piece, handle and all. Some primitive perfectionist must have spent half his life on that job.

We also uncovered the remains of several houses with sides and entrance halls consisting of the skulls of large bowhead whales. And from a long-buried icehouse came the whole skin of a musk-ox, along with one horn—all embedded in the ice. I dried the skin and sent it, with the horn, to Dr. Hornaday, director of the Bronx Park.

Fascinating work! Even the Eskimos grew enthusiastic. The result was that I had acumulated and catalogued a really fine collection of Arctic specimens—which led to my first meeting with Vilhjalmur Stefansson.

He came sledding in from the east so nonchalantly one summer day that it was hard to believe he'd been traveling towards me all spring. But it had taken him that long to come from far-off Coronation Gulf where he had been studying the new Eskimos. What he wanted now was to dig up old implements and other specimens such as we had been excavating around our neck of the world.

"How long can you stay?" I asked.

"All summer."

"Fine. Make yourself comfortable. We can't do much till the snow melts."

I told him of a place on the shore of the lagoon two miles from Berinak where I always went duck hunting about July tenth but where specimen hunting might also be good. He finally persuaded me to go a week early this year in order to help him dig.

Armed with picks and shovels, he and I pitched camp there one evening and next morning went to work. By the time we'd skinned the sod off a spot twenty feet square, noon had come. He was taking an after-dinner nap when I got him on the job again. We shoveled dirt all afternoon. By supper I was ready to call the whole thing off, but since Steff had talked me into coming there a week ahead of time, I wanted to show him that I wasn't a quitter. Around eight that night I poked into his tent and after an argument dragged him out. Both of us then dug till midnight—with no results.

Next morning Steff eyed me thoughtfully across the campfire.

"I think," he said, "maybe I can do better buying the things your Eskimos are finding."

In the end I took charge of the purchasing for him since I had been doing this in a small way for some time. When he went out on the "Bear" that fall he had some twenty thousand specimens that I had bought for him from the natives.

CHAPTER XLV

THAT was the last I heard of Steff for several seasons. But his enthusiasm lingered with us, renewing the Eskimos' interest in excavating all the old buildings around Utkiavie and at Nubook, too.

Occasionally their finds revealed customs and practices as old and forgotten as the relics themselves.

One of the men brought me what he called a suit of armour. Made from the flattened ends of bear ribs laced together with seal-hide thongs, it could easily have turned aside a bone arrowhead.

Examining this specimen, the village ancients recalled hearing how young men had been bred as gladiators in the early days. They couldn't even marry until after fighting age—around thirty, perhaps. Their main job in life was to meet the fighting men of other tribes with bows and arrows, knives and clubs, and put on a show to the death.

These clubs were evil-looking weapons of bone with one-inch saw teeth along the edge and a thong attached to prevent the owner from losing it during the height of battle. The best war club I ever had I sent to the American Museum. It was found near Cape Halkett at a place supposed to have been famous for such contests.

I have sometimes wondered what my old friend down at Tigara, the late, terrible Attungowrah, could have accomplished with such a skull-cracker.

The winter after Steff left happened to be one of those occasional periods when lynx migrate from inland and appear along the coast by thousands. It's goodbye then to fox-trapping. The crafty lynx go from trap to trap eating foxes as fast as they are caught.

Not that lynx are bad eating themselves, according to my notion. The trouble that winter was that so few of the men shared my taste. Fred in particular. The only thing that ever seriously came between Fred and me was a nice fat lynx that I had killed and

245

asked him to cook. His lip began to curl before my request was out.

"If you're down to eating a damned cat," he roared, "you can cook it yourself."

Although we shot and trapped a lot of them, their small fur value never made up for all the fox-skins they cheated us out of.

Later, foxes were to furnish us some of our most profitable trapping; especially the white foxes which breed from thirty to fifty miles inland and come trooping out on the ocean ice as soon as it makes in the fall. Here, far from land, they spend most of the winter, subsisting on dead seals or walrus or even dead whales drifting in the pack, or else following the polar bears about to eat whatever these animals leave of their kill.

But along towards spring their favorite dish consists of baby seals which they dig out from under the snow, since seals don't go into the water until they are over a month old. Should all other food fail, white foxes can always dine well on the small marine animals frozen fast to the bottom side of young ice. This may require a bit of waiting. But as soon as a pressure forms the young ice will turn over and expose everything.

After a nourishing winter spent on the bleakest floe, white foxes come ashore and wander inland as spring advances. Around July they have their young, four to ten in a litter. Many of these are killed by white owls always hanging around the dens waiting for the new arrivals to come out and play. But those that survive this ordeal are now ready for the next winter migration out on the ocean ice, thus starting the fox cycle all over again.

When the lynx let us alone we went after white foxes in a big way. Finally word got around the country that we were a surefire market. This brought natives from all over the east and far inland. All came loaded with skins which we bought. It didn't hurt my feelings a bit. Prices of white foxskins were rising and I needed all I could catch or buy to pull me out of the hole I'd got into from trying to sell bone when none was wanted.

Despite occasional setbacks our business in furs increased so that the time came when I opened up a branch station at Wainwright, to the south, then another far east of us at Beechey Point.

Polar bears, of course, were always a substantial source of profit. We had one unusually fine season, although it ended in tragedy. The ice made early that fall, coming in great sheets from the north, grinding along the beach without an opening anywhere. Long before it would support the weight of a man, half a dozen polar bears could always be seen from the top of the Station moving southward over the ice, the condition of which never bothered them at all.

Their instinct was marvelous. On thin ice they spread themselves out so as to cover a large space; if very thin, they lay flat on their bellies, hauling themselves along with their claws. When the ice was too thin even for this, they swam underneath, breaking up through with their heads to breathe.

This remarkable exhibition of bear versus ice kept up for days until the surface was strong enough to bear the weight of a man. Then all hands went hunting.

Konnettowra, one of the men from the village, happened to be out sealing one day. Dragging his seal home at dusk, he felt something tug at it every little while but thought it was the rough ice he was traveling over. Finally, feeling a harder tug than usual, he looked back and found a polar bear following him and trying to eat the seal.

Konnettowra slipped the harness from his shoulders in a hurry. The bear started for him. With no time to get his rifle out of its sack, he used the ice pick on the end of his spear and with one lucky thrust forced the sharp point into the animal's brain. Although not a large polar bear, it could have given him a nasty mauling.

A few days later, another native came in with two polar bear cubs which he wanted to sell me.

"Where's the mother?" I asked.

He'd shot her a long way out on the pack. The cubs, he said, wouldn't let him come near at first. So he waited to see what would happen. Finally they ventured closer and closer to where their mother's skin lay on the ice. After a while they began nosing it all over looking for the teats, then finding nothing to eat, calmly curled up on the skin to rest. When he started home dragging it over the ice, they followed as if nothing were the matter. But even the native thought it rather pathetic when, growing tired, they allowed themselves to be dragged along curled up on their mother's skin.

I bought both cubs and sent them out later on the "Herman."

A great year for polar bears!

The Eskimos killed sixty before the ice went off with a change of wind. That was when our good luck turned to sudden tragedy. For the wind hauled offshore one morning while most of the hunters were far out on the pack. Those who noticed the shift instantly turned shoreward and managed to get back on anchored ice in time. Six others, however, failed to make it and were carried out. We gave them up. It was like a return from the dead, therefore, when two of them showed up a couple of days later, having finally got to land about forty miles south of us.

The other four we never heard of again. Those lost belonged to Point Barrow, and all were young men.

In 1913 Captain Pedersen of the power schooner "Elvira" put in with brief but interesting news. Stefansson, he said, was on his way north, this time with the Canadian Arctic Expedition. Steff himself had headquarters aboard the "Karluk" which was commanded by Captain Bob Bartlett. Two other boats belonging to the Expedition, the "Mary Sachs" and the "Alaska," would be coming along later. Pedersen said that Steff expected to be in the ice for several years.

"Several *years?*" I exclaimed.

"That was the idea when I left them outfitting at Nome. If I were you, Charlie," Pedersen advised, "I'd get extra supplies together, in case they're expecting to add a few last items here."

Some time later we sighted the "Karluk" a long way south of the village and apparently stuck so fast that it might be days before she'd get through to us. I certainly wasn't looking for Steff when almost at once he and Dr. McKay came walking up the coast.

Could I furnish the Expedition with two oomiaks, several sleds and considerable gear? Also, how about recommending a couple of good Eskimo men, one of whom must be willing to take his wife along to repair clothing? I'd have plenty of time for all this, said Steff. The ship was tied fast to the ice and no telling when the wind would move the pack out and let her through.

After I had agreed to do the best I could and found the necessary Eskimos for him, Steff took me aside.

"One thing more, Charlie. We need another white man. Can you loan us Hadley?"

"It's all right with me if Jack wants to go."

So Jack Hadley joined the Expedition, too.

When we had everything nearly ready, I called Steff's attention to the fact that his ship looked closer than before.

"I can't understand that," he answered, squinting at the distant "Karluk." "Bartlett had her tied to ground ice when we left."

She was drifting, though. No doubt of that. And the prospect of the pack sweeping her right past the Station worried Steff considerably.

When the vessel had reached a point almost abreast, he suddenly decided that he'd better get his crowd aboard, as well as all the stuff they could carry in one trip. The "Mary Sachs" could take the rest when she came along.

For a while the Station was in an uproar. I got all the natives with their sleds to help over the ice and across the narrow leads. It looked like the start of a tremendous whaling outfit.

"Goodbye, Steff!"

"Goodbye, Charlie. See you in a few years. Thanks for all—" The wind carried the rest away.

After they were safely aboard, we followed along the beach for several miles. The ship began drifting faster as the increasing current drove the pack north until, once past the tip of Point Barrow, she finally managed to work herself free. The last we saw of the "Karluk" she was steaming east through an almost open sea.

In a week or so the "Alaska" went by. Later, the "Mary Sachs" stopped to take on a boat and other equipment that Steff had wanted put aboard. More farewells, more waving of hands. Then the last of the Canadian Arctic Expedition took off for its projected "few years' " sojourn in the ice fields.

We heard nothing more about the three ships until the end of September when a party of Eskimos came in from the East to report the "Alaska" and "Mary Sachs" safe in winter quarters off Collinson's Point.

"Isn't the 'Karluk' there too?" we asked.

No one had seen or heard of the "Karluk."

We thought this strange. The Arctic played curious tricks on men and ships, but how account for two vessels of an expedition being visibly safe, the third vanishing into air? I should have given a lot for a few personal words with Steff just then.

I had them—and more—one morning a month later when he and three other members of his party appeared at the Station. But instead of clearing things up, their visit deepened the mystery. They'd lost their own ship!

"That 'Karluk' is unlucky," said Steff, dolefully. "First she gets caught in the ice here. You remember. Then off Cross Island she sticks again and we drift east all the way to Camden Bay."

"Hundred and fifty miles?"

He nodded. "That's not all, Charlie. The pack carried us *west* again as far as Return Reef. There the 'Karluk' froze in for good." He paused and added: "At least we thought so."

Confident that their ship was fast for the winter, he and the three now with him had walked over to Jones Island for a little hunting. That night it blew a gale from the east. When they looked seaward next morning the "Karluk" was gone. About all they could do was to get across to the mainland at the first chance, then walk along the coast trying to catch up with her.

Steff went on to describe the crazy game of hare and hounds the old ship had been playing with them ever since.

At Point Tangent some Eskimos told of seeing such a vessel drift past in the ice not long before their arrival. Now she wasn't even in sight. It had been that way for days as they hurried along, always hopeful of sighting their ship around the next point, always disappointed.

The final word came from a native on the tip of Point Barrow itself. A while before, this man had seen the same ship drifting west about ten miles out. Now he could only point in the general direction of Wrangel Island off distant Siberia. There, he said, was where she was headed.

So it seemed the "hare" had won. And now nothing for the "hounds" but to head east again and try to rejoin their other two vessels still frozen in at Collinson's Point.

There was no further word of the "Karluk" until the following summer. Then, when the "Bear" came in with Captain Bob Bartlett himself aboard, we gathered in her wardroom to listen to his firsthand account of the "Karluk's" end.

His ship, said Captain Bartlett, had never got clear of the ice but had drifted across the Arctic Ocean to a point north of Herald Island. There, some time in January, the ice finally crushed her.

Bartlett and most of the crew managed to reach Wrangel Island over the ice. Then he crossed to the mainland of Siberia, making his way south to East Cape where he was picked up and taken to Nome. The "Bear" was to try and rescue the men still on Wrangel Island as soon as she could get back to Nome for coal.

We knew now that Jack Hadley and our Eskimos had at least reached Wrangel Island. We hoped all those there could stick it out until the "Bear" took them off. There was no time to spare. We heaved a sigh of relief when the Cutter headed for Nome to coal.

But it wasn't to happen that way. The "Bear" had hardly left when up from the south came a little power schooner, the "King and Wings," whose skipper, Swenson, was destined to do two excellent turns that summer.

I was the first beneficiary. As soon as Swenson revealed that he wasn't too anxious to go farther east, I made a good deal for all the merchandise he had aboard. Next, hearing about the "Karluk's" wrecked crew, he volunteered to see what he could do about it.

Skirting westward along the great floes, it was Swenson, with his little schooner and unbelievable luck, who reached the men on Wrangel Island during the one short period of that entire summer when the ice opened up enough for a ship to get through.

Not all the men were alive. As we knew from Captain Bartlett, two parties had been lost on the ice while sledding away from the "Karluk." Others had since died of exposure.

But all the rest Swenson brought out safely—among them Hadley and our natives.

CHAPTER XLVI

WAR in Europe!

The "Bear's" wireless had picked up the flash while we sat in her cabin listening to Captain Bob Bartlett describe the last of the "Karluk." For the moment we felt as close to world events as though Point Barrow were New York. Then the "Bear" left and, deprived of her wireless, Point Barrow once more became—Point Barrow.

Luckily, the telephone operator down at Candle on Kotzebue Sound had the bright idea of copying the daily news reports he got from Nome and sending them up along the coast as often, and by such means, as he could. It was well worth the five dollars a month I paid him for what was probably the world's most northerly "syndicated news service."

I would have paid ten times as much after the United States went in. Now the war became personal. My two sons had enlisted, Jim in the army, Bill in the navy. How eagerly I watched every living speck coming up the coast! You never could tell who might be bringing late news from Candle.

But no skeletonized dispatches were so satisfactory as flesh-and-blood Archdeacon Stuck who spent two weeks with me in February of 1918. His news, while old, was enhanced by the practical views of a thoughtful man.

Here was my chance, too, to show someone in authority our need for a hospital at the Point. I told him how sick natives journeyed here from all over this part of the country expecting us to cure them, and pointed out our lack of facilities. He agreed that it was the logical spot for a hospital. But when he promised, on leaving, to get the Mission Society to put one up immediately—well, I took that with a large grain of salt. A hospital at Point Barrow cost money.

He left in March to strike east for Herschel Island and I furnished a capable native to accompany him as guide and helper. This man returned in April. He told of their reaching Herschel in twenty-one days only to learn that Stefansson, who had been quite sick there with typhoid fever, had just been sent out to the hospital at Fort Yukon. With twenty-one days of difficult going behind him, the Archdeacon, nevertheless, had immediately turned south, hoping to overtake the party and help them get Steff safely over the mountains.

There, it seemed, was a *man*.

Long after it was news to the rest of the world, I was thankful to hear that the war was over, and that both of my boys were home at my sister's in New Jersey. It seemed that Jim, who had served as bayonet instructor at Camp Fremont until he went across, had come back a second lieutenant. All that was fine.

I wasn't so pleased to learn of a severe flu epidemic they were then having at Nome, with more Eskimos dying every day and the mail carrier quarantined at Kotzebue for fear he'd bring it north to us. When further word filtered in that hardly a native was left alive at Wales, I felt the time had arrived for somebody to take defense measures in our own village.

The things I thought should be done were these. First, clean our houses and *keep* them clean. Second, prevent all strangers from entering the settlement.

Such simple precautions would have been easy a few years before. The difficulty now was due not so much to a change in the natives as to the attitude of some of the teachers and missionaries who had brought it about.

With dancing and story-telling out, a lugubrious gloom pervaded the once carefree populace. They no longer welcomed friends to their houses as in the old days, nor took much interest in outdoor games like football. Everything centered in the religious meetings now held almost nightly.

They had been told that it was wicked to strike a whale on Sunday, even if that were the one chance to secure their year's supply of vital whale meat and blubber. When our commercial whaling went by the board, the missionaries had tried every way to prevent families from moving farther out where fur-trapping was good. They wanted them nearer the church. They even urged the people of Nubook to abandon their homes at one of the best hunting and whaling spots on the coast and move to Utkiavie to be handier for church services.

That was once when I stepped in, going to the people of Nubook direct and finally persuading them to stay where they were and let the preacher come to them. For this I was never quite forgiven.

No doubt it was natural enough for certain of our more transient missionaries and teachers to feel a bit jealous of an old-timer like Charlie Brower. For however changed the Eskimos were, they continued treating me like one of themselves and seemed to think they still had a right to come to me in any difficulty.

It was a confidence I valued highly. In return, I did everything practical that I could for them. If they were hungry or hard up, I always helped. I gave them medicine when sick, or a coffin if they died—and never charged for these things the way certain missionaries had been doing.

Of course the newcomers were jealous of me at times. In a way, I can't blame them. But some of the missionaries and schoolteachers we had couldn't even get along with each other. That made any united effort between us almost impossible.

Take, for example, this flu emergency. First, I tried to get our teacher to do something, for, besides teaching school, he was supposed to be health officer, too.

Nothing happened. Then I tackled the missionary.

"What's the use?" he answered, helplessly. "Whenever I try to do anything for the natives he always opposes me."

Finally, by getting both men together, each promised to help if I would take the initiative. So I took it that same night.

Calling all hands together at the church, I explained the flu situation from every angle, the missionary and schoolteacher standing in the rear of the meeting, watching me like hawks.

After a while I noticed that hardly any of the older people were following my English, so I switched to Eskimo. At this the teacher broke in to demand that I talk in a language a white man could understand. But I had all the natives with me now, and just for meanness went on in Eskimo. I was about fed up with petty nonsense.

I named certain natives to inspect every house and report to me weekly. Others I appointed official lookouts to see that no strangers came in from any direction without first being examined.

It was all very simple, yet tinged with an official importance which the Eskimos loved and understood. By the time we broke up I felt certain that my orders would be carried out.

They were—strictly.

Whether or not these two measures—housekeeping and isolation —were wholly responsible for keeping the epidemic away from us that year, I'm morally certain that our missionary-teacher contingent had little to do with our good luck.

Which isn't to say that these good people didn't mean well enough, or that I held a rather poor opinion of all missionaries and schoolteachers who came my way. Some, like Mr. Stevenson to whom I had entrusted my small daughters years before, not only *meant* well, but possessed the right combination of sincerity and horse sense to back it up.

Mr. Hoare, the missionary at Tigara, was another fine, capable man. We had long been close friends. Only that spring he and Mr. McGuire, the District Superintendent of Schools, whose son taught school at Tigara, had made me quite a visit. Then I traveled back with them as far as Wainwright, where I had some fur business to attend to. All of which made the news brought by the "Herman" a few weeks later particularly shocking.

The bare facts were these. As Mr. Hoare and the Superintendent neared Tigara, Hoare hurried ahead to see how everything was at the mission. He had just started to get off the sled when young McGuire stepped out of the door and in cold blood shot and killed his father's friend.

The Superintendent then came on the run but halted at seeing the gun pointed at him, too. A lot of persuasive talk was all that saved him from being shot by his own son. Young McGuire then took to the hills and made his way as far as Cape Lisburne before being captured by some Eskimos who had followed. They sent him down to Candle and from there, eventually, to Nome.

It turned out that while the two older men were away visiting me, he had taken an Eskimo woman to live with him, and suddenly finding himself caught with her in the mission, had acted on an insane impulse.

"A bad mess, Charlie," the "Herman's" skipper called it. The sort of thing too often blamed on the Arctic alone, although in this case the bleak solitudes probably had had an unbalancing effect on the young schoolteacher.

But it was my old friend I was thinking about, and how the Arctic had far too few missionaries like Mr. Hoare.

As though to balance such tragedy, the skipper brought me good news, too, declaring that the schooner "Fox" would soon be along with all the lumber and equipment for our new hospital.

Now, I had considerable faith in an Archdeacon who, on completing a twenty-one day winter jaunt to Herschel Island, would immediately head for Fort Yukon to help a sick man across the mountains. When such an Archdeacon promised to do all he could to push our hospital project, I really had hopes of seeing it built in a few years. But for material and equipment actually to be on the way—well, I'd have set it down as a baseless rumor except for three passengers whom the "Herman" had landed in our midst.

One was a Mr. Brown sent here to erect the hospital during the coming winter. Another was his wife who had come along to keep him company. The third, a capable young woman named Miss Jordan, offered the most convincing proof. For what would a hospital nurse be doing on this God-forsaken coast unless a hospital were soon to follow?

By the time the lumber and equipment arrived on the "Fox" I was willing to admit to the world that Archdeacon Stuck had indeed "put it across."

CHAPTER XLVII

I DON'T say that our new hospital turned Point Barrow into a popular summer resort, but its erection did seem to usher in a period marked by arrivals of scientists or explorers who found Barrow a handy stopover for everything from emergency supplies and repairs to just plain talk.

Shortly after my return from a leisurely business and vacation jaunt that took me all around the United States, the "Bear" arrived with a party of young men on a collecting expedition for the Colorado Museum of Natural History. The naturalists, Alfred M. Bailey and R. W. Hendee, were with the party and Captain Cochran took them clear to Demarcation Point—as far east as the old "Bear" had ever ploughed. Bailey and Hendee paid us numerous visits that fall and winter, Bailey completing his own collection at Cape Prince of Wales where he went by dog team in the spring.

Late the next October I enjoyed a fine three-day visit from Captain Amundsen whom I hadn't set eyes on since he anchored his little "Gjoa" off the Point several years before. He and Lieutenant Omdahl, of the Norwegian Navy, had come to Wainwright with a plane, built themselves a house christened Maudheim and now were busy planning a spring flight to Spitzbergen.

There was only one thing that Amundsen didn't like about my home. The man who could navigate the Northwest Passage, who could calmly risk his life in both the Arctic and Antarctic—was completely upset by some lemmings I kept in a cage. Eyeing me with a gaunt look that first morning, he declared he'd commit murder if those animals kept him awake again by scratching on the wire screen around their cage. It wasn't quite clear on whom he'd wreak his vengeance,—me or the lemmings. But for fear it might be both, I hastily replaced the wire sides with glass, thus insuring sound sleep and stimulating conversation for the rest of his stay.

Another guest whose visit proved particularly welcome was the Danish explorer, Knud Rasmussen. Dropping in during May of 1924, he brought with him Hansen, the photographer of the expedition, and two Greenland Eskimos. One reason Rasmussen's stay gave me so much satisfaction was because—I admit this frankly—*his Eskimo theories agreed with mine.*

I had always argued that our Alaskan Eskimos originally hailed from the east coast of America, bringing with them the ancient soapstone lamps, cooking utensils, copper and so on that we were finding in old dumps and dwellings. I knew, too, that their hunting implements and tools used in tanning hides were strikingly similar. Also, there was a deepseated tradition among our people that these things all had been "brought along" at some dim, distant time.

Rasmussen and I thrashed these matters out with remarkable spirit, considering we were both on the same side. And if further proof were needed that that side was the right one, we had only to point to the ease with which his Greenland Eskimos and ours had understood one another from the start.

A couple of months after Rasmussen went south along the coast, leaving Hansen to get pictures, our tender, the "Arctic," took shelter behind some ground ice five miles south. Another vessel, the "Lady Kinderly," had already arrived. She lay outside a ridge off the Station. When the pack ice came in, the ice inside the ridge moved north, permitting Captain Joe Bernard to bring his small powerboat, "Teddy Bear," along the beach and tie up to ground ice.

Rasmussen had met the "Teddy Bear" near Point Hope, and hearing that she was walrus hunting, had chartered her to get Hansen at Barrow and have him take walrus pictures. Unfortunately, ice conditions prevented the "Teddy Bear" from leaving, once she'd reached us.

Early in August, the wind hauled northeast and the "Lady Kinderly," trying to get under way, broke her rudder and began drifting northwest with the ice packing solidly around her.

With vivid recollections of how the ice had gradually swept us away on the old "Navarch" in '97, I watched anxiously for the

"Arctic" to steam to her aid. She didn't budge. Upon reaching her an hour later I saw why. She couldn't. But as I neared her, the crew started blasting in an effort to get free of the surrounding ice and help the "Lady Kinderly" before it was too late.

When we finally blasted the "Arctic" clear, the "Lady Kinderly" was so far into the pack that we couldn't get within twelve miles of her, and it began to look like another "Navarch" episode, only with this difference. Both the "Arctic" and "Lady Kinderly" were fitted with wireless. At least we could keep in touch.

As there was little else that could be done at the time, we turned back to the Station and went about the prosaic business of discharging cargo. Only the first few lighters of gas and oil had been put ashore, however, when a shift of wind and ice sent the "Arctic" scurrying back to her old position for safety.

There she stayed until August eleventh, her crew coming and going over the ice, her wireless talking with the "Lady Kinderly" which kept in sight for several days but was being forced farther into the pack all the time.

Early the morning of the eleventh, the "Arctic's" protecting ice ridge was suddenly driven inshore and the ship herself jammed hard and fast. Then at five o'clock—the end.

With her whole starboard side crushed, we routed out all the able-bodied men of the village and put them to work salvaging whatever they could. By afternoon I had the ship's crew ashore and taken care of at the Station—the men and their personal effects.

Despite this, some had helped themselves generously to whatever they could lay their hands on before quitting the ship. I didn't mind so much except for the example it set the natives.

Coming up from the wreck that night, I met an Eskimo woman who had been working all day in the storeroom, passing out cloth and small articles.

"What's that you've got in your bag?" I inquired.

It was nothing, she said, staring ahead. Just a few little things of no value.

"Let's see."

Her "valueless" items consisted of eleven telescopes and one barometer, all new. Another bag being dragged home by a man yielded six dozen wood pipes and a miscellaneous assortment of woodworking tools.

All this plunder was given up with placid smiles. When I explained that it was my goods they had been stealing, both the man and woman insisted on lugging the stuff clear to the Station for me. That night several other Eskimos came trailing in to give up what "few little things" they, too, had thoughtlessly appropriated. None had considered his actions as stealing. It was just that some of the white men had helped themselves, so why shouldn't they?

Meanwhile we set up the "Arctic's" wireless receiver in the Station and kept in touch with the "Lady Kinderly," now somewhere off Cape Simpson. Those on board announced several times that they were planning to abandon her. We hoped they wouldn't, but could only hope, our means of communication being of the one-way variety.

Learning from our receiving set that the Bureau of Education's ship "Boxer" was on the way north to help her, I quit worrying about the "Lady Kinderly" and determined to get to Nome somehow for more supplies. We were fixed all right at the Point but had our eastern stations to take care of, now that the "Arctic" had failed us. If things went smoothly, I thought I might even go on to 'Frisco.

A northeast wind finally opened the ice and I started south on the "Teddy Bear," taking our shipwrecked crew along as well as Hansen, the photographer. He got a fine picture of the listed "Arctic" as we passed—her stern held up by surrounding ice and all the Eskimos still working around in the water. At eleven that morning we met the northbound "Boxer," and came alongside to discuss with her skipper the best way for him to get the men off the "Lady Kinderly." Later, off Cape Lisburne, we passed the big "Bay Chimo" also going north. Between them all, chances looked good for the "Lady Kinderly's" crew.

The "Teddy Bear" was small, and with ice to fight most of the way, it took us nineteen days from Barrow to Nome. We had hardly anchored when Tom Ross of the Coast Guard informed us that the "Boxer," with the "Lady Kinderly's" crew aboard, was due at Nome in just a few hours, having made the run from Barrow in five days.

I felt ten years younger. But long before the first boat left for Seattle a wireless reached me that piled the years back on again. The message, relayed by the "Bay Chimo," was from our Dr. Griest at the hospital, saying that there was smallpox at Barrow and asking for vaccine.

No way then existed of getting anything to Barrow except by the first winter mail, and the thought of what might be happening made me sick. The one bright spot was my confidence in Dr. Griest himself.

It developed later that after the "Bay Chimo" had been there a while, with our natives mingling freely with the crew, one of the officers told Dr. Griest that they had smallpox aboard and he'd better come out and examine the men.

Now, Dr. Griest was the most conscientious man we'd ever had at Barrow. As minister, he was absolutely sincere. As physician and surgeon, there were few his equal, even in civilization. When he learned the true situation on board, I can well understand that he was a very angry man as he slapped down a belated quarantine and tackled the disease with what old and probably worthless vaccine he had on hand. At any rate, no deaths occurred, and only a few light cases developed on shore, mostly among children.

Not knowing of this happy outcome at the time, I was more than glad to have Knud Rasmussen arrive at Nome and divert my mind.

He had come to collect Eskimo stories and folklore, but wanted badly to cross to Siberia and study the people at East Cape. When a reply to his wired request to the Soviet Government failed to arrive, he decided to take a chance, using letters he had from the Danish Government as well as from the Ambassador at Washington.

So he chartered the "Teddy Bear" and finally reached Emma Harbor, on the south side of East Cape. There a soldier first ordered

Courtesy Arnold Liebes

THE "ARCTIC" TIED UP TO THE ICE

Photo by Arnold Liebes

NATIVES, IN A WALRUS HIDE "OOMIAK," GOING OUT TO THE SHIPS TO TRADE him away, then, impressed by the official looking papers he flashed, escorted him twelve miles across the Cape to Whalen, where he explained what he wanted to the Soviet Governor.

Fine! Would he stay for dinner?

All seemed to be going well. But during the meal the Governor meditated deeply. At its end he pushed back and cleared his throat.

He could understand, he said, a man wanting to mine gold or trade in furs, but since Rasmussen's only wish was to study a lot of dirty, lousy Eskimos, it was clear that he must be crazy. Whereupon, he ordered him deported at once.

Poor Knud had to walk twelve miles to the "Teddy Bear" with his escort, and when at last he got back to Nome I never saw a more thoroughly disgusted man.

He made up for it a few days later, though, when a bunch of woebegone Eskimos from Nunavak Island reached Nome under a marshal's charge. They were the most primitive of people, and the dirtiest. But after they were clear of the court, Knud had the time of his life, practically living with them in order to get information at the source. Despite my anxiety over conditions at Barrow, I nearly died laughing at sight of Rasmussen trailing all over Nome with this pack at his heels dressed in every sort of outlandish skin garments—the women with huge beads hung through their nostrils. The recollection continued to cheer me up clear to San Francisco.

Much Company business awaited me here, chiefly the purchase of a tender to replace the wrecked "Arctic." For this we bought the motorship "Caroline Frances," one of the strongest built vessels of her size I had seen and needing only certain alterations to adapt her for use in the ice. While these were going on, I made another of my "grand tours" through civilization, starting in Denver with a delightful visit with my friend Bailey, of the Colorado Museum of Natural History, and his wife.

In New York I ran into Stefansson who insisted on giving me a dinner and introducing me to a number of well-known scientists. I had a fine visit, too, with Dr. Hornaday, of the Bronx Park, to whom I had been sending specimens for years. Finally, I went to Washington for a conference with Dr. Taggert of the Bureau of Education.

He thought that our schoolteacher at Barrow had enough to do without the postmaster's job tacked on. I agreed. Since there seemed no one else to take it over I ended by applying for the position, and eventually received my commission as postmaster after returning to Barrow.

In going back, the Company planned for me to travel to Nome from Seattle on the "Victoria" and there board our new tender, the "Caroline Frances," which meanwhile had been on an initial trading expedition to St. Lawrence Island. At Nome we were also to pick up Dr. Newhall and his wife who were bound for Barrow to relieve Dr. Griest.

I had long since heard of our good luck there in escaping a serious smallpox epidemic, and with a fine vacation behind, looked forward eagerly to the trip north in our reconditioned tender. But when she hove in sight, I didn't recognize her.

Her lines were familiar, but my glasses searched in vain for the former name on her bow. It didn't look like "Caroline Frances" to me.

Suddenly a wave of almost childish pleasure swept over me so that my eyes watered and I felt all the emotions of a kid with his first birthday cake.

In my absence they'd decided at 'Frisco to rechristen our new tender the "Charles Brower."

CHAPTER XLVIII

LATE the following January I received a wire at Barrow dated "New York, November thirteenth," and asking me to reserve for the sender all the aviation gas I had here and at Wainwright. It was signed, "Wilkins."

George (now Sir Hubert) Wilkins had spent a few weeks with me in 1913 along with Stefansson. Since he also had been a member of the Canadian Arctic Expedition, I felt that I knew him quite well. But his reference to gas had me guessing until I remembered mentioning to Steff in New York that I had several drums of the stuff here and at Wainwright which belonged to Amundsen's expedition. I still wondered what Wilkins was up to.

Another wire arrived. He would be at Barrow the end of February. Would I mark out a landing field and have clothing ready for three men? He added that his plane would be fitted with wheels.

The end of February came, but no plane. I had begun to think he'd changed his plans when on March eleventh a representative of Wilkins named Hammond came in from Kotzebue with a load of supplies.

The party, then at Fairbanks with two planes, was larger than I had supposed. It included, according to Hammond, two old friends of mine, Alex Smith and Earl Rossman, who were coming overland with snow motors hauling additional gasoline and a wireless outfit with which to keep in touch with the party when they flew out over the ice.

That was the first word I'd had as to what the expedition was all about. I heard the rest three weeks later when a plane named the "Alaskan" appeared out of the northeast and landed in fine style, coming to a stop a few yards from the bank of the small lagoon south of our Station.

Everybody gathered around to greet Wilkins and his aviator,

Ben Eielson, as they climbed out. The pair had left Fairbanks that morning, flying over mountains "at least eleven thousand feet high." But instead of hitting Barrow on the nose, they had wandered out over the Arctic Ocean, then doubled back to Point Tangent and finally come in, as we had seen, from the northeast.

We thought them lucky to get here from any direction. So, apparently, did they. One of their first acts was to rig up a wireless set which they had brought. It was only a little bit of a thing with a hand-operated dynamo, but it informed the world, via Fairbanks, of the safe arrival of Barrow's first airplane.

Wilkins told me that his Detroit Arctic Expedition was being financed in Detroit by the North American Newspaper Alliance, with Stefansson, Dr. Bowman, himself and others as directors. Their purpose, he said, was to fly out over the ice and try to discover new land. Failing that, they would keep on across the pole and land at Spitzbergen. Either seemed to me to offer a fairly formidable program.

What concerned me more immediately was when Wilkins said that Smith, Wasky and three other white men, including Rossman, now with the Pathé Company, were coming over the John's River Pass bringing a motion picture outfit and two more wireless sets— one a very large one. He thought they'd get through all right, but he didn't know when.

"What about those snow motors?" I asked.

He shook his head. "No good. Got to bring our gas by plane. I'm going to fly back and forth between here and Fairbanks carrying all the fuel I can each time until we have enough to go out over the ice."

Knowing that he was to start back for the first load next morning, everyone turned out early. I think nothing better illustrates the difficulty of Arctic take-offs than what we went through the next few days while Wilkins tried to get into the air.

First, the oil was too cold, requiring a tent rigged over the motor with a stove inside to keep everything warm all night. Next, we dug a path several hundred yards long going down to solid ice. With time out for stormy weather, all this took several days.

However, he got away at last, carrying letters and packages and commissions to buy this and that. Nearly everybody wanted something that had been brought over the mountains by plane. A few days later he flew back bringing thirty-five five-gallon cans of gas. Two more successful trips accumulated quite a supply.

Meanwhile, Hammond, who had struck out eastward to meet the overland party, returned with Wasky and the smaller of the two wireless sets. The rest of the party, he said, would be in later but had had to leave the big set "somewhere on the Anaktuvuk River."

That night Wasky erected his smaller outfit in the Station and I sent the first message over this set to Fairbanks. Then, with the solemn feeling that the world was shrinking fast, I sent another to San Francisco.

Late next day Smith and Rossman, badly snow-blinded, stumbled into Barrow and accused Hammond of leaving them with nothing to eat, not even food for their dogs.

Wilkins was bitterly disappointed over the probable loss of the big set. He said it made the whole trip a failure.

"Sure we left it behind!" snapped Smith and Rossman. "Why not? Our dogs were starving, and so were we—thanks to Hammond here."

Voices rose high and it looked for a time like a rough-and-tumble, with no holds barred. I kept out of the row myself, seeing no use mixing in a situation where snow-blindness, frayed nerves and physical exhaustion undoubtedly had played their part. I think Wilkins felt the same. At any rate, he succeeded in smoothing things out between the men to the point where Smith agreed to go back for the big wireless set as soon as his eyes were better.

Then Wilkins ran into trouble himself. Flying to Fairbanks for another load of gas, he got through all right but wirelessed us that in taking off for the return the "Alaskan" had smashed one of her wings.

As we all sat around the stove, our thoughts on Wilkins at Fairbanks, exciting news came through from another direction. Amund-

sen was at Spitzbergen awaiting good weather to fly over the North
Pole in the dirigible "Norge." If successful, he hoped to land here
at Barrow before continuing down the coast to Nome.

It appeared the open season for explorers was on us.

A week later we were arguing over the proper etiquette for receiving dirigibles when word came that Byrd had just hopped off
from Spitzbergen, flown to the Pole and returned safely, thereby
beating Amundsen to it. No dirigibles for Barrow this year! So we
thought.

But on the eleventh of May Amundsen himself announced that
he'd left Spitzbergen for Nome.

Not knowing when to expect him, we had someone watching
constantly until the next evening when a native rushed in about
seven-thirty, yelling:

"Airship! Airship!"

It had been cloudy all day. Now, luckily, the northern sky was
clear. Silhouetted against it, the "Norge" made an impressive picture as she floated silently above the lead of water six miles out,
slowly drawing closer but apparently not intending to land. The
hour she remained in sight is fixed in my memory for all time.

Of course, we all felt personal disappointment that the "Norge"
never quite reached Nome, a storm forcing her down at Teller
where she was deflated and later shipped outside.

Not that we'd forgotten Wilkins. We were still waiting to hear
if he'd got the "Alaskan" fixed, when one day a terrific clatter
overhead brought us out pell-mell in time to see a three-motored
plane pass north over the house and continue out to sea. Then,
circling around, it came in and landed at Wilkins' regular place on
the lagoon. When we made out the name, "Detroiter," we weren't
at all surprised to see Wilkins climb out.

He had a new pilot, Wisley, and had brought Major Lamphere
along with him. None of them wanted to stay long.

"Just long enough to look for land out there, Charlie," said
Wilkins, sweeping his arm in the general direction of the Pole—
"then back to Fairbanks—and home."

I'll say this. Never did a man try harder. I don't know how many times he attempted to take off for his flight over the ice. It just wasn't in the cards. Somehow, the engines, when they ran at all, turned at different speeds, forcing the plane out of the track we'd built for it and into deep snow.

This happened so often that at last there wasn't enough gas left for both a flight over the ice and a return to Fairbanks. Wilkins now faced the problem of getting his plane back home.

We decided on another runway, a big gang shoveling one out forty feet wide and eleven hundred feet long. After waiting six days for a favorable weather report from Fairbanks, Wilkins decided it was now or never.

The runway certainly looked fine. But I had seen them try so often that this time I never went near the place. Instead, I climbed up on top of the warehouse to watch from afar.

I could hear the motors start. Then they stopped. Presently they started up again. Everyone going climbed aboard. The plane moved down the runway, gathered speed, and just at the very end managed to get off the ice in time to clear a rack used for drying bearskins. Circling once, she headed southeast and up through a hole in the clouds.

A pretty sight! But one which I was sure marked the end of Wilkins' attempts to fly out over the ice. Not even the message he sent me later from Fairbanks changed my opinion. He said he was coming to Barrow next spring sure, and would have a new supply of gasoline shipped up here in my care.

We all had a good laugh at that—until the "Charles Brower" got in in July. Along with our regular supplies she brought Wilkins' gas and oil, which he never would have shipped without meaning business.

Our tender brought an even bigger surprise to me in the person of Harry Riley, whom I had known back at San Francisco.

"Hello, Charlie!" he sang out. "I'm here to relieve you!"

"You're *what?*"

"Yep. The Company wants you to come outside."

Now, I liked going south every once in a while. The only trouble was that each trip meant being away from home a whole year. A month or so would have suited me better. The winters always seemed so cold down there in the States. Nevertheless, I welcomed Harry's news and began to get ready to catch the "Charles Brower" after she came back from our eastern stations.

But by the time I left on her in August, Harry's continued vagueness as to *why* the Company was calling me back at just this time had me frankly worried.

CHAPTER XLIX

TOUCHING at Unalaska on the way down, we found the "Bear" in port but, like ourselves, intending to sail for 'Frisco in a day or so. I went over to pay my respects to Captain Cochran.

"You and I haven't been shipmates in a good many years, Charlie," he reminded me, with a rare burst of sentiment. "What's the matter with sailing the rest of the way with me?"

"Off-hand, I can't think of a thing," I grinned.

When he added that this was the "Bear's" last trip as Coast Guard Cutter in these waters I got sentimental myself. I had been along the first trip she made under Captain Mike Healy, so it would be like helping round up her long career on the Alaskan coast.

During our eleven-day run to 'Frisco, if the feeling came over me that this might be a rounding-up time for the Company, too, a hurried call at the office confirmed it.

Everything was upset. Tired of the whole Alaska enterprise, H. Liebes seemed determined to liquidate the business any way they could, despite the difficulty of digging up a purchaser for a string of fur stations on the edge of nowhere. But a few of us objected to any such sweeping sacrifice. So again the directors were called together. After several days' talk, and the burning of much good tobacco, I suggested,

"Let's send the tender north again with just enough outfit to fill the holes in our merchandise, and stick it out for another season."

More talk and smoke. At last, somewhat to my surprise, it was so ordered. I felt fine. What matter that I'd have to cut our expenses to fit a greatly reduced budget? It was enough to know that I'd soon be on the "Charles Brower" going north again where I belonged.

We sailed the middle of June. In all the excitement of getting

271

under way I often had to stop and regard with quiet satisfaction a couple of young men we were taking with us—my own son Dave, from San Diego, and the son of my old partner, Tom Gordon, who had been in San Francisco. It seemed fitting that this younger generation should carry on the old friendship.

By July third we had left Unalaska and were heading for St. Lawrence Island to pick up a few furs before going on to Nome. The trip had been routine to the point of monotony. In fact, I had hoped secretly for just a bit more excitement in order to show our boys what their dads had to go through in the old days.

Nearing St. Lawrence Island, a fog caused our skipper to slow down and keep the lead going constantly. It seemed perhaps I'd have my wish, after all. But about four o'clock the weather cleared enough to reveal land dead ahead three miles away. With a sigh of relief the skipper called in the leadman, altered his course and rang for full speed ahead. He said he knew exactly where we were.

Dinner was at five-thirty. As we sat placidly eating at the first table, all at once we shot out of our seats and sprawled on the floor, along with crashing crockery and spilled food. There was no "second table" that night.

The ship had struck a sloping rock, slid up half her length and hung there, bumping every time a roller came in. Already pieces of her keel were ripping off. We could see them as they floated away. Our luck lay in the fact that the weather was light, with only a ground swell on at the time. The big job was to get afloat again before the sea kicked up.

After lowering the boats to lighten us as much as possible, we ran out the kedge anchor and tried to haul off. Nothing doing. The kedge wouldn't hold. But we did discover that there were only two and a half fathoms of water under our stern. Had the lead been going we never would have got into such a fix.

Meanwhile, our wireless sent out S.O.S. calls which were answered by the Coast Guard Cutter "Algonquin" and the yacht "Northern Light." The "Northern Light" belonged to Captain Borden of Chicago who, with his wife and a party of friends, happened to be cruising in the vicinity on a hunting expedition. However serious the mess our skipper had got us into, we knew that help wasn't too far away in case we couldn't get off by ourselves.

Night came on with fog, and the light breeze freshened to a wind which kicked up a nasty swell that made us pound alarmingly. There seemed to be a ridge of rock right under our mainmast. Each time the ship raised and came down it looked as though the mast actually lifted, then dropped back into place. If the old "Charles Brower" hadn't been built like a battleship she'd never have stood that punishment.

When all efforts to haul off astern only caused the kedge anchor to drag more, it seemed worthwhile trying it out ahead. So we shifted it to some deeper water off the port bow, ran out all the good hawser we had and got busy at the winch. It may have been that the south wind raised the water a bit. All we knew—or cared —was that at the first turn of the winch the ship came off almost of her own accord.

At the same time one of our small boats broke adrift and disappeared to leeward in the blackness and fog. The mate made preparations to go after it with our launch. When he needed a couple of men to go along, Dave and Tom Gordon's boy jumped forward.

"Come back here, you boys!" I yelled. "Let the crew—"

Neither paid me the slightest attention, and, mad clean through, I heard them chug off into the fog. Then gradually my anger turned to nervousness, finally to fear. What chance was there of locating a small drifting boat out there in the night? Or even of finding their way back to the "Charles Brower"? For an anxious hour I paced the deck listening to the intermittent blasts of our whistle and doing a little "whistling in the dark" myself.

Suddenly the launch wallowed out of the blackness and nosed alongside with the lost boat in tow. I don't know how they ever found it. But now that the boys were safe I got ready a few forceful remarks on disobedience. Then when they came over the side followed by the grinning mate, what I really said was: "A good job— men!"

In my time I should probably have done the same thing exactly.

The "Northern Light" reached us shortly afterwards, and coming as close as he dared Captain Borden asked if we needed help.

We thanked him but answered no. Our hull, we explained, didn't seem to be badly damaged and the pumps were handling what few leaks had developed.

Just the same he stayed close by the rest of the night as we stood slowly offshore with our lead now going constantly.

Next morning, limping into Gamble, the village at the northeast end of the island, we anchored and took a daylight look under the stern. The rudder was twisted. Outside of that it was impossible to see much wrong although we knew from the crazy way she'd been steering that something must be hanging loose beneath.

What this was remained a mystery until we limped slowly into Nome and secured the services of an ex-diver then working for a mining company. His report wasn't reassuring. The skeg under the rudder was completely gone, the rudder, twisted and split, hung only in the pintles and all that remained of the after part of the keel were several large pieces which stuck out and made her steer hard. A little more pounding on that rock would have stove in her bottom sure.

While having a general survey made we communicated with San Francisco, and they with the insurance people. Their final decision: we could proceed cautiously if we first made certain temporary repairs and promised at no time to get into the ice.

So we constructed a makeshift rudder out of planks and spars, strengthened by a couple of chains on each side, and on July twenty-sixth once more turned north along the coast. . . . Five days later the "Charles Brower" crawled slowly past Utkiavie and anchored off our Station.

That nerve-racking trip was something new for me in the line of Arctic mishaps. It would have been for Tom Gordon, too, had he been along. But our sons took it in their stride.

CHAPTER L

AMONG the unopened letters awaiting my return to Barrow was one from Captain Wilkins. It stated that he and Ben Eielson were planning to arrive in March for another try at flying out over the ice. They might go on to Spitzbergen if conditions looked good.

I glanced at the date. It had been mailed seven months before!

"What about Wilkins?" I asked. "Did he get here?"

"Sure did," several answered. "He and Eielson."

After everyone had put in his two cents' worth I pieced together as thrilling a vignette of Arctic adventure as anything I'd heard.

Their arrival in March had ushered in the usual long train of preparatory mishaps. But about six o'clock on the morning of March twenty-ninth they took off from Barrow and flew northwest on the old quest for new land. Engine trouble forced them down a long way out, but they got aloft again.

Five hundred miles from land further engine trouble brought them down on the ice, this time at about latitude seventy-six north, longitude one hundred seventy-five west. Here Wilkins took soundings. If I remember correctly he found a depth of five thousand four hundred forty meters, or nearly three and a half miles—the deepest water ever recorded in the Arctic Ocean. With an anxious look at their diminishing gas supply, the two men tinkered their engine into running smoothly, then headed straight for home.

They might have made it without incident except for two things —more engine trouble, and a shift of wind to the northeast which held them back like a giant brake.

I could imagine them sitting up there watching the gauge as darkness closed in and the wind increased to a gale and the universe turned bitterly cold. There came a moment when they knew it was no use.

With only a few drops of gas left, Eielson turned, inquiringly, and heard above the sputtering engine:

"All right, bring her down."

Ben let her glide into the wind as both men braced themselves for a blind landing without power. So they dropped through the dark, trusting to the one chance in a hundred that they wouldn't hit some high ice and wreck everything.

They didn't. It was a close shave, though, one wing clipping a jagged peak which swerved the plane so that when they spun to a landing all they broke was a ski.

Daylight revealed this "landing field" to be a small piece of level ice completely surrounded by high ridges which discouraged any take-off even if the tanks had been full. It looked like a case of walk —or die.

Bad weather kept them penned up in their icy crater for several days. They spent the time building a small, makeshift sled, in the course of which Ben froze the fingers of one hand. The wind finally hauled northwest, then west. Realizing that they must start now or never, they loaded all the food and extra clothing the sled would carry and set out from the plane, traveling south.

As I sat there in comfort listening to the boys repeat Wilkins' account of their trip over the drifting pack, I could visualize my own shipwrecked crew that terrible summer of '97. How well I recognized all the details! Coming unexpectedly to an open lead— searching for a way around—finally ferrying across on bobbing ice—perhaps breaking through, just as Ben had done at one place, only to be fished out by Wilkins after considerable trouble. And I could appreciate Ben's ordeal of trying to change his wet clothing in the open with the thermometer below zero.

I was with them in spirit, too, when heavy pressure ridges forced them to abandon the sled and carry their stuff in packs. I remembered those ridges; how all the ice slabs seemed set on end, with soft snow between into which you plunged to your neck; how you had to crawl on your belly at two miles a day, never sure the pack wasn't carrying you faster in the opposite direction.

All this was the price Wilkins and his pilot paid the Arctic for the privilege of hunting new lands. And Ben's frozen fingers must have added exquisite agony to the cost. Wilkins' ability to build snow shelters and eat over a small lamp undoubtedly saved Ben's life and probably his own.

On April fourteenth, twelve days after quitting their plane—and at least a hundred miles farther east—the pair reached land near Beechey Point.

"Doc Newhall had to amputate Ben's little finger," someone explained, "otherwise both men were fine. Captain Wilkins went right back to Fairbanks. Said he was going to fix up his big plane and hire another pilot to try it again next spring."

But much was to happen at Barrow before that.

Early on the morning of January eighteenth our schoolhouse burned down. Mr. and Mrs. Vincent, the teachers, awakened by smoke, had done their best to check the flames which probably started from a defective chimney. In fact, he'd been seriously gassed, and his wife almost perished ringing the bell before they left the building. The assistant, Ethel Sage, barely escaped being trapped; and once out, she had to make her way through sub-zero weather to the nearest house clad only in her night clothes.

By the time I got there the building was doomed. Practically nothing could be saved. Even the bell cracked from the heat. I felt mighty sorry for the teachers in particular because all three lost everything they owned.

The fire, together with an unusual influx of red foxes which made white ones scarce that winter, left me facing spring in a rather somber mood. I almost regetted having ordered enough supplies on my own hook to keep Barrow going another year. But the return of Wilkins on March nineteenth put a sudden end to this sickly brooding. His enthusiasm made me ashamed of myself. When he and Eielson swooped out of the sky, it was like a breath of cold, brain-clearing air.

Not even the letter he brought me from the Company seemed very important. If they had sold the "Charles Brower" to a Russian company, and refused to send any more outfits up here, and insisted that I dispose of the other stations as best I could, it was no more than I had expected. Perhaps I could arrange somehow to take them over as an independent operator.

I stuffed the letter in my pocket and turned to examine the fine new Lockheed Vega plane with which I'd fallen in love at first sight.

"Well, what's your program?" I asked Wilkins, as we walked up to the Station.

"Charlie, this time we're going to Spitzbergen or bust."

Late in March I had a crowd of men clear a four-thousand-foot runway on the small lagoon, but bad weather prevented any take-off attempt until April seventh. That ended with a broken ski and the discovery that four thousand feet was too short a run to get them into the air with their three-thousand-pound load. So we pumped the gas from the wing tanks, hauled the plane back with dog-teams, substituted wooden skis for the iron ones, and within a few days had the Lockheed ready for another try.

Again she failed to rise at the end of the runway and piled up over the far bank as before. Fortunately, nothing broke. But twice in the same place was enough for Wilkins. That same afternoon he had the plane hauled to the big lagoon and all hands pitched in building a new and longer runway. Since the big lagoon ran clear to Point Tangent, a good thirty miles east, Wilkins came in for some kidding.

"Just keep 'er in the runway, Captain, and you'll be at Spitzbergen before you know it."

The men worked late into the night. Next day we put on a larger crew. The runway grew so long that even Wilkins was satisfied and decided to take off the following morning. When I pointed out that that would be the thirteenth of the month, hence unlucky, he laughed and went ahead getting ready, anyhow.

The thirteenth *was* unlucky. Same old story—too short a runway.

Getting Wilkins off the ground now became a challenge to all of us. I sent twenty-three more men out there, and next day another thirty-five in addition to all I could muster farther out on the Point.

We'd get him into the air if we had to shovel a path to Tangent!

It was slow, back-breaking labor, clearing that fifteen-foot runway of snow two feet deep. Most of it had to be cut out in blocks with saws, carried far enough back to prevent the wings of the plane from hitting, then the rest of the surface cleaned with shovels. Wilkins worked along with the rest, and harder than most, until the runway stretched out a mile and a quarter.

This, he said, was long enough. They'd start in the morning.

When morning came the spirit was willing but Wilkins was still so exhausted from his labor that I persuaded him to get another day's rest.

Before turning in that night, he took the receiving set out of his plane and gave it to Mr. Vincent, asking him to listen in each hour from ten in the morning and try to catch the messages he'd send.

We were all up early. Fred had a big breakfast ready and their thermos bottles filled with something hot. At six o'clock they left for the plane with dog-teams. It was ten, however, before they taxied down the runway, the rest of us craning our necks as the plane roared along the narrow strip of cleared ice and grew small in the distance. We expected them to rise any second now. When they didn't I thought sure we were in for another session of road-building.

But at the very end, instead of piling up in the snow they rose clear with all their load, headed out over the Point, then turned east for their flight towards Greenland and elusive Spitzbergen far beyond.

Mr. Vincent went to church that day, so failed to listen in until afternoon. But from four o'clock on he heard Wilkins almost every hour until the plane neared Greenland. Some of the messages he didn't get right, but most, I think, were correct. At any rate, here they are, just as he put them down.

4 P. M. K.Z.D. ONE HOUR. NO CLOUDS. NOT YET OVER MOUNTAINS.
5 P. M. K.Z.D. ABOVE CLOUDS, SKINNING THE TOPS. NOW IN LATITUDE 80. ALL O.K.

6 P. M. K.Z.D. OVER (SOMETHING) CLOUDS AHEAD. K.Z.D.

6:20 P. M. K.Z.D. CLEAR NOW, BUT COLD. FOG AHEAD.

7 P. M. K.Z.D. O.K. SO FAR. 300 MILES FROM GRANTS LAND.

8 P. M. NO MESSAGE.

9 P. M. WE ARE O.K. WILKINS ARCTIC EXPEDITION. 100 MILES FROM GRANTS LAND.

10 P. M. K.Z.D. CLEAR BUT CLOUDS AHEAD.

11 P. M. CLOUDS. STORMY HERE BUT WE ARE NOT FAR FROM COAST.

12 M. NO MESSAGE.

1:20 A. M. K.Z.D. WILKINS ARCTIC EXPEDITION. GREENLAND STORM.

2 A. M. MESSAGE TOO WEAK TO BE TAKEN—GOT TWO WORDS—OUT TANKS.

3:30 A. M. HEARD TOO FAINTLY TO UNDERSTAND.

3:50 A. M. SILENT TRIP TO HERE. 17½ HOURS.

That three-thirty message, too faint to be understood, was the last we heard from Wilkins for nearly a month.

All the while we went about telling one another that since they'd made Greenland, why, of *course* they'd got the rest of the way. Privately, some of us had our doubts. Those phrases like "Greenland storm" and "out tanks" took on ominous significance as the weeks passed.

When a plane appeared at half past two the afternoon of May fourteenth our first thought was that Wilkins had returned. Instead, two strangers climbed stiffly out—the aviator, Noel Wien, and a Mr. Hart.

But if a shade of disappointment tinged our welcome it didn't last long. The package of mail Hart handed me contained something that brought a yell from all of us. It was a long-delayed wire from Wilkins himself announcing their safe arrival at Spitzbergen weeks before.

The hilarity of the occasion was hardly lessened when Hart innocently informed us that "none of the messages Wilkins sent during his trip got through."

CHAPTER LI

As soon as our first excitement had died down, the new arrivals explained that they were part of a group coming to Barrow to get motion pictures of the Eskimos' spring whaling. Would we help?

"Hollywood is a little out of our line," I grinned, "but we'll do what we can. Where are the others?"

"Well, we don't exactly know," Hart admitted. "You see . . ."

The party had left Fairbanks the day before in two planes, but after getting over some high mountains had been forced down by fog. Besides a pilot named Merrill, the other plane carried a couple of camera men—Charlie Clarke from Hollywood, and a Captain Robinson who once had made a picture in southeastern Alaska called "Alaskan Adventure." Luckily, said Hart, the planes had come down together "on a frozen lake with high bluffs all around."

"About a hundred miles from here," the other added. "That's where we spent last night."

In the morning they had tried repeatedly to take off, but with such heavy loads all they accomplished was to burn up a lot of good fuel. When only enough remained for one plane, Hart, who was in charge, decided that they'd transfer it all to Noel's plane, the larger wheel tires of which didn't sink into the snow so far. This enabled Noel and Hart to get into the air. The plan agreed on seemed simple enough at the time. They'd fly to Barrow for gas, then return and get the others.

Not knowing just where Barrow lay, Noel and Hart flew north until they saw a herd of deer near the coast. After that they followed the coastline west, finally spotted several houses—and here they were.

"So if you'll let us have some gas," said Hart, "I'd like to get those fellows out of there today."

The cook fixed them something to eat while their plane was

being fueled, then off they went, expecting to locate their friends without much trouble. At eleven-thirty that night they returned—alone.

"We picked up the reindeer camp all right," Noel reported, "but hanged if we could find our lake anywhere. Well, they'll have to wait till tomorrow, that's all."

They tried again next afternoon, and after flying all over that part of the country got back around ten—again alone.

I questioned them carefully. Were they *sure* it hadn't taken longer to reach the deer camp than they had thought when they first came out? And how about the wind? That would make a difference, too.

From what they said now it seemed to me that the lost plane might be farther south than they had estimated; perhaps even south of the Tashicpuk River and near the Colville.

Fog prevented any more attempts for several days. But we put the delay to some use by replacing their landing wheels with Wilkins' broken skis which we managed to patch up. Then when this job was done and everything ready for another try, a howling gale set in from the northeast and held them on the ground until the twenty-second.

By this time all Barrow was worked up over the plight of the lost party. They had clothing of a kind, and rifles, and there were deer in the country, but would a pilot and two camera men ever guess how easily a fire can be kindled from moss dug up under two feet of snow? Probably not.

I had another long talk with Hart. At its close he jumped at my offer to send some natives and dog-teams to the deer camp, having them spread out from there and cover as much ground to the south as they could.

Six teams left on May twenty-third. Early that evening Noel and Hart, restless, took to their plane again and tried to get off with a considerable load of gas. They couldn't make it. Finally, Hart climbed out, after which Noel managed to get aloft and started to hunt by himself.

We sat up that night. We scanned the sky all next day. Noel failed to return. So now we had Noel to worry about, too. Around nine in the evening the sudden hope raised by the roar of a motor coming in from the south was short-lived. It wasn't Noel's plane but a smaller one piloted by Matt Nieminen. Hearing nothing from the expedition since it left Fairbanks, those remaining behind had hired Matt to fly up from Anchorage and send back word if anything was wrong. To this end Matt had brought along a wireless outfit as well as an expert to set it up—for all the good that did. The equipment had something wrong somewhere. Not a message went out.

In the midst of all these successive disappointments a message came through from Kotzebue announcing that Nobile had just started on his flight and might even then be at the North Pole.

I don't believe the news of any historical event ever caused less stir among men who should have been vitally interested. Matt and Hart hardly glanced up when I told them. They were planning flights of greater importance to themselves and all of us.

Later, they made several—one as far as the east side of Smith's Bay—but found no signs of Noel or any of the others.

Then, the evening of the thirtieth, when Noel had been gone a week and we'd about given him up, back he came flying low through the fog.

That was when I made a solemn resolve never to worry again about *anything*. The way he described them, Noel's adventures had consisted mostly in waiting comfortably for fogs to lift.

When he left us the week before, he located the deer herd but was grounded there four days before being able to circle south through the Colville River district. There the fog closed in again. This time, instead of landing, he got back to the coast and holed in at Cape Halkett. He made one more flight inland, then came back to Barrow without, as he thought, accomplishing a thing. But in this he was wrong. At Halkett he had met an Eskimo who gave us our first real lead.

This native said that while camped at the east end of the Tashicpuk nearly three weeks before, two planes had passed overhead bound for the coast. Pretty soon they came back and disappeared into the south. It was on a Sunday. He remembered that distinctly because the members of his party were all in camp. So this checked with my own theory that the two planes had come down farther south than Noel and Hart thought.

On the strength of the Eskimo's report, John Hegness, who ran the Station at Halkett, promised Noel that he'd send several natives inland and would himself search all along the coast. John was convinced that the men, if alive, would have tried long since to reach the coast on foot.

I thought so, too. Some of the others still favored another search inland as soon as weather permitted.

When June second broke clear, Matt and his wireless man took off in one plane, Noel and Hart in the other. Their plan was to zigzag far to the southeast, at the same time keeping together for fear of getting lost themselves.

After several hours of flying, Matt sighted the lost plane resting on a small frozen lake with high bluffs, just as Noel and Hart had described it. He landed at once, the other crew coming down near by.

They found the plane abandoned. But on top of the cameras and other equipment lay a note dated May twenty-fourth and signed by Merrill:

"Clarke and Robinson left May nineteenth for coast and Barrow. I am leaving today. Following the same course."

While Matt and the others stood talking things over, the first Eskimos that I had sent out from Barrow with dog-teams suddenly appeared at the lake. These boys had seen the planes a mile or so away, watched them land, and now came hurrying up to learn what had happened.

After transferring the cameras and other stuff to the high banks of the lake and covering them up so as to save at least something in case the lake ice thawed, the four white men took off for the coast again, leaving the Eskimos to follow with their dog-teams.

This time the planes separated in order to cover more ground. Noel and Hart weren't even in sight when Matt picked up the tracks of two men going north. He followed them quite easily for a while, then kept losing and finding them in a tantalizing manner until they disappeared for good. He and the wireless man continued on to the coast anyhow, and turned west as their gas was getting low.

Skirting the coastline, they had reached a point about halfway between Cape Simpson and Point Tangent when all at once Matt saw something beneath them that made him swing back in a U-turn and fly low for a closer look. . . .

Next moment he landed his plane within twenty-five yards of where two men staggered along blindly, helping each other as best they could.

It was Clarke and Robinson. Both were snow-blind and so blistered that their noses and lips would have made them unrecognizable to their closest friends. Besides this, Robinson had frozen two toes, while Clarke had so injured the tendons of his leg that only a small piece of driftwood lashed under that foot enabled him to hobble at all.

Matt turned to the wireless man:

"She won't carry the whole crowd."

"That's all right. I'll stay here."

"Good. I'll be back to pick you up soon's I can make it."

So they bundled the injured men into the plane and Matt made a quick flight to Barrow and the hospital.

Dr. Newhall found that while Robinson's toes weren't badly frozen, Clarke had wrenched his leg tendons so severely that he'd lost all control of that foot. Without the driftwood brace, it flopped around any old way. Aside from this and the frightful condition of their faces which cracked and bled profusely from the indoor warmth, the men weren't so badly off.

That they seemed only moderately hungry surprised us as much as anything until they mentioned the leftover food in a trapper's cabin on Smith's Bay which they reached four days after quitting the plane. Here they ate and rested for quite a while before starting west along the coast.

Had they just kept on, we might have found them much sooner. But, coming to some low mud flats, they figured that they had wandered out to sea on the ice. This turned them back inland for a needless four-day detour before coming out on the coast again. They kept up their strength in the meanwhile with food brought from the cabin, supplemented by eggs which they found in the nests of snowy owls.

It was their blistered faces and Clarke's bad leg that caused their greatest suffering. And according to Dr. Newhall, these were things that would take careful nursing.

As Matt climbed into his plane to fly back for the wireless man, I caught him grinning to himself.

"A good job, Matt," I said.

He tossed it aside with something about "luck," and went on,

"I was thinking of the first words Clarke said to me when we found him. 'This,' he said, 'is the first time I ever gave the Grand Hailing sign, and I hope t'hell I never have to give it again!' We're both Masons. See?"

CHAPTER LII

LOCATING the wireless man where he'd been left cooling his heels on the beach—literally cooling them, too—Matt brought him back to Barrow, and an hour later Noel and Hart flew in with faces a yard long.

Their relief on learning that Clarke and Robinson were here safe affected the pair in opposite ways. Hart, half sick with anxiety for days, now acquired so terrific a headache that it knocked him out completely. To Noel the good news was like a shot in the arm.

"Give us some more gas, Charlie," he pleaded. "Fill 'em up— both planes! By God, we're going back and find Merrill or know the reason why!"

"But Hart's all in," someone reminded him.

At this my son, Dave, elbowed to the front and insisted on going along as Noel's observer. For once I kept my mouth shut.

Both planes, refueled from the hospital warehouse, left around midnight.

I had my own doubts about a fast-flying plane spotting Merrill on the beach. Assuming that he had followed the others to the coast, I doubted if he could get much further after days of tramping through the same soft deep snow that had left Clarke and Robinson in pitiful condition. Half hidden in some rough shelter was where I felt the man would be found, if at all.

And so before the planes took off I sent out a couple more sleds along the sandspits, telling the boys to investigate all sheltered places with special reference to the ragged shores of Dease Inlet.

At three in the morning the planes got back. From the strained faces of their crews and Noel's cryptic, "Lucky this country of yours is level," it was soon clear why they brought no word of Merrill. They'd run into thick fog and had had to fly so low that most of the way home they were barely clearing the ground.

On June fourth three dog teams approached from the east. Two we recognized in the distance as the ones I had sent out last. Suddenly we all started on the run to meet them. The third team, we now saw, was being driven by John Hegness from Halkett Station, and on the sled was a bundled up form resembling a dead man.

He had Merrill, all right. But Merrill wasn't dead by a long shot. After looking him over at the hospital Dr. Newhall announced that except for snow-blindness Merrill seemed in far better shape than either Clarke or Robinson when they were brought in.

This, we all thought at the time, was probably due to the calmness with which he had faced a dangerous situation, taking things easy and apparently never doubting that he'd reach Barrow if he kept walking long enough. I thought perhaps a lack of imagination had helped. And Merrill's experience, as he described it, seemed to bear this out.

Before leaving the grounded plane he had written his note and made sure that everything was properly protected against the weather. Then he started north with some bedding and a rifle. After wading through the deep snow a couple of miles, he figured he'd do better traveling light. So he returned to the plane, neatly deposited his bedding and rifle with the other things and started out again.

A day or so later—he wasn't sure how long—he found the tracks made by Clarke and Robinson after they had turned north the second time. He followed this trail clear to the coast, then west until the tracks ended.

"I was pretty sure the others had been picked up," he explained. "It was quite a help to know that somebody had been looking for us."

Still he kept taking things easy on the chance that he might have to walk all the way to Barrow yet. The only thing that got him down, he said, was once when a plane flew almost directly overhead without seeing him. That, he admitted, was hard to take.

Like the others, Merrill had been finding occasional nests of snowy owls and eating the eggs. But he varied this by catching some lemmings and eating these, too. "Lemmings," he explained, "aren't so bad if you're hungry enough. 'Specially the hind quarters."

Finally he came to a small cabin on a sandspit and rested there quite a while, making several leisurely meals off some old whale meat he found before plodding west again.

"I must have gone three or four miles," he said, "when it struck me that the hind quarters of a couple of lemmings that I'd brought along might not be enough to last all the way to Barrow. There was some whale meat left in the cabin and I couldn't decide whether to go back for it or not. Funny I couldn't decide, wasn't it? But it didn't matter because just then along came John, here, and picked me up."

According to Merrill that was all there had been to the rescue. He didn't mention one small detail that I got from John later.

When he came up with his team, John said that Merrill didn't seem to realize that his troubles were at an end. He looked the outfit over and asked, rather hesitant,

"I wonder if I can hire you to take me to Barrow?"

It was the first time in a good many years that John had come so close to bawling. He said he couldn't say a word for a minute. Then it made him sore to choke up that way and first thing he knew he blurted out:

"Get aboard, y' damned fool! Who th' hell d'y' think I'm looking for, anyway?"

From his excellent physical condition I felt sure Merrill would have got here all right afoot if nobody had found him. We all thought so. That was why Dr. Newhall was as puzzled as any of us by the way matters turned out.

Excerpts from my diary tell the rest, so far as facts are concerned. The reasons behind them? Your guess is as good as mine—or Dr. Newhall's.

June 5 Noel and Hart flew to lost plane. They brought back all the cameras, also the propeller. Men in hospital doing fine.

June 8 Clarke and Captain Robinson walked over to the Station. Both very thin, otherwise getting along all right. Merrill not so well as the others. Seems weaker than at first.

June 14 Noel, Hart and Matt made another trip and brought in lost plane. Now that everything belonging to party is safe, Hart plans to leave for outside. Will take some of party along. Nothing they can do here, as whaling is over. Maybe Robinson will go to Wainwright later and get walrus pictures. Queer about Merrill. He's getting weaker all the time—simply wasting away. Nobody knows what ails the man.

June ? Two planes left this evening, Matt for Anchorage, Noel for Fairbanks. Noel took Clarke along. Merrill in bad way. Losing strength. Can't even sit up now.

July 4 Noel Wien and his brother Ralph, also an aviator, arrived from Nome to take Merrill home. Only place he wants to go. Talking continuously about wife and baby.

July 5 Fine weather. Both planes tuned up. Noel left for Wainwright with Robinson to get walrus pictures. Ralph took Merrill to Kotzebue in his own (Merrill's) plane. We bundled him up and put him aboard on a stretcher. So weak and helpless now that it was decided the nurse, Miss Morgan, would have to go along. All hands down to see him off. Afraid that's the last of Merrill. But why? A strange case.

CHAPTER LIII

TONY EDWARDSON ran our Beechey Point Station where he lived with his Eskimo wife and their two small boys. I thought a good deal of Tony. I had for years.

When a native came through from the East in the early spring of 1929 with word that both Tony and the woman were in a bad way it gave me something of a shock.

"Who's taking care of them?" I asked.

An Eskimo boy and girl.

Now, Beechey Point is east of Harrison Bay, and while it served us well as a fur station, I could think of no worse place for a family with small children to be sick. As quickly as possible I sent one of the men with a good dog-team to bring them all to Barrow where they could be looked after properly.

Our man got as far as Cape Halkett only to meet a party of Eskimos bringing Tony and the little boys to me. The mother, it seemed, had died the first day out from Beechey Point. They had buried her somewhere along the shore of Harrison Bay. And here sat Tony on the sled, staring straight ahead, paralyzed, unable to move hand or foot.

I knew nothing of all this, of course, until John Hegness, in charge of Halkett, appeared at Barrow with the remnants of the Edwardson family.

"Figured I'd better bring 'em along myself, Charlie," he explained. "His wife's dead, and Tony's pretty bad off."

We put the sick man in the hospital at once, and though they tried every way to make him comfortable nothing seemed to do much good. Later, when capable Dr. Griest, who had been outside, returned to take up his duties with us again, he and the doctor from the Coast Guard Cutter held a long consultation.

Both came away shaking their heads. The man, they agreed, had a blood clot on the brain. Then I knew as well as they that it was only a matter of time.

When Tony died in September, it seemed the least I could do was take his two boys into my home until a place could be found for them with some family in need of children.

That was the fall when the great depression began wrecking fortunes overnight. By 1930 enough news had come through to convince all of us that the rest of the country was in for a mighty serious time. But Barrow, we thought, was so many thousands of miles away from the panic that all we need do was go about our hunting and trapping as usual and forget the foolishness of civilization. That was the advantage of dealing with dumb animals who didn't know a depression when they saw one, instead of being dependent on dumb financiers. So we patted ourselves on the back and got ready for a new season which we hoped would prove our best.

It turned out to be the worst we'd ever experienced since going into the fur business. When I think back to that spring of 1930 I'm ready to believe that world conditions exerted some strange "hedging" effect on every Arctic animal that normally yielded us a living. They just weren't there. Afraid to come out of their holes, perhaps, like the rest of the universe! Even the Eskimos' whaling went by the board. Thus the depression was brought squarely home to the natives themselves who still depended on whale meat and blubber to see them through.

A dismal air still hung over Barrow when the "Paterson" put in that summer and my old friend Captain Pedersen came ashore for our usual "gamming" session. I'm afraid it wasn't much of a success.

"What *you* need," he said, at last, "is to come outside a while and see for yourself that the United States is still afloat. I'm going straight to 'Frisco. What d'y' say, Charlie?"

I threw some duds—mostly soiled—into a bag and was aboard the "Paterson" long before she sailed.

We landed at San Francisco. That winter I indulged in another of my leisurely "grand tours" of the country, renewing old acquaintances and making it a point to soak up new experiences like a sponge.

One of these was not without its long-remembered moments of excitement. Some well-meaning friends in Chicago had arranged for me to give my first talk over the radio. I did. But in retrospect it proved an experience notable chiefly for the vast sense of relief it brought me at the close. No doubt my listeners felt the same.

Before leaving San Francisco homeward bound for Seattle, there to catch the steamship "Victoria" to Nome, I had read newspaper accounts of Lindbergh and his trip across the northern part of Canada. This meant that he might well skirt the Arctic coast as far as Barrow before heading south. So I let him know that if he wanted any gas landed there I'd be glad to take care of it for him. He thanked me and accepted the offer.

Reaching Nome, I transferred to the cutter "Northland" which sailed after taking aboard the gas I had ordered for Lindbergh. We heard nothing more from him direct, and I only hoped I'd get home in time to meet him. But on August eighth the "Northland" picked up a wireless message from Morgan, our operator at Barrow. Lindbergh, it said, was leaving the Mackenzie River that same day.

Near midnight came further word from Barrow. The Lindberghs had just arrived safely and their ship was lying in the small lagoon near the Station. How simple it sounded coming over the ether—Mackenzie River to Barrow! A thousand or more miles of Arctic wilderness in only a few hours!

I didn't know until afterwards that he had run into thick fog near the mouth of the Colville River and flown blind the rest of the way; or that at the very end he had come close to missing Barrow entirely.

The trouble was that while he found Point Barrow in the fog, he was stumped by the lack of anything resembling a wireless station. Like most people, he'd thought that Barrow was the same as *Point* Barrow, instead of being the name given to the postoffice at the settlement around our Station nine miles south.

Luckily, one of our men happened to be at the Point with his boats, and as Lindy circled overhead he waved him south to our lagoon.

What tickled our operator, Morgan, the most was Mrs. Lindbergh's delight at finding that he'd picked up a message she had sent on their short wave set while the plane flew blind through that Colville River fog.

Next day, as we on the "Northland" continued steaming up the coast, Lindy sent us word that he had plenty of fuel so wouldn't need any of the gas we were bringing. Nevertheless, when it was apparent that the "Northland" could never make Barrow before the plane left, the captain decided to put in at Wainwright and wait.

Two days later, while we were approaching Wainwright, Morgan wirelessed that the Lindberghs were leaving for the south, and a little later their plane passed us, flying low just offshore. Finally it turned in towards the beach ahead of the "Northland" and circled over Wainwright. All hands crowded the rail to watch. We had a fine close view, but it wasn't until they squared away for Nome that I had sense enough to grab my camera. Then the plane was too far off.

Their arrival at Barrow had stirred up plenty of excitement. Our boys did everything they could to make their stay enjoyable, so I think the Lindberghs must have had a pretty good time.

I felt fresh and fit myself, and glad to be home again in spite of the responsibilities that went with it.

One of my immediate problems was deciding what on earth to do with Tony's two orphan boys who had been at my house ever since their father's death. Why some childless family hadn't wanted to adopt the likely youngsters was beyond me.

All at once such a simple solution flashed across me that I kicked myself for not thinking of it before.

So I arranged to adopt them and raise them myself.

CHAPTER LIV

WHEN I say that the next three or four years passed without incident I mean only that they furnished none of those shattering events which stir the emotions and highlight the memory.

It was a busy but "routine" period at Barrow. Our fur business ranged from good to bad and back again, according to the mysterious dictates of ice and the animal kingdom. We had our human tragedies and comedies. As United States Commissioner, I recorded births and deaths, performed marriages in a pinch, and tried to play Solomon in settling disputes.

But on the whole it was one of those uneventful periods which I have often noticed about life in the Far North; an interlude so suspiciously calm that after a while you find yourself bracing for the crash to come.

I hadn't quite reached that point on August thirteenth, 1935, when Morgan hurried over to the Station and handed me a message from Fairbanks.

"Here you are, Charlie," he beamed. "Looks like we're due for visitors."

I read the message and grinned back. Nothing could have pleased me better. Will Rogers and Wiley Post were planning to drop in on me, and how was the weather up here?

We flashed word back and began discussing their probable arrival.

No plane appeared that day nor the next. When a spell of particularly bad weather followed, with snow and sleet and no visibility whatever, we resigned ourselves to an indefinite postponement.

On the morning of the fifteenth Morgan got another message. The men, still at Fairbanks, asked again for weather at Barrow. There was nothing surprising about this. You never can tell what is happening in one place from conditions in the other. But it was lucky, we told ourselves, that they checked up in case they'd had any idea of taking off today. We'd seldom experienced a meaner storm. At times you couldn't see fifty yards.

So Morgan sent the information warning them of what was going on in the Barrow district. After which all hands dropped back into the routine work of a nasty day.

About nine that night, while I sat at home working on some specimens to be sent outside, there came a sharp knock followed immediately by the headlong entrance of a panting Eskimo named Claire Okpeha. I knew Claire well, but had thought him away on a hunting trip. Whatever had brought him in on the run, it was plain from his face that something pretty serious had happened. There was nothing to do, however, but wait until he'd caught his breath. Then it came out that a plane had crashed in the lagoon.

"You mean in our lagoon—here at *Barrow?*"

No, no, the lagoon twelve miles south. At Walakpa. He'd run all the way and had told Frank Dougherty, the schoolteacher, and Frank had sent him to me.

Recovering his wind, Claire explained that he and some others were camping on a small stream at Walakpa when this plane, carrying two men and flying low in the storm, came overhead and passed back and forth several times. Then noticing the stream, they followed it to where it emptied into the lagoon only a short distance away. This apparently was when they first spotted Claire standing on the bank because a moment later they brought the plane down on the water, waded ashore and asked him how far they were from Barrow.

On learning that it was only twelve miles, the two immediately went back to their plane and took off.

Claire told me that everything seemed to go all right until they were up four or five hundred feet. Then suddenly their engine sputtered and died completely. As Claire watched, the plane went into a nose dive, hitting the shallow lagoon with the speed of a rocket, and turning completely over, so that engine and fuselage were buried under three feet of water.

Claire said the whole thing happened so quickly that he just stood there a minute hardly able to believe his eyes. Coming to, he began yelling to the men to see if they were alive. There was no answer. Convinced now that he had just witnessed a terrible tragedy, Claire started for Barrow on the run to get help, and so far as I could make out, he never stopped until he reached the settlement and met Frank Dougherty.

"Tell Charlie, quick!" Frank directed. "Tell him a plane's crashed. Tell him I'm getting a launch in the water. I'll notify Morgan."

That was how the first news of the tragedy reached Barrow.

Strange, it seems to me now, that nobody thought of Will Rogers and Wiley Post in connection with the crash. Increasing use of planes was bringing strangers up to the north coast more frequently than before and few came this way without making Barrow a sort of headquarters. My immediate thought, therefore, was that it was probably a couple of hunters who had neglected to get weather reports from our side of the mountains.

At any rate Claire's story called for quick action.

Morgan and the schoolteacher had left for the wreck already. But since my motor launch was faster than theirs, I loaded it with blankets, sleeping bags, tackle and whatever else I thought might be needed, and sent it after them, with Dave in charge. Dave's party was also towing a light oomiak so that they could get into the shoal water of the lagoon.

Neither Dr. Griest nor I thought there was much chance of the men being found alive after what Claire Okpeha had said about the crash, but there was some satisfaction in knowing that we had a hospital ready for anything—even preparing the dead.

Around three in the morning both launches returned with the oomiak in tow. The fact that their motors were throttled down to normal speed seemed ominous. A glance at two heavily blanketed forms lying in the bottom of the oomiak offered mute proof that the worst had happened. And yet I was hardly prepared for the shock that Dave's first words brought.

"Dad," he said, "it's Will Rogers and Wiley Post."

It *couldn't* be! The weather report we'd sent—

"How do you know it's Rogers and Post?" I asked, forgetting that the two would be quite as familiar to Dave as to thousands of other countrymen all over the world.

"We found out on the way down," Morgan explained, stepping heavily ashore. "We knew it soon as Claire said something about one of the men wearing a patch over his eye. . . . I better notify Fairbanks. My Seattle office, too."

Since my job as United States Commissioner put the bodies officially in my care, I had them carried at once to the hospital. There Frank Dougherty, Dr. Griest and I prepared them for removal to Fairbanks as soon as a plane, already summoned, could get here.

Both men had been killed instantly. There was no doubt of that. We found Will Rogers' legs completely crushed, the bones protruding everywhere. These had to be placed back inside and the flesh sewn up. He had a deep gash across one hip, with a lot of smaller cuts on the arms. Apparently, his back had received none of the impact. The top of his head, though, was crushed.

Post's body, though terribly bruised, with several bad cuts on the arms and a deep gash across the throat, was in somewhat better shape in that no bones protruded.

A terrific strain, those three hours it took us to get the bodies in shape!

Poor Dr. Griest was all in, and for once so nervous that he could hardly work. This left most of the sewing to me. I worked until six o'clock, with Mrs. Griest threading the needles and warning me not to stick the needle into myself.

Before we had finished, messages were pouring in from all the news agencies in the United States demanding details. I answered one briefly and let it go at that. I had no wish to commercialize on the tragedy of two such nationally famous men so soon to have been my guests.

The famous pilot, Joe Crosson, and his assistant mechanic must

NATIVE WHO CARRIED SAD NEWS

Claire Oakpeha, Eskimo who ran 12 miles to Barrow to carry word of the plane crash which killed Will Rogers and Wiley Post. Part of the wreckage visible is in the water in the background.

Associated Press Photo

MEMORIAL ERECTED TO THE MEMORY OF WILL ROGERS AND WILEY POST AT WALLIPI, ALASKA

Associated Press Photo

"KING OF THE ARCTIC"

Charles D. Brower has lived at Point Barrow for 57 years and is known throughout the Alaskan territory as the "King of the Arctic."

have left Fairbanks not long after we finished our work early in the morning for they were at Barrow by eleven o'clock.

About five that afternoon we lifted both bodies into Crosson's plane, along with all the personal effects belonging to the men. Joe took off at midnight, flying directly to Fairbanks. Eventually he flew the bodies all the way outside.

A few days after the accident I sent twenty-five men with a couple of lighters and a launch to try and save what was left of the wrecked plane. It was a two-day job, but in the end they came back with the plane, engine and propeller. At the request of Pratt & Whitney, who claimed that the engine was their property, I cleaned it up and shipped it to them later in the summer. The Standard Propeller Company notified me that the propeller belonged to them. That, too, was duly crated and sent out.

The body of the plane, however, belonged to Mrs. Post, and at her request we destroyed it completely as she didn't want any part of it sent outside as a souvenir. But she was anxious to have all the instruments. These were the same that Post had used in the famous "Winnie Mae," and their possession would enable her to complete the sale of the "Winnie Mae" to the National Museum. So I collected every part of these instruments that it was possible to find and packed them in a case, and shipped them to Mrs. Post in April, 1936.

The tragedy threw a pall over all of us. It seemed so needless. Whether our weather warning ever reached the men is something I have never been able to discover. One finds it hard to believe that so experienced a pilot as Wiley Post would have started out in the face of it. And yet, who can guess what personal reasons may have prompted them to take the risk?

Once over the mountains, and into the storm, the latter part of their flight through snow and sleet was clearly indicated by a later checkup. We had only to piece together several reports that filtered through. For example, some natives tending a deer herd, three times detected the sound of a plane flying about as though lost over the tundra. Once they even caught a glimpse of it, but not long enough to wave any signals. Since their camp was some ninety miles from Barrow it is certain that Rogers and Post had been groping their way long before they got anywhere near Barrow.

Some of the territory they covered was indicated by the report of a trader, Gus Masik, who was crossing Smith's Bay that same afternoon and heard them clearly but was unable to catch sight of the plane. A similar report reached us from a native who had heard the plane above Point Tangent. So evidently the lost fliers had skirted the north coast for a while, working northwest—in the general direction of Barrow, had they only known. But from Tangent they must have veered off west across country since nothing more was heard of them until they got close to Okpeha's camp near the small lagoon at Walakpa.

When our two parties, which included Claire Okpeha, arrived at the scene of the accident, Morgan took charge. They found that some of Okpeha's friends had reached the upside-down, partly submerged wreck and already removed Rogers' body through an opening in the side, but hadn't been able to get the other one out.

Taking a flashlight, Dave then went into the plane himself, but with no better luck. Post's body was jammed fast between the engine and one of the pontoons. Finding all ordinary methods useless, they finally rigged a tackle and, with all hands helping, succeeded in tearing the pontoon and one wind entirely off the plane. Even then it was only with great difficulty that they extracted the body.

Before leaving, Dave examined the plane carefully to try and discover why it had crashed. That was easy. Not only did none of the tanks contain so much as a drop of gas but there was no sign of any on the surface of the landlocked lagoon. Add to this evidence the sudden sputtering and dying of the motor which Okpeha had mentioned, and it seems certain that the men were entirely out of gas when they landed on the lagoon the first time. Perhaps they thought they had enough for a bare twelve miles more. Perhaps they didn't even check their gauge. We shall never know.

Not that this detail is important now, any more than knowing the exact time at which the crash occurred. Post's valuable gold watch had stopped just a few minutes before eight o'clock.

Rogers' timepiece, still running when the bodies were brought to Barrow, seemed somehow to symbolize all that made Will the simple, beloved man-of-the-people that he was.

It couldn't have cost over a dollar and a half. He wore it tied to the end of an old string.

CHAPTER LV

I FEEL like knocking on driftwood when I say that in all these years Barrow has had only three really bad fires.

The first, when the ill-starred "Navarch" burned on the beach in '98, cost us eighty tons of coal when needed most. Later, education at Barrow temporarily went up in the smoke of the schoolhouse. Early in 1937, at six in the evening while the personnel ate dinner, our hospital took fire from defective wiring.

Luckily, only three patients were in it at the time and the nurses and hospital force got them out unharmed. Had the beds been filled, as was often the case, we should have had a holocaust on our hands. Dry and weathered, the structure burned so fast that by the time outside help arrived any mass rescue would have been impossible.

The Arctic usually does things in a big way. Once the elements get out of hand, Nature goes the limit. The hospital embers were hardly cool when Nature showed what could be done with frozen water. As if jealous of all that its fiery rival had accomplished on the hospital, suddenly ten million tons of sea ice, driven by a southwest gale, came surging in to finish the rest of Barrow. They thundered against the anchored ice along the shore. They shoved it across the sandspits and up the slopes beyond. They squeezed and pressured it into fantastic masses which towered seventy-five feet high.

All in twenty minutes! Then, when there seemed no hope left for any wooden structure, the pressure ceased as abruptly as it had started and the fleeing populace, not yet adjusted to loss by fire, came back to survey its loss by ice.

We were lucky. Except for native boats crushed and buried, Barrow escaped—the Station itself by a matter of yards. But it remained for mere *man* to keep us stirred up and anxious the rest of the year.

Due to Barrow's location at the jumping-off place, we had long been used to keeping a sort of international open house for travelers, explorers, naturalists and what have you. As yet, however, nothing Russian had come our way. So, on receiving a hot tip from the press in June, 1937, that a Russian expedition proposed to fly over the Pole on a non-stop trip to San Francisco, I gladly agreed to relay any newsworthy angle that we might pick up.

But I didn't know my Russians. After waiting for days to flash the first word to a breathless world, we learned that the Russians had landed at Vancouver long before.

In July came rumors of a second group about to attempt the same flight. Again we watched and waited—only to discover, when all was over, that this crew not only had completed their flight but had come down at San Jacinto, California, thereby establishing a new world record for distance.

Apparently, we were destined to be dismal failures as reporters—at least when things went well.

But a few weeks after that record-breaking flight another Russian, Commander Levanevsky took off on one, and suddenly Barrow became the center of rescue attempts which for persistence beat anything I had ever seen.

Levanevsky left Moscow on August thirteenth with five companions in a four-motored plane, planning to hit Barrow and go on to Fairbanks to refuel. Reports showed that they passed over the Pole at one-fifty A. M. next day. An hour later they were heard from again with one motor missing and ice forming on wings. That was the last message ever received from the men.

On the nineteenth Barrow began to hum. First Bob Randall arrived, having skirted the coast from the mouth of the Mackenzie. Next came a plane from Fairbanks with Harold Gillam as pilot. Presently, a big Russian Fokker swooped down out of nowhere and landed on the lagoon. As if that wasn't enough for one day, the same evening we sighted the Russian icebreaker "Krassin" stuck fast in the heavy ice offshore. She, too, had come to help.

After drifting around in the pack a few days, she smashed her way through and one evening anchored directly off the Station. Anxious to be of any possible service—curious too, I admit, to see what life on a Russian icebreaker was like—I tactfully waited until their dinner was over, then went aboard.

Captain Michael Belousov proved to be the only one of the whole lot who spoke English. The main thing he wanted was to turn over to me a number of drums of fuel for future use of the rescue fliers. So I sent ashore for our lighters, and while his crew was loading them with the drums, all my men were treated to a picture show.

Life on the "Krassin" was simple and wholesome. I don't know how many women were aboard besides the three who waited on the captain's table, but what impressed me as much as anything was the school they ran on the ship, with daily classes.

"Most of the crew attend," explained Captain Belousov, with a touch of pride. "On that we insist. It is good for—what you call it?—morale."

But if the evening I spent on the "Krassin" opened my eyes to Russian morale and organization, it also introduced me to Russian reticence. Apparently, Captain Belousov possessed no charts of the Alaskan coast. So we gave him all the definite information we had. But if we asked the simplest questions about his own movements, he'd manage to tell us exactly nothing. Belousov certainly was an artist in polite evasion.

For that matter, so were most of the Russians, who seldom let slip the slightest bit of information unless specifically authorized by Moscow. Perhaps they were justified, so far as releasing official statements to the world. But to us at Barrow, too close to the center of things to be fooled, it seemed rather silly—particularly when they got their wires crossed.

For example, when the pilot and navigator of the Fokker wrecked their plane on a jagged ice floe far from land, the story given out was that they had come down right alongside the "Krassin," had been taken aboard and the plane easily saved.

"Those Russians sure have luck," we thought.

The true story came out later. After crashing on the ice a good ten miles from help and nearly drowning trying to save their radio, the aviators barely got their rubber boat inflated before the plane sank under them. Their luck consisted in ever managing to reach the "Krassin's" side at all.

Again the Russians got their wires crossed when a crew of six, headed by Gracianski, flew a big Sikorski from Siberia to Barrow. On a subsequent flight out over the ice they reached latitude seventy-seven degrees and fifteen minutes—the farthest north any-one had ever flown from Barrow. Returning safely, Gracianski excitedly let slip that they had discovered new land seventy-six north and one hundred fifty west. He described it minutely; a sandy island about a mile and a half long.

Here at last was news! And out it went to the Associated Press.

Next day the Russians made a blanket denial of the whole thing —which certainly put us in the doghouse so far as the press was concerned. It took several embarrassing days before the discovery of new land, solemnly confirmed by Gracianski, was permitted by the Russian Government to be officially announced.

All this time the search for luckless Commander Levanevsky and his five companions was being carried on by various planes as well as by the "Krassin." A lively spot, Barrow, while the search was on!

About the only familiar face I missed among those persistent airmen was that of my old friend Wilkins who, no doubt, would have relished a job like this. But Wilkins was a long way from Barrow, and with winter just around the corner, the hopeless search must soon end without him.

At last the "Krassin" left for good, one by one the planes quit and Barrow gradually settled down for a normal winter. The last time Gillam took off for Fairbanks I suddenly decided to go that far with him, just for the change, but I ended by flying all the way outside.

It was during a layover in Juneau that a wire reached me from Stefansson. Captain Wilkins, it said, was coming to Barrow to keep up the search all winter. He would bring some Canadian fliers with him, and could I take care of a party of twelve?

I wired back that I was on my way outside but that my son Dave would do everything possible for the party.

Wilkins' belated entrance into the picture gave me peculiar satisfaction. Not that I thought he'd accomplish anything. During the winter we have only five full-moon days in which you can do effective flying *even if the sky happens to be clear*. And besides, I was convinced like everyone else—except Wilkins, apparently—that the lost men had long since died. But such persistence seemed, somehow, to set things right. It was characteristic of the man.

While I spent the next few months in the States, Wilkins and his Canadian fliers wintered at bleak Barrow, poised and eager to take up the search again at the first chance. Only twice did he have the right kind of weather. On one of these occasions he made a wonderful flight out over the ice by moonlight from Barrow to Aklavik, reaching eighty-two degrees of latitude.

His last flight zigzagged back and forth across the mountains and to the coast between Barrow and Aklavik for a distance of three thousand miles. But he never found a trace of the lost men. After that Wilkins returned to New York with his plane just about the time I was beginning to get homesick again for the North.

It had been fine to motor around the country with my son Bill, visiting old friends, talking shop with naturalists to whom I had been sending specimens these many years, rubbing elbows with the crowds in San Francisco, Washington, New York. I don't deny liking a go at such things now and then. I always have. Luxuries, soft living, so-called civilization—there's nothing better to make me appreciate Barrow.

And so, as usual, spring brought back the old lure of the Arctic with its wideopen spaces, its plain living, its deep but exciting peace in which man can think things out while he works.

By March twenty-sixth I was sailing from Seattle bound for Anchorage a week away. There followed a quick trip to Fairbanks by plane; then, on Saturday a flight over the mountains with my pilot friend, Harold Gillam, who had worn this air route smooth while flying for the Russians the year before. Dusk was falling when Alatna hove in sight ahead of us and far below.

"We can spend the night here or go on," said Harold. "How about it, Charlie?"

Up to that moment you couldn't have got me to Barrow too soon. Suddenly a queer notion struck me.

"Let's stay over," I said.

"Plenty of gas," he reminded me.

"I know, but—"

Why try to explain that a sentimental old idiot, homeward bound, wanted to prolong the thrill by making an extra night of it?

Next morning we landed on the small lagoon near the Station just as Sunday services were getting under way.

Now, I had no intention of breaking up that meeting. I swear it. But what could I do when the Mission door banged open and the native congregation, having heard our plane, swarmed out—men, women, kids—shouting and waving as they came on the run to welcome Charlie home?

EPILOG?

AND so comes an intermission in this colorful drama which the Arctic has been unfolding for me these many years. It began at the end of that brief, hazy prolog when I went to sea. The main performance is still going strong. There can be no real epilog. Nothing is ever finished along these bleak, exciting coasts where Stone-Age oomiaks meet the four-motored planes of a Flying-Age.

I inch forward on my chair, so to speak, watching breathlessly to discover what the next scene will reveal. Something new in natural history, perhaps. A snowbird driving a full-grown lemming, squealing, beneath the porch of one of my warehouses.

I've never seen *that* happen before.

Or the mystery of myriads of Ross gulls drawn inshore by the "crack" of my gun. Habitually, these birds feed far out on the floe, listening for the noise of leads opening up in the ice where their food lies. Then why did they come inshore? A strange phenomenon! I puzzle over the thing all day, unmindful of native sleds arriving with excellent new furs. Suddenly the answer comes and I score one more victory over the Arctic. Those fool birds mistook the "crack" of my rifle for a lead opening up and merely followed the sound, anticipating food.

Well, I've never seen *that* happen before.

Or it may be some long-forgotten tragedy suddenly recalled by a tin canister cast up on the beach, such as happened in the spring of 1937.

An Eskimo boy found it near Beechey Point and cut it open in search of food. Instead, the can contained a number of documents, all so carefully sealed that the youngster, impressed, sent them on to me intact.

When I started to open them up, I got as far as reading the name of the British man-of-war "Enterprise," then quit. The papers were too old to stand amateur handling. The slightest careless movement, and they would have fallen to pieces. I ended by mailing them sealed as they were, to the British Admiralty Office in London, together with a letter telling how and where they had been found.

Several months later back came photostatic copies of the restored documents; also letters of appreciation from both the Admiralty and the National Maritime Museum. It seemed that eighty-two years before, the British Government had sent out two ships, the "Enterprise" and "Endeavor," to try and find some trace of Sir John Franklin's lost expedition in search of the North Pole.

After depositing food and clothing at definite points, the captain of the "Enterprise" recorded the locations of these caches on sixty identical documents, sealed them in tin canisters and scattered them to the four winds, each attached to a small balloon. In this way he hoped that eventually some might be picked up by members of Sir John Franklin's luckless crew.

Since ours was the only one ever recovered, those papers have great historical value. The photostats and original letters of appreciation from London now rest in the archives of the University of Alaska at Fairbanks, with copies deposited in the American Museum of Natural History, the Smithsonian Institute and in the Valuable Documents Department of the Library of Congress.

Well, let them stay there to catch the tourist's hasty glance and make him speculate, if only for a moment, on just where those papers may have drifted during eighty-two years.

But what, after all, are eighty-two years in the Arctic compared with all the centuries of sameness that rolled by before the white man came with his guns and ships?

True, much has happened at Barrow since, particularly in these last few years. Electric lights! Radios! Short-wave sending station! "Daily" papers six times a year! First-class air mail oftener! No wonder our white population has grown until at the end of 1940 Barrow boasted ten women, nine men and six children. Sometimes I think we're getting a bit too crowded for comfort.

And yet I wouldn't have missed these last few years, nor the chance they've given me to keep open house for great names like Stefansson, Wilkins, Rasmussen, Amundsen. The little "Gjoa" creeping out of the east and anchoring at the Point after Amundsen had completed his Northwest Passage—this alone was the sight of a lifetime.

When I look farther back through long years of tragedy and comedy, other sights and people come to mind as clear-cut as though it were yesterday. Shall I ever forget my last view of terrible Attungowrah as he stood, apelike and silent, among the rotting corpses of his murdered victims to wave me an affectionate goodbye?

Not that I have too much time for retrospection these days, with a good-sized business to look after, and the functions of United States Commissioner to perform, as well as Postmaster—not to mention being on our Selective Draft Board which covers a district of sixty thousand square miles.

It's the long winter nights that bring the past to life. Nights when the North Pole sends a gale howling around Barrow and I sit snugly working on my specimens, or writing, or carving a bit of ivory. Or perhaps saying to myself, as we used to in the old days, "But just wait till *next* spring!"

For on such a night familiar echoes come easily to the ear of memory; ghostly sounds which, nevertheless, will always typify the Arctic to me. I hear them plainly as I work—the rhythmic beat of the devil-driver's drum, wind-swept shouts of a triumphant crew, or, mingling with the boom of ice, the dying *swis-s-sh* of a bowhead whale.

THE END

Courtesy Photo Archives, Denver Museum of Natural History

CHARLES D. BROWER
PHOTOGRAPH BY ALFRED M. BAILEY

INDEX

change of, 124, 152, 165, 181;
rites, 44; rules, 230; taboos, 45-
46, 59, 104-106,149. *See also*
Eskimos; Eskimo customs;
Whaling industry

Fairbanks, 267-69, 281, 283, 290,
295, 298-299, 303, 305-306
Fawnskin clothing, 193-194
Fearless (steamer), 201-202, 205
Fish, 39-40; man-eating fish, 167
Flaxman Island, 211, 221-222
Fleetwing ("crowbill"), 127-129, 132
Flints, 88-89, 91; flint knives 58, 91
Flu epidemics, 228-229, 254-256
Fort McPherson, 206
Fort Yukon, 254, 257
Fox: red, 277; white, 246, 277; skins,
25, 41, 78, 133, 141, 246;
trapping of, 95-96, 245-246
Fox (schooner), 257
Franklin, Sir John (lost expedition),
309

Gage (captain of the *Beda*), 7-10
Gamble [sic] (village on St.
Lawrence Island), 274
George, Tom (boat-steerer from the
West Indies), 219-220
Gilley (mate of the *Grampus*), 77-79,
119
Gillam, Harold (pilot), 303, 305-307
Gjoa (sloop), 238, 258, 310. *See also*
Amundsen
Gold, 215-216, 235; miners 235
Gordon, Tom (of Cape Smythe
Whaling and Trading Company),
134-135, 139, 140-141, 151-153,
155-157, 159-161, 198-199, 202-

203, 205, 212, 215, 220-222, 225,
228, 233-234; son of, 272-273
Graber, Charlie (prospector), 233
Graciansky (Russian navigator), 305
Grampus (whaler, former Coast
Guard cutter *Rush*), 73-74, 77, 79-
81, 107-109, 133, 198
Grants Land, 280
Greenland, 279-280. *See also*
Wilkins
Greubin, John, 215, 225
Grey, Patsy (Irishman), 75, 82, 84-
85, 104, 126, 128-132, 134-135,
140, 145, 147, 152, 223
Griest, Dr. Henry (minister and
surgeon at Barrow Hospital), 262,
264, 291, 297-298
Griffith, Ned (of the Pacific Steam
Whaling Company), 157
Grub, 22, 83, 85, 126-127, 189, 203;
grub-staking 112
Gulls: ross, 308, seagulls, 18, 65,
165

Hadley, Jack, 215, 223, 225; with
Canadian Arctic Expedition, 249,
251-252
Halkett, Cape, 171, 197, 245, 283;
whaling station at, 284, 288, 291
Hammond (with Detroit Arctic
Expedition), 265, 267
Hansen (photographer of Rasmussen
expedition), 259, 261
Hanson (boatsteerer), 197
Harrison Bay, 71, 108, 166-167, 169,
171, 291
Hart, Mr. (member of a film crew),
280-285, 287, 289-290
Haverside, J. J., 7, 13, 16

McGuire (District Superintendent of Schools), 256-257

McGuire's son (teacher at Tigara), 256-257

McIllhenny, E. A., 201-202, 206, 209, 214, 228

McKay, Dr. (of the Canadian Arctic Expedition), 248

McKinley, William, 212

Magnetic Observatory at Utkiavie, 31

Mary Sachs (Canadian Arctic Expedition), 248-250

Marsh, Dr. H. Richmond & Mrs. (teacher-missionaries at Utkiavie), 201, 214, 230-233

Masik, Gus (trader), 300

Mason (captain of the *Jennie*), 179-180

Mauri, Jack (New Zealander), 82, 108

Measles, 232-234

Merril, Russ (aviator), 281, 284, 287-290

Mission Society, 253

Moggs, Billy, 103-104

Morgan (wireless operator at Barrow), 293-298, 300

Morgan, Miss (nurse), 290, 293-298, 300

Mosquitoes, 169

Mountain, Cape, 9

Muctuc [sic], 30, 50, 227. *See also* Whale blubber

Mungie (headman of Utkiavie, author's hunting partner), 89-92, 96-97, 99-100, 106, 109, 127, 136, 140, 142, 144, 146-148, 182, 211, 225-226

Murders, 146-148, 223. *See also* Joe, the Portuguese; Pisa

Murres, 65-66

Musk-Ox, 243

Nagaroo (assistant of devil-driver Owaina), 95, 99, 102-103

Narwahl, 109

Natives. *See* Eskimos

National Maritime Museum, 309

National Museum [sic], 299

Navarch (whaler), 183, 185-190, 199-200, 202-205, 209-210, 259-260, 302

Naverin, Cape (Siberian coast), 74

Nelakatuk (Eskimo dance/game), 61-62

Nelson (boat header), 175

New Bedford (home of the whale-bone market), 141-242

Newhall, Dr. Albert (of Barrow Hospital), 264, 277, 285, 286, 288-289

Newport (steamer), 201-205

Newth (captain of the *Alton*), 150-151

Nieminen, Matt (pilot), 283-287, 290

Nobile, Umberto, 283

Nome, 235, 248, 251, 257, 261, 262-264, 268, 272, 274, 290, 293-294; flu epidemy [sic] 253-254; gold rush, 216

Nome, Cape, 212, 216

Norge (dirigible), 268. *See also* Amundsen; Nobili

North American Newspaper Alliance, 266

North Pole, 266, 268, 283, 303, 309-310